The United States and the Americas

Lester D. Langley, General Editor

*This series is dedicated to a broader under-
standing of the political, economic, and
especially cultural forces and issues that have
shaped the Western hemispheric experience—
its governments and its peoples. Individual
volumes assess relations between the United
States and its neighbors to the south and north:
Mexico, Central America, Cuba, the
Dominican Republic, Haiti, Panama,
Colombia, Venezuela, the Andean Republics
(Peru, Ecuador, and Bolivia), Brazil, Uruguay
and Paraguay, Argentina, Chile, and Canada.*

The United States and the Americas

Chile and the United States

William F. Sater

Chile and the United States: Empires in Conflict

The University of Georgia Press

Athens and London

The map on page xiv is reprinted from Latin American History:
A Teaching Atlas, edited by Cathryn and John Lombardi.
Copyright © 1983 by the Board of Regents of the University
of Wisconsin System.

The map on page 74 is reprinted from The Cambridge Encyclopedia
of Latin America and the Caribbean. Copyright © 1985
by Cambridge University Press.

The paper in this book meets the guidelines
for permanence and durability of the Committee on
Production Guidelines for Book Longevity of
the Council on Library Resources.

Printed in the United States of America

94 93 92 91 90   5 4 3 2 1

Library of Congress Cataloging in Publication Data

Sater, William F.
    Chile and the United States : empires
    in conflict / William F. Sater.
        p.   cm. — (The United States and the Americas)
    Includes bibliographical references (p.).
    ISBN 0-8203-1249-5 (alk. paper).—ISBN
    0-8203-1250-9 (pbk. : alk. paper)
    1. United States—Foreign relations—Chile.
    2. Chile—Foreign relations—United States.
    I. Title.   II. Series.
    E183.8.C4S27   1990
    327.83073—dc20   90-35055
                                              CIP

British Library Cataloging in Publication Data available

To Elise and her daughters, Audrey and Joanna,
and to my brother, Jim,
and his sons, Gregory, Marc, and Anthony

Contents

Acknowledgments

Various individuals have generously provided both their counsel and their time helping me complete this work. Professor Jaime Rodriguez, Dr. Harold Blakemore, and Professor Christon Archer not only kindly read this manuscript but they, in addition to Dr. Joseph Natterson and Professor Colin Maclachlan, also tolerantly endured my ad nauseum discussion of this topic. Professor Ricardo Couyoumdjian always sent the latest material from Chile. Sharlene LaForge and Catherine Lewis-Ida of the interlibrary loan section of the library at California State University, Long Beach, invariably obtained copies of arcane books and articles with both speed and good humor. They as well as Joan McCauley and Roman Kochan, associate director of the University library, certainly facilitated my research, for which I am most grateful. The series editor, Dr. Lester Langley, worked at great length on this manuscript, and his efforts certainly enhanced this volume.

Chile and the United States

PERU

Arica

BOLIVIA

Iquique

Antofagasta

Atacama Desert

CHILE

La Serena

KEY

Roads

Railways

International
boundaries

0   320 km

0   200 miles

Viña del Mar
Valparaíso

Santiago

Concepción

Central Valley

Valdivia

Puerto Montt

ARGENTINA

Punta Arenas

Introduction

When Chilean revolutionaries declared their independence from Spain in 1810, the United States expressed a cautious neutrality. In truth, American officials seemed fearful to acknowledge officially, let alone to endorse publicly, the Chilean independence movement. As the War of 1812 demonstrated, the United States could ill afford to antagonize Europe's imperial powers. Sandwiched between two colonial millstones, Canada and New Spain, Washington confronted its more immediate need—safeguarding its western frontier. As part of this plan, the United States hectored Madrid to cede Spanish Florida. Even after this transfer occurred in 1819, Spanish outposts in the Caribbean still threatened America's Gulf Coast.

Because Washington did not wish to antagonize Spain, its early diplomatic ties with Chile remained unofficial. The United States withheld recognition until it became clear that Spain would not, or could not, reassert its control. Washington's fears were not groundless. Spain had reconquered large portions of Gran Colombia after Simón Bolívar proclaimed that area's independence. Common sense, therefore, dictated caution. This policy was vindicated in 1814: after approximately four years of chaotic self-rule, Spain subdued the rebellious Chileans. Three years of harsh repression elapsed before the rebels drove the Spanish from the central valley and occupied the capital, Santiago. Not until 1826 did the royalist troops, holed up in the south, finally abandon Chile.

The reluctance of the United States to commit itself to an independent Chile, while prudent, distressed Santiago. The fact that the first American diplomatic agents to Chile invariably allied themselves with the factions that lost the postindependence struggle for power only exacerbated this budding hostility. Thus, by the time that Diego Portales restored order to Chile in 1830, the United States had already alienated the nation's leaders.

1

This anti-American animus lingered. Since Chile became the first nineteenth-century Latin American nation to establish internal order, it considered itself an exemplar of progress. Indeed, Santiago saw itself, like Rome, as a white enclave in a colored continent. Chile's leaders concluded, therefore, that because they represented a racially more advanced nation, they should impose their will upon their Indian/mestizo/black neighbors. Certainly Chile's victory over the Peruvian-Bolivian Confederation in the 1830s reinforced the country's sense of superiority. It seemed proper, if not natural, for Santiago to impose its own vision of international order on the Pacific Coast.

Predictably, the Moneda, Chile's equivalent of the White House, regarded with suspicion any nation that challenged its self-declared hegemony. The United States, however, acutely aware of its own Manifest Destiny, was ill disposed to acknowledge Chile's ambitions in South America. Thus, conflict between the two nations seemed inevitable.

Santiago regarded the North American republic with almost the same disdain that it felt for Chile's colored neighbors. Although obviously white, the United States was nonetheless flawed because it was culturally deficient. "To see the typical Yankee," wrote one Chilean intellectual, "is to see the old Saxon."[1] Thus, just as Rome triumphed over the barbarians by virtue of its superior culture and morality, Catholic, Hispanic Chile would vanquish the materialism and greed of Anglo-Saxon, Protestant America.

Chile changed dramatically after the 1838 war with Bolivia and Peru. Its economy expanded when silver and copper were discovered in the north. Not content with laboring in their own nation, Chileans migrated to Bolivia, where they worked in the silver mines and *salitreras* (nitrate fields). Santiago's farmers dominated the wheat markets of Peru, Bolivia, Ecuador, and Polynesia. Following the collapse of the California market, Chilean *hacendados* exported grain to Australia, which, like California, enjoyed a brief gold rush in the 1850s. When Australia's mining fever subsided, Chileans began selling their cereals to England and the other North Atlantic nations. But while the agrarian sector prospered, it did not contribute as much to the national treasury as did the mines. Henceforth, Chile's farmers existed on the margins of the world economy, requiring a natural catastrophe, like locusts or drought, to allow them to compete successfully against their competitors.

Other significant changes occurred. Although Chile had embraced free trade in the 1860s, the nation slowly repudiated this economic doctrine. During the next ten to fifteen years, the Chilean congress passed legislation encouraging the development of domestic industries. The Moneda spurred the establishment of industries to process not only locally produced raw materials but also those of Chile's neighbors. In the early 1870s, for example, Chile gave favorable tax treatment to smelters that refined imported ore from Bolivia, Peru, and Argentina into pure ingots. Similarly, the legislature implemented measures encouraging Chilean manufacturers to process raw materials imported from Oceania into soap or burlap cloth. In a limited fashion, Santiago saw itself as an emerging industrial power, providing the mining enclaves of Peru and Bolivia with domestically produced manufactured goods as well as grain. The Chilean economy dominated Peru, Bolivia, and, to a lesser extent, Ecuador and even Argentina. Not without reason did Chileans come to believe that they should dominate these nations politically as well.

Americans also possessed a sense of national destiny. Beginning in 1840, they saw themselves as the paladins of the Anglo-Saxon race that, by virtue of its racial purity, should dominate the mongrel people of the south. "The law of progress," expounded the nationalist organization Young America, "of national growth, of very necessity, that has carried us to the Gulf of Mexico and to the Pacific Ocean, will continue to impel us forward."[2] Clearly the threat from the north caused the Moneda concern. Although political skirmishing began in the 1840s, the first confrontation did not occur until the late 1860s, when Spain futilely attempted to annex portions of Peru. Madrid's lamentable attempt at imperialism revealed Washington's ambivalence. The United States had widely trumpeted that its Monroe Doctrine would protect Latin America from the grasping hands of the Europeans. Yet, Washington selected when and over whom to throw this mantle of protection. When Madrid moved against Lima and its navy bombarded Valparaíso, the United States refused to act, in part because of the distance and in part because it did not wish to alienate Spain.

American reticence infuriated Chile, a curious reaction given Santiago's earlier denunciation of the Monroe Doctrine. It became clear, however, that the Moneda had adopted a paradoxical posture: while it excoriated the United States for arrogating to itself the role of hemispheric policeman, it nonetheless expected Washington to help repel Spanish aggression. When it did not act, Santiago became both disenchanted and disdainful. Having imposed its vision of a balance of power upon its neighbors, Chile considered the refusal of the United States to stand by its declared policies as craven and immoral. The Spanish intervention clearly demonstrated the United States's spiritual inferiority and lack of integrity.

Chilean antipathy increased in the 1880s when, during the War of the Pacific, Washington naively attempted to prevent Chile from annexing portions of Peru and Bolivia. Enjoying an enormous naval superiority, the Moneda forced the United States to retreat. Santiago retained the territory, and Washington reaped the ignominy of an abortive intervention. This diplomatic victory merely reinforced Santiago's sense of superiority vis-à-vis the United States. The materialistic Americans, led by the venal James G. Blaine, failed, while the more resolute Chileans triumphed. Twice, in the 1860s and in the 1880s, the United States demonstrated that it lacked the will to enforce its rhetoric. For the remainder of the decade, Chile ruled the hemisphere's Pacific Coast.

Eventually, the Moneda had to acknowledge geopolitical reality. A tiny nation containing a small population and limited natural resources, Chile won a succession of diplomatic confrontations because it possessed superior organizational abilities, while its opponents did not. By the late nineteenth century, however, Chile lost this advantage. The central government in Buenos Aires, Argentina, finally tamed its dissident provinces after years of unrest. Once peace reigned in that rich nation, large numbers of European immigrants flocked to the Platine republic, and by 1900 Argentina's population, wealth, and military capability exceeded those of Chile. The Moneda no longer controlled the Southern Cone.

To compound Santiago's problems, the United States had also changed dramatically. Possessing the will, the military infrastructure, and the economic resources to finance any foreign adventure, Washington reached beyond its boundaries, even to the Pacific. As the United States began to expand into the West, Chile endured a costly civil war in 1891. Thus, at precisely the confluence of domestic crisis and growing external pressure, Washington and Santiago clashed over the maltreatment of some sailors from the USS *Baltimore*. Ravaged by the 1891 civil war, facing the increasingly truculent, well-armed Argentina, and lacking European friends, Chile capitulated to the United States. This confrontation marked a watershed in Santiago's relations with Washington. After 1891, Chile went on the defensive, limiting itself to protecting its borders and the territory it had acquired as a consequence of the War of the Pacific.

Chile abandoned any idea of confronting the United States, whose population and resource base had expanded as Chile's economy stagnated. Santiago's venal and inefficient parliamentary regime had lost its administrative skills, the same abilities that had guaranteed its early triumphs. Incapable of resolving its domestic problems, the government could not rival the United States. Although the Moneda eventually settled Chile's most vexing border dispute with Argentina, Chile became a second-class nation, not merely when compared with the United States but also when compared with the more powerful Latin American nations. No longer able to challenge Washington directly, Santiago nonetheless waged a successful diplomatic campaign to frustrate any U.S. attempt to force Santiago to resolve the status of Tacna and Arica—a legacy of the War of the Pacific. When the Moneda, not the White House, decided, Chile resolved this dispute. The friction continued after 1930. During the Great Depression, Santiago cleverly whittled down its debts to foreign, largely American, creditors, increased taxes on U.S. copper corporations, compelled Washington to pay higher prices for Chilean copper, and asserted more control over American multinational corporations. At perhaps the high point of its campaign of passive resistance, Santiago successfully deflected American pressure to declare war on the Axis powers.

After World War II, Chile attempted to regain its past glory. Discovering that traditional political solutions were inadequate, Chileans turned to strongmen who presumably knew how to return the nation to the path of greatness. When they failed, Chileans embraced new doctrines: Christian Democracy, socialism, and, finally, military rule. None of these solutions has restored Chile's political unity and self-esteem. Understandably, Chileans refused to accept their country's decline. While they happily attributed earlier successes to their superior skills or racial heritage, they invariably blamed their subsequent failures on external forces. Not surprisingly, the United States emerged as the principal culprit for Chile's underdevelopment. By exploiting Chile's copper, American citizens had looted Chile's natural resources. By lending Santiago money, Wall Street had indentured Chile's future. By refusing to fund programs, Washington had stymied Chile's plans for economic independence. Chileans, in short, held the United States responsible for their nation's inequitable social system and economic stagnation.

Chile's eventual fall from power can be ascribed more easily to its rivals' greater populations and superior resources than to Santiago's domestic deficiencies. It was only a matter of time before rivals' strengths and Chile's limitations reduced the Moneda's international influence. Rather than accept such banal explanations, Chileans instead have fabricated a complicated scenario of betrayal, ultimately attributing their nation's political and economic decline to capitalism and its principal practitioner, the United States. Curiously, this search for foreign demons has united the traditionally disparate Right and Left. The former believed that Americans, by introducing alien values and materialism, shattered Chile's supposed cultural unity. The Left, conversely, flayed Washington for perpetuating an exploitive socioeconomic and political system. Because the United States was responsible for Chile's plight, both political extremes also expect it to provide a solution. This book will examine how these two nations and cultures arrived at this disturbing junction in their relationship—one demanding respect, the other gratitude, which neither believes the other deserves.

1   Imperial Republics

While Chileans, virtually from the onset of Chile's independence, saw their nation as unique, if not superior, among its neighbors, the passage toward self-rule was neither easy nor simple. Four years after the 1810 proclamation of independence, Spanish troops reoccupied Chile, putting to flight the rebel leadership. Bernardo O'Higgins fled to Argentina to regroup, and José Miguel Carrera, O'Higgins's more radical opponent, traveled to the United States to buy equipment and to raise support to continue the struggle against Madrid. In 1817, O'Higgins and the Chilean-Argentine army, under the command of General José de San Martín, expelled the Spaniards from Chile's central valley.

For six years O'Higgins ruled Chile as "supreme director." Because he advocated reforms, including the abolition of titles of nobility and the entailed estate, his administration alienated the nation's elites. Only the oligarchy's fear of the more radical Carrera deterred them from turning on O'Higgins. When the pro-Carrera elements were defeated, latent hostility toward the Supreme Director erupted into civil war in 1823. Rather than permit his nation to tumble into a fratricidal bloodbath, O'Higgins resigned.

For the next seven years, Chileans wrangled, sometimes violently, over the political institutions of the new nation. Conservatives yearned for a restoration of traditional order and institutions: a union of church and state, centralized government, and, most of all, political stability. Liberals sought to extirpate the vestiges of clericalism and authoritarian rule, proposing in their stead a federal and secular democratic republic. This ideological confrontation, exacerbated by regional jealousies, roiled Chile's political waters until 1830. Initially, the Liberals held power, but their political experiments, including a short-lived attempt to make Chile into a federal republic, alienated a majority of the political elites. In 1830, the Conservatives, led by General Joaquín

Prieto of Concepción, turned on the Liberal government. At the battle of Lircay, Prieto's forces defeated the opposition, transforming the general from rebel to president. Officially, Prieto ruled Chile for the next decade, but its de facto leader was Diego Portales, who occupied every seat in the cabinet room except that of the president, and who made Chile into the area's most powerful nation.

The Portales Years

Portales was a businessman who believed that republican institutions bred domestic unrest. Chile would not enjoy political tranquility, he believed, until the nation's elites accepted the authority of the central government. In exchange for their acquiescence, he allowed the oligarchy to control the nation's political institutions. Thus the new Chile closely resembled its colonial predecessor: a highly centralized state, combining limited democracy with traditional Spanish authoritarian institutions. Atop the political pyramid stood the president, indirectly elected by the oligarchy, who virtually controlled the state. The president had the authority to suspend already limited civil rights in times of national emergency and to select the judiciary, cabinet, and high-ranking episcopal officials. Under certain circumstances, the congress could refuse to fund the government, but this power constituted the only legislative check on the president's power. Not without reason did one historian describe Chile's president as the reincarnation of an absolute monarch.[1]

The indirectly elected senators, who had to be literate, mature— if not aged—and economically comfortable, served for nine years. Only repesentatives to the Chamber of Deputies, who had to meet progressively less stringent property, age, and educational requirements than did senators, were popularly elected. Precisely for these reasons, a deputy's term of office lasted only three years. By enfranchising only literate, affluent, and mature men, the political system successfully prevented the overwhelming majority of Chileans from participating in the political process. Exclusion, of course, was the oligarchy's intent: the fewer Chileans who voted, the elites believed, the more stable the nation. They succeeded beyond expectations. In the 1840s, only twenty thousand of the nation's million citizens were enfranchised.

Chile's rulers were white, but those whom they governed were not. Like the former Spanish colony, republican Chile remained, in the words of George McBride, divided into two classes, the Master and the Man: the small, landed oligarchy and the mestizo-Indian majority, who lived under an institution—*inquilinaje,* a form of tenant farming—that bore an uncomfortable resemblance to slavery.[2] Landlords, the *terratenientes,* granted to their resident laborers a squalid hut, firewood, and barely enough land to graze some animals and raise food. The *terrateniente* virtually owned the *inquilino* and, in some cases, his wife and daughters. If the tenant protested, then the landlord exiled him from the farm and blacklisted him as well. In a nation in which land was in short supply, evicting an *inquilino* condemned him, and his family, to a life of itinerant poverty. The landlord possessed additional powers: he could have the *inquilino* beaten or jailed, and he could take his bride on his wedding night. Below the *inquilinos* were the *afuerinos,* rootless casual laborers who worked only when landlords required it, generally during sowing and harvesting.

Despite *inquilinaje's* obvious inequities, as an economic system it functioned smoothly. Chilean farmers successfully exported large quantities of wheat, barley, and flour to Peru, Bolivia, Ecuador, and Polynesia. In the 1840s and 1850s, Santiago also sold its cereals to Californian and then Australian gold miners. When these markets evaporated, Chile expanded into the Atlantic economy. For a time even Argentina, which subsequently emerged as a major agrarian nation, imported wheat from Chile.

Chile, however, did not have to rely exclusively on agriculture. The discovery of enormous silver deposits in 1832 in Chañarcillo invigorated the Chilean economy. Subsequent finds of silver and copper prolonged the mining boom. Within ten years, Chile had become the world's leading producer of copper. A railroad—the nation's first—connected the interior of the northern mining province with the port of Caldera. In the south, Chileans used domestic coal deposits to process locally produced copper ore. Consequently, a metallurgical complex developed in the south, in Guayacán, where refineries equipped with the latest European technology smelted Chilean ore as well as minerals imported from Argentina, Bolivia, and Peru.

As Chile increased its mineral and agrarian exports, its urban-based economy also prospered. The process accelerated when the government began to develop Valparaíso. Relatively near the Strait of Magellan, Valparaíso stood astride the trade routes to the Pacific. Anxious to make the port into a major entrepôt, the Moneda built facilities for ship repair, and bonded warehouses, where traders could store their merchandise, duty free. In the 1830s the number of ships docking in Valparaíso and the volume of trade increased dramatically. Merchants, mostly British but occasionally American, flocked to Valparaíso, where they established trading houses that exported Chile's raw materials and imported consumer goods. The completion of a rail line between Santiago and Valparaíso allowed the nation's farmers to export more easily their wheat and barley. Indeed, exports of these products rose some 500 percent during the early 1840s.

The economic boom stimulated the creation of new towns and increased the population of existing coastal cities: about sixty thousand people lived in Valparaíso, slightly more than half the number of Santiago's inhabitants. Local industries, albeit somewhat primitive, developed in order to satisfy the commercial and mining centers' need for consumer goods. To foster development, Chile began to protect, selectively, certain industries.

The nation's mines provided the Moneda an ample, if not generous, income. Indeed, Chile became one of the few Latin American nations to balance its budget and to service its foreign debt, achievements that endeared it to the international banking community. The government used its revenues to construct roads, canals, and telegraph lines and to develop the nation's elementary and secondary educational institutions. In 1842, for example, the state founded the University of Chile. During the late 1840s, Chileans began to push back the Indian frontier, encouraged foreign immigration, and staked a claim to the Strait of Magellan.

Clearly the 1833 constitution served Chile well. True, the nation twice, in 1851 and 1859, stumbled into civil war. But with these two exceptions—indeed, perhaps because of them—the political system became porous enough to allow the newly emerging elites to share in the power. Thus, while its richer neighbors wallowed in civil war, Chile, possessing less wealth but a viable political system, became South America's most progressive nation.

Chile's Foreign Policy

Portales not only brought domestic order to Chile but also conceived its international policy. Just as Portalean Chile was theoretically a democracy, its foreign policy was officially reactive, if not passive. Santiago, according to stated policy, would neither intervene in its neighbors' internal affairs nor meddle in their international disputes. President Joaquín Prieto (1831–1841) observed: "An exact neutrality has been and will continue to be the role of our conduct."[3] The conduct of Portales's foreign policy proved more vigorous than Prieto's pious disclaimers. Rather than cultivating their own garden, Portales and his successors used diplomatic intimidation to pursue aggressively Chile's economic and geopolitical goals. When that tactic failed, the Moneda did not hesitate to use force to achieve its international objectives.

Nowhere was this tendency more clearly demonstrated than in Chile's relations with Bolivia and Peru. In 1835, Bolivia's new president, General Andrés Santa Cruz, persuaded Peru's ruler, Agustín Gamarra, to create a confederated republic encompassing much of the old viceroyalty of Peru. The proposed confederation, with its large population and enormous land mass, jeopardized Chile's hard-won economic gains.

The Santa Cruz government, for example, abrogated Bolivia's 1835 commercial treaty with Chile. This ostensibly innocuous act caused enormous anger in Santiago. When the Moneda made Valparaíso a commercial center, it reduced maritime traffic to Callao, a Peruvian port that previously dominated the Pacific trade routes. Lima, of course, wished to woo the merchants back to Callao. By annulling the 1835 treaty, the confederation increased the duties on imports entering Peru via Chile, thereby reducing any economic advantage of using Valparaíso's facilities. Worse, when the confederation abrogated its agreement, it limited imports of Chilean wheat. Since these new policies devastated Santiago's merchants and cereal producers, the Moneda saw its economic prosperity disappearing. To compound the problem, a group of dissident Chileans launched an expedition from Peru to depose the Prieto government. The Moneda managed to quash the potential coup, but it doubtless concluded that the confederation, in addition to waging economic war, had abetted the abortive rebels.

Without warning, Portales ordered the Chilean fleet to sail into Callao harbor, where it captured three Peruvian naval vessels. In reprisal, a furious Santa Cruz jailed Santiago's diplomatic envoy. Recognizing his mistake, the general ordered the official released. To make amends, the Bolivian leader agreed that Santiago should retain the Peruvian ships it had captured, and he even promised to prevent Chilean exiles from launching other expeditions. He also sent a special delegate, Casimiro Olañeta, to Santiago to reassure Portales.

None of Santa Cruz's attempts to placate the Moneda succeeded. Indeed, by 1836, Portales—who described the Bolivian leader as a *cholo*, a vulgar term for someone of Indian extraction—argued that it would be suicidal for Santiago to tolerate the Peruvian-Bolivian Confederation. The Chilean leader warned, "the incorporation of the two republics into one . . . places in manifest danger the security of the neighboring states, [hence] it is not possible to consent to it without leaving the future destiny of the community to the mercy of the most dismal contingency."[4] Alleging that the Peruvian-Bolivian Confederation threatened the stability of Latin America's Pacific nations, the

Moneda insisted that Peru quit the confederation, repay the money it borrowed to finance its war of independence, limit the size of its fleet, and sign another commercial treaty with Santiago that benefited Chile. While Santiago claimed that it sought to restore the stability of the area, the Moneda clearly intended to assure Santiago's hegemony over its neighbors. As General Santa Cruz noted, "Chile . . . intervened in our internal affairs solely for the purpose of preventing direct trade with all the peoples of the earth by states of the Confederation, and in fear that Valparaíso would lose the mercantile supremacy that it had possessed for years as a consequence of Peru's disorders and . . . economic errors." Santa Cruz had repeatedly but unsuccessfully tried to avoid the conflict: Santiago insisted that Peru secede from the confederation. Portales explained: "Any system in which the population, wealth, and resources of Peru and Bolivia be at the disposition of a single government, and of a government that has given us incontestable proof of its ill will, is incompatible with the security of this Republic."[5]

In October 1836, Lima rejected Portales's conditions. Fearing that the confederation would "smother Chile," Portales ordered his navy to attack the Peruvian fleet as it lay at anchor.[6] Although the aggressor, the Moneda's first expedition fared poorly. An invasion force of 3,500 men landed in Peru, only to be quickly subdued by Santa Cruz's army. To escape annihilation, the Chileans surrendered to the Bolivians, who graciously allowed them to return home. The price for such generosity was an agreement, the Treaty of Paucarpata, signed by the Chilean commander, Admiral Blanco Encalada, committing the Moneda to return the ships seized by the Chilean navy and to recognize the Peruvian-Bolivian Confederation. In return, Santa Cruz pledged to pay Peru's war debts to Chile and granted Santiago a new trade treaty. Both nations, moreover, vowed not to intervene in the other's internal affairs or to allow its territory to be used as a launching site for revolutionary activity. Once troops returned home, Santiago promptly repudiated the Paucarpata agreement, raising another army to pursue the war against the confederation. At Yungay, the Chilean soldiers, under the leadership of General Manuel Bulnes, routed Santa Cruz's army. The hapless Bolivian fled to La Paz only to suffer a second humiliation when his political opponents forced him into exile.

By destroying the Peruvian-Bolivian Confederation, Chile restored its hegemony on the Pacific Coast. It had also demonstrated its willingness to employ force to impose its will. This aggressiveness, born out of a sense of racial superiority and reinforced by success—Chile constituted, after all, South America's only stable republic—strongly influenced the Moneda's relations with the United States.

The Conflicted Relationship

From the beginning, formality, not cordiality, characterized Chilean-American relations. At first glance this tepid association seems incongruous. Americans, after all, had fought against Spain in Chile's army and navy. America, moreover, had inspired some of the new nation's actions: Chile deliberately convened its first national congress on 4 July 1811. Subsequent administrations copied many American institutions and customs, notably the republican form of government. Chileans even briefly adopted a constitution written by a U.S. diplomat, William Worthington.

The sharing of republican political institutions could not create a basis for a lasting friendship. Despite its statements advocating hemispheric solidarity, the United States waited until 1822 to recognize Chile's independence. Strategic concerns dictated this American policy: Washington hesitated to recognize Santiago, fearing that such an action might delay the Spanish withdrawal from Florida, which, one Chilean angrily charged, seemed "a matter a thousand times more important to the United States than the redemption of Spanish America."[7] When Washington belatedly granted recognition, many Chileans concluded that economic, not moral, considerations had inspired Washington's change in policy. In part, the cynics were correct: commercial relations had historically taken precedence over political considerations in U.S. foreign policy. Washington's policies, however, did not appear unique. Great Britain, which yearned to become Chile's trading partner, also hesitated before bestowing diplomatic recognition upon Santiago. But the difference in priorities, understandable in the American diplomatic tradition, raised suspicions of U.S. motives that have persisted in Chile, and elsewhere in Latin America, to our day.

If Washington expected diplomatic recognition and a presumed ideological affinity for republicanism to smooth the way for improved economic relations, then it quickly became disillusioned. Chile did not want what the United States produced. As Henry Clay noted, "Chile had nothing to give us, nor have we anything to give her."[8] Clay underestimated the political implications of the economic asymmetry. Because both Chile and the United States exported cereals and minerals, they were not only economically incompatible, but they were also rivals in the quest for markets. Conversely, since the more industrially developed and wealthier Great Britain complemented the Chilean economy, it easily won the brief Anglo-American economic race for Santiago's pocketbook and its heart.[9]

Trade disagreements continued to complicate an already difficult U.S.–Chilean diplomatic relationship. In the late 1820s and 1830s, as its envoys vigorously pressed Latin American governments for commercial treaties, the United States collided with Chilean economic goals. In 1835, for example, Chile signed a commercial treaty with Peru that permitted the products of each nation, traveling in the ships of their respective merchant marine, to enter the other country after paying only 50 percent of the duty normally imposed upon countries enjoying the status of most favored nation. Because Chile produced large quantities of wheat, the new treaty reduced American grain exports to Peru and effectively prevented the Americans from selling their sugar and rice to Chile. The U.S. minister to Santiago vigorously but unsuccessfully protested the treaty's provision.

The trade competition continued. Anxious to capitalize on the new market created by the California gold rush, Chilean *hacendados* cultivated more farmland and constructed flour mills. For a few years they prospered, but the good times quickly ended. Americans began shipping their cereals to California, and eventually California's farmers started to raise grains as well. Ultimately these western farmers displaced Chile as the major provider of wheat for the Pacific nations.[10] Having lost its once-secure market, Chile's agrarian sector managed to survive only by exporting its wheat to North Atlantic nations, particularly England.

Economic rivalry constituted the most visible manifestation of the developing antagonism between the two imperial powers, Chile and the United States. Chile, fresh from its victories over Peru and Bolivia, saw itself as the Southern Cone's premier power. Possessing a strong government and a vibrant economy, the Moneda created a delicate balance of power, which it alone regulated. Clearly, unruly Bolivia, Peru, and Argentina could not dispute Chile's hegemony. The United States, whose citizens were occasionally vilified as the "garbage of the world," merited disdain, not respect. American leaders, wrote the Chilean intellectual and politician Benjamín Vicuña Mackenna, lacked "honor, patriotism, or intelligence" and were consumed by a "depraved selfishness . . . a cancer" that endangered the continent. "Mercantilism," he argued, permeated every aspect of American culture—"religion, family, the tomb, the marvels of creation." A former Chilean diplomat described the northern republic as a nation whose Protestant religion could not prevent rampant promiscuity, alcoholism, and abortion. Although a republic, Catholic, Latin, and racially mixed Chile had little in common with the Protestant, predominantly northern European, white United States. Spain, despite its history of exploitation, remained the *Madre Patria*, the mother country. The United States was the Anglo-Saxon, disparaging Latin America in the same way that the Vandals despised Rome.[11]

Chile's foreign policy mirrored these attitudes. The éminence grise of Chilean stability, Diego Portales, suspected that the United States sought "to conquer America, not only by force but by influence in every sphere," an eventuality, he predicted, that "will occur, perhaps not now but certainly some day. Take care," Portales warned, "not to escape one domination to fall under another! One has to distrust these gentlemen who approve of the work of our champions of liberations, without having helped at all." [12]

Portales's assessment exaggerated his nation's importance to the United States. Contrary to the Chilean leader's worldview, Santiago mattered little to the U.S. State Department. (Generally months passed before Washington filled its diplomatic postings to Santiago, and even when it had a minister in place, the State Department forgot him.) Various U.S. diplomats reciprocated Portales's ill feelings. Most Americans—including the envoys—felt uncomfortable in ultramontane Chile. The highly centralized government's severe limitations on political and personal freedoms chafed them. "The old Spanish Party," observed one diplomat, "is inaugurating a reign of terror. . . . Corruption and bribery fill the land. Spaniards exiled from other countries have come to Chile and hold high offices. The old monarchists are returned to full force." [13] Contempt for Chilean political practices did not abate. The American envoy, seeing "volunteers" in chains after being press-ganged into the army, wryly noted: "Such is the evidence of liberty in this new land; such are the fruits of free government here." The War of the Peruvian-Bolivian Confederation did not improve Santiago's reputation in Washington. Richard Pollard, Washington's envoy, favored the confederation—its economic policies, unlike those of Portales, benefited the United States—and denounced Chile for precipitating the conflict in order to make "itself the Guardian for the South American states." [14]

Although disapproving of the war, Washington did not intervene in the struggle. London, however, did. The British fleet repeatedly carried supplies for Santa Cruz's army. English naval officers tried to force the Chilean army to evacuate Lima, and the local British naval commander, Commodore Charles Ross, even threatened to bottle up the Chilean fleet until the Moneda apologized for maltreating a British citizen. Eventually London forced Santiago to accept its mediation in order to settle the war as well as to liquidate British financial claims. London's blatant intervention should have antagonized the Moneda. But to Pollard's chagrin, when President Prieto attended a victory celebration, he insisted that Ross occupy the seat of honor while the American, who ranked higher in the diplomatic hierarchy and who had remained neutral, occupied a less-favored place at the banquet table. Furious at the insult, Pollard stomped out of the victory celebration.

Not surprisingly, postwar relations between the United States and Chile worsened. American property and citizens had sustained substantial damages during Chile's struggle against Spain and the subsequent civil disturbances. Yet, despite Washington's repeated entreaties, the Moneda refused to provide compensation. One incident, the *Macedonian* claims, dragged on for decades. What galled Washington was that Chile often settled the less valid claims of French or British citizens while ignoring those of Americans.

While problems with private claims were vexing, the two nations' contemporaneous territorial expansion in the 1840s engendered the most problems. Believing that they represented a superior culture, Americans became intent upon fulfilling their Manifest Destiny. "History warrants us in believing in inferior races of men, as well as inferior animals," noted one American. "The Anglo Saxon race, from which we Americans trace our descent, is surpassed by none other that ever existed." [15] Thus, while the United States did not target Chile for conquest, by implication the "progressive" South American country nonetheless fell into the same category as those Hispanic nations that Santiago itself despised.

Not without reason, therefore, did one Chilean fret that "the Spanish race will perish in America, if it remains in the *status quo*, while the Anglo Saxon takes a greater vigor and growth." [16] Clearly, Yankee individualism threatened to absorb Latin America. "We have already seen fragments of America fall into the Saxon jaws of the boa constrictor which fascinates us and unwinds its tortuous sinews. Yesterday it was Texas . . . now we are beginning to hear the footsteps of the colossus who, fearing no one, stuns his neighbors more and more every year with his diplomacy, with the spawn of adventurers that he spreads around, with his growing influence and power." [17] Events in California subsequently confirmed these fears. In July 1849, a band of angry San Franciscans attacked a makeshift settlement, dispersing its inhabitants, many of them Chileans, and destroying their property. Vicente Pérez Rosales, a Chilean residing in California at the time, attributed the incident to American hostility toward "colored" people. Americans, noted Pérez, believed that "Chileans were descended from Spaniards; [that] Spaniards were of Moorish ancestry; [and that] therefore a Chilean was at the best something of a Hottentot." [18] The following year, other disgruntled Californians expelled Chileans from the local gold fields, even driving them from some cities.

The reports of ill treatment so inflamed "the slumbering enmity which seems so inherent in the Spanish race towards our people," that certain Chileans advocated expelling any American residing in their nation. A few enraged deputies urged the Moneda to dispatch a warship to California in order to protect Chilean lives. Although the Moneda refused to make a formal demand, it did retaliate. When the U.S. Senate rejected a request that Washington protect Chilean citizens involved in mining, Santiago refused to renew its commercial treaty with the United States. [19]

These incidents, in conjunction with Washington's annexation of Texas and its war with Mexico, frightened distant Chile. As Santiago's minister to Washington, Manuel Caravallo observed, "What today they are doing to Mexico by taking over California, they will do to us tomorrow for frivolous reasons if it occurs to them." Neither distance nor the presence of a more tempting target would distract the colossus of the north from Chile. "Our government should be aware of the fact that sooner or later Chile's turn will arrive because a nation so rich in agriculture and minerals cannot escape the insatiable greed of the Americans." [20]

Chile did not have long to wait. In 1854, Washington offered three million dollars and a guarantee of territorial integrity to the Ecuadorean government. In return, it requested General José María Urbina, Ecuador's ruler, to grant U.S. citizens the right to mine any guano found on the Galápagos Islands. Believing that agreement might deter possible Peruvian aggression, Ecuador welcomed the American presence. The suspicious Moneda, however, interpreted Washington's offer as an intrusion into Santiago's sphere of diplomatic influence and consequently as a threat against Chile. Fearing that Ecuador might become a "North American colony," the Moneda launched a vigorous campaign calling for hemispheric cooperation to stop U.S. imperialism, while alerting various European nations of the American plan.[21]

The Moneda faced some unpleasant choices. It could confront the U.S. directly or alternatively try to depose Urbina in the hope that his successor would withdraw the general's offer to Washington. Fortunately, Santiago did not have to take this step. When the Americans discovered that the Galápagos contained only turtles, not guano, their interest waned, and eventually the proposal lapsed. This issue demonstrated that Chile, despite Portales's dictum, was ready to intervene in Ecuador's internal affairs in order to assert its hegemony on the Pacific Coast.

A few years later, the Chileans found other reasons to fear U.S. expansionism. The invasion of Nicaragua in 1856, led by a band of Americans commanded by William Walker, increased anxieties. After the Mexican-American War, Latin American nations could not be expected to view calmly the interventionist activities of any American, including the clearly deranged Walker. The Peruvian government dispatched warships to the Caribbean, urging Santiago to join Lima in containing the filibustering expedition. But the Central Americans raised an army and, with the aid of the British and Cornelius Vanderbilt (who was losing money by Walker's domination of the Nicaraguan transit route), drove the filibuster from the isthmus.

Although the Walker episode did not officially taint the Moneda's relations with the United States, many Chileans privately considered the filibuster a symbol of the northern republic. "Walker," wrote the radical intellectual Francisco Bilbao, "is the invasion, Walker is the conquest, Walker is the United States . . . the prophetic voice of a filibustering crusade which promises to its adventurers the regions of the South and the death of the South American initiative." Thus, even though it failed, Walker's raid demonstrated the possibility of American involvement in the hemisphere. *El Mercurio* described the United

States as a "threat to everything that you touch and surrounds you because you cannot live for much time in peace. This is the danger for Chile and all of the Spanish American republics."[22]

The fear of U.S. imperialism outlasted Walker. In 1859, President James Buchanan stridently proclaimed Washington's right to intervene in any Latin American nation that tolerated the destruction of American-owned property. His words caused concern in Chile, where they were viewed as a prelude to the eventual annexation of civil war–ravaged Mexico. Even the American minister noted that Chileans believed that the United States "is maturing plans for the forcible annexation of Mexico and all of the Central and South American States." Chile, warned *El Mercurio*, had no alternative: either it must imitate the United States by becoming a developed nation or suffer the same wretched fate as hapless Mexico.[23]

Chile and the U.S. Civil War

If some Latin American nations might have enjoyed the spectacle of the United States immersed in a domestic bloodbath, their pleasure was not completely pathological: as long as the Union and the Confederacy clawed at each other, the hemispheric countries could rest easy. The Confederate cause, however, did not enjoy much popularity in Chile. Many Chileans disapproved of slavery, likening it to a cancer that threatened the foundations of the democratic state. They feared, moreover, that a Confederate victory might precipitate a new surge of American imperialism.

Happily, the diplomatic relations between Santiago and Washington improved when, in 1861, Thomas Henry Nelson became America's envoy to the Moneda. A lawyer and personal friend of Lincoln, he successfully capitalized on the emerging pro-Union sentiment in Chile to enhance diplomatic ties. Unlike his irascible predecessor, Nelson gladly attended Chilean functions, where he delivered countless speeches emphasizing the grandeur of Lincoln, the Union, democracy, the Monroe Doctrine, and republican institutions. Nelson, moreover, stressed that the Lincoln administration had inaugurated a new diplomatic era in which Washington harbored no territorial designs upon its neighbors. Various sectors of the Chilean press increasingly came to believe Nelson, generously choosing to blame earlier acts of American imperialism on the slave states and the Democratic party. Nelson won additional public support when he helped to reconcile an argument between Chile and Bolivia. He even managed to resolve some of the vexing U.S. financial claims that Chile had incurred as a consequence of the 1859 revolution. The minister also became quite popular when, at great personal risk, he helped rescue some church-goers trapped when Santiago's Iglesia de la Compañía caught fire. Both the Moneda and private citizens thanked Nelson as well as the other Americans for their personal heroism and their help.

In some ways, fighting fires proved less onerous than Nelson's diplomatic duties. The Confederacy's capacity to survive made it extremely difficult for Nelson to convince the Chileans that Lincoln and the Union would eventually triumph. It is for this reason that Nelson, at the behest of Secretary of State William Seward, tried to prevent the Moneda from removing its Washington legation. Seward feared that some nations might interpret such an act as indicating the Chileans' lack of confidence in the Lincoln government. While Nelson reassured Seward that his fears were overblown, he nonetheless communicated the secretary's concern to then president José Pérez, who eventually decided to retain the minister, Francisco Astaburaga, thus providing Washington with a demonstration of Santiago's loyalty.

Despite the Union's initial defeats, Santiago supported Lincoln throughout the war. Not surprisingly, news of the fall of Richmond sparked spontaneous victory celebrations in Valparaíso; the entire nation rejoiced when the Confederacy finally surrendered. Conversely, Lincoln's assassination caused great sadness. The Moneda ordered the flag of the national congress lowered to half mast and declared a day of mourning, decreeing that certain naval vessels and forts fire salutes. Private citizens organized processions and commemorative ceremonies.

But even Nelson could not easily explain Washington's refusal to intervene when, in October 1861, France's Louis Napoleon installed Archduke Maximilian as his surrogate ruler of Mexico. Chile's new minister of foreign relations, Manuel Tocornal, inquired if Washington would oppose France's involvement in Mexico. Fearful of antagonizing neutral Europe, Secretary of State Seward responded cautiously. It fell to Nelson to deliver the unpalatable message that although Washington could not afford to break relations with France, it adamantly opposed European intervention in the hemisphere. Whether this rationalization pacified Tocornal remains unclear; it did relieve the pressure on Nelson. Perhaps Chileans recognized that the Civil War prevented Washington from enforcing the Monroe Doctrine. Santiago, of course, could afford to be generous: Napoleon's intervention occurred so far from Chile's shores that it had little to fear.

But France was not the only European nation that entertained imperial aspirations. In 1861, a Spanish flotilla appeared off the coast of Peru. While the fleet was presumably engaged in scientific research, Madrid secretly authorized the squadron's commander, Admiral José Manuel Pareja, to act on behalf of Spanish citizens claiming property damages against any Latin American nation. Seizing upon a dispute between the Peruvian owner of the hacienda Talambo and his Spanish workers, the admiral occupied Peru's Chincha Islands. These desolate isles, which were coated with nitrogen-rich guano, provided Lima with most of its income. Hence their loss threatened to bankrupt Peru. Lima, therefore, opened negotiations with Madrid in order to regain the islands. It also simultaneously called for an inter-American conference in order to forge a hemispheric response to the Spanish incursion.

Chileans disliked Peru, but they resented more Spain's arbitrary intrusion into a neighbor's affairs. Not surprisingly, Chileans organized meetings that raucously condemned Spain's seizure of the Chincha Islands. The Moneda reacted no less forcefully, although slightly more politely, publishing a statement criticizing Spain. Public outrage became so vitriolic that it forced the Moneda to dismiss Tocornal as minister of foreign relations, replacing him with Alvaro Corvarrubias. Responding to the same public outcry, the government prohibited the sale of Chilean coal or victuals to any Spanish naval vessel. It also sent a delegate to the inter-American meeting in Lima in order to lend more weight to the hemispheric complaints about Spanish imperialism. By the time the Latin delegates met, the crisis had eased because Madrid had renounced its territorial claims to the Chincha Islands. But the Spanish refused to evacuate the islands until Peru satisfied its nationals' financial claims.

Facing Spanish intransigence, the delegates to the conference urged Peru to attempt to negotiate a peaceful settlement with Spain while simultaneously preparing itself for war. The arrival of a second Spanish fleet so cowed Peru's president, Juan Pezet, that he agreed to settle the claims and even reimbursed Madrid for the cost of the expedition. Infuriated by the president's supine attitude, the Peruvian congress refused to ratify the treaty. Peru's populace became so incensed that it overthrew Pezet.

Convinced that they had humiliated Peru, the Spanish focused their anger on Chile for refusing to coal Spanish ships, for permitting aid to reach Peru, and for not censoring a Santiago newspaper, the *San Martín*, that printed irreverent, if not indecent, editorials about Spain's Queen Isabel and her subjects. Madrid's envoy was a truculent naval officer who demanded that Santiago atone for its earlier insolence by paying an indemnity of five million pesos and firing a twenty-one gun salute to the Spanish flag. The officer gave the Chilean government four days in which to reply, threatening reprisals if it refused his conditions. The Moneda, unlike Peru, rejected the Spanish ultimatum. When Spain retaliated as expected by blockading Chile's coast, the Moneda declared war.

The U.S. Reaction

Despite its earlier denunciation of American materialism and imperial foreign policy, the Moneda nonetheless turned to Washington for assistance. Eluding the Spanish blockade, Benjamín Vicuña Mackenna traveled to the United States, where he tried to procure military equipment and generate American support for Chile. Although strapped for funds, Vicuña Mackenna purchased four ships—which, unfortunately, arrived after the Spanish fleet had departed Chile's waters—and tried to recruit an expeditionary force of Chileans and Peruvians who, he hoped, would use the United States as a point of departure for an invasion of Cuba. This plan failed, as did Vicuña Mackenna's attempts to purchase weapons. New York Customs officials stopped the sailing of the *Meteor*—one of the ships that Vicuña Mackenna had bought. Worse, the U.S. authorities jailed Vicuña Mackenna when he tried to hire the services of an American torpedo expert. Only a statement by the Chilean minister to Washington, certifying that Vicuña Mackenna enjoyed diplomatic immunity, saved him from prosecution.

Vicuña Mackenna enjoyed more success as a publicist than as a quartermaster. To publicize Chile's plight, he founded a Spanish language newspaper, *La Voz de America*. He also organized a meeting at Cooper's Union in January 1866 that attracted such notables as William Cullen Bryant, James Garfield, Horace Greeley, and the Civil War hero General William Rosecrans. Most of the participants denounced Spanish imperialism while describing the Monroe Doctrine as a "responsibility toward our sister republics, and an obligation to defend and protect them," even, as one speaker stated, "if need be . . . at the mouth of the cannon." [24]

Regrettably for Chile, Secretary of State Seward did not share these sentiments. On the contrary, he seemed to resent that Chile and Spain stumbled into a state of hostilities. "The war has no object," he observed. "Spain has no reason to cause it nor Chile any motive to accept it. For reasons of etiquette, great harm will befall commerce." [25] Seward certainly wanted the Spanish to withdraw, but he feared that Madrid, if pressed, might retaliate by granting the Confederacy belligerent status or, worse, diplomatic recognition. Rather than invoke the Monroe Doctrine, the secretary of state waffled. U.S. support for Latin America, he argued, did not preclude the right to wage war. Hence, European nations could intrude into the Western Hemisphere, providing that they did not intend to seize or occupy land. Thus, because Spain entertained no territorial designs against Chile, it had not violated the Monroe Doctrine. Washington, therefore, could remain neutral.

The conclusion of the Civil War did not alter Seward's attitude. Indeed, the secretary so feared offending Spain, whose cooperation he now required to construct a trans-Caribbean telegraph system, that he attended a diplomatic banquet in Cuba where he indiscreetly but lavishly praised Spain as "the only European power that has any right to a footing in America."[26] Presumably this desire to appease Spain led Seward to replace Nelson with Judson Kilpatrick, a former Civil War general. Ironically, although Kilpatrick, like Nelson, became a convert to Chile's cause, he could not convince the State Department to intervene. When Santiago requested U.S. assistance, Nelson and Kilpatrick could only offer America's good offices. Chile refused to negotiate until the Spanish fleet abandoned the blockade and Madrid dropped some of its more outrageous preconditions. Eventually, thanks to Anglo-American mediation, the Spanish reduced their demands to one: both nations must exchange reciprocal salutes. But Madrid's delegate insisted that Chile must fire the first cannonade. When Santiago refused, the Spanish navy threatened to bombard Valparaíso on 31 March 1866.

Chile's principal port did not possess adequate coastal fortifications. Hence Valparaíso's only salvation lay in the presence of the Anglo-American naval squadron lying at anchor in the harbor. These eight vessels could easily have repelled the Spanish fleet. Initially it seemed that they would do precisely that: when the U.S. flotilla reinforced its armor, it appeared that the Americans were preparing for battle. The U.S. naval commander, however, refused to act unless the British joined him. But London's minister to Santiago would not permit the Royal Navy to act. Thus, the allied squadron ignominiously fled Valparaíso, leaving the undefended port to its unhappy fate: a savage bombardment that inflicted damage costing approximately fifteen million pesos, mainly to foreign-owned property. Its heroic work done, the Spanish fleet returned to its home port.

Chile's Reaction

The Spanish attack on Valparaíso, literally before the eyes of the American navy, dissipated most, if not all, of the good will that Nelson had so painstakingly accumulated. Chileans could neither forgive nor forget the United States's seemingly supine acceptance of Spain's aggression. Predictably, Washington became almost as despised as Madrid. The press turned first on Kilpatrick, then on the U.S. naval commander, and finally on Seward, accusing them all of betraying Chile. Vicuña Mackenna, once an advocate of the Monroe Doctrine, henceforth denounced it as a cruel illusion. A journalist and deputy, Justo Arteaga Alemparte, professed not to be surprised by the White House's craven policies: the selfish Americans considered Latin Americans as inferiors and hence unworthy of assistance.[27]

Certainly the Chileans had ample reason to be disillusioned. Washington's strident evocation of the Monroe Doctrine had convinced Chile that the United States would protect it from European aggression. Consequently, when the White House chose not to react, Santiago became understandably angry. American inaction confirmed a prevalent Chilean attitude: the United States would aggressively defend its nationals' property but not the nation's principles. In contrast, Chile preferred to endure a devastating bombardment before repudiating its convictions.

The Spanish intervention, however, pointed up a curious ambivalence in both the United States and Chile. Washington might proclaim the Monroe Doctrine as a fundamental diplomatic policy but choose to enforce it selectively. Conversely, Chileans attacked the doctrine as a unilateral and unwanted intrusion into hemispheric affairs. Nonetheless, they expected Washington to enforce it when Chile was weak or required assistance.

Chileans emerged from the 1860s disdainful of the United States. Santiago's dealings with Washington reinforced its belief that the Latin nation was morally superior to the republic of the north. After decades of loftily disparaging Latin Americans for what seemed to be their congenital civil unrest, the United States had to endure a brutal civil war. If the War Between the States demonstrated that the United States suffered from the same political malaise as its Latin neighbors did, then Washington's failure to respond to the Spanish in Valparaíso showed that it lacked moral commitment. The United States was a braggart that would collapse when confronted by another nation. The Monroe Doctrine, although crafted in forceful language, lacked substance. Conversely, Chileans saw themselves as a progressive nation. They had vanquished Peru and Bolivia; they had emerged as the moral victors in their conflict with Spain. Only Santiago seemed capable of restraining Washington, which was advancing "like a growing wave whose waters are poised to empty a cataract on the south." [28]

2   The War of the Pacific

Chile's 1879 decision to declare war on Peru and Bolivia demonstrated that its imperial pretensions in South America equaled those of the United States in the north. Beginning in the 1840s, Chileans penetrated their nation's southern rain forests, pushing back the Indian frontier. To the north, so many Chileans migrated to labor in the silver and copper mines of Bolivia's province of Atacama that by 1879 Chileans outnumbered Bolivians residing in that arid coastal plain. This situation proved to be potentially volatile. Bolivia's governments, isolated in the Altiplano city of La Paz, ruled an area rich in minerals but capitalized and peopled by foreigners. Even a strong administration would have encountered problems in retaining control of such an economically important but geographically distant province. Continually ravaged by political upheaval, La Paz possessed neither the bureaucracy nor the military strength to control its capital, let alone a region located hundreds of miles away. Just as Mexico's administrations, isolated in the central valley, could not prevent the creation of a rebellious American enclave in Texas, so Bolivia could not stop Chileans from usurping its littoral.

The frontier separating Chile and Bolivia lay in the largely uncharted wastelands of the Atacama Desert. Given the barren nature of the area, neither nation initially seemed willing to quibble over the location of the boundary stakes, until the discovery of guano in the 1840s altered this situation. Chile began to demand the land up to the twenty-third parallel; Bolivia claimed territory south to the twenty-sixth. The dispute over the Atacama became so bitter that only Madrid's 1866 intervention in Peru prevented Santiago and La Paz from going to war. Faced with the Spanish threat, the two nations agreed to fix the boundary at the twenty-fourth parallel. This settlement might have endured, but the Bolivian congress subsequently disavowed the 1866 treaty. After years of acrimonious discussions,

31

Santiago and La Paz signed a second treaty in 1874. The new arrangement reaffirmed the twenty-fourth parallel as the border. Chile, however, no longer shared in the area's tax revenues. In return, La Paz agreed not to increase taxes on Chilean corporations operating in the Atacama for twenty-five years.

Bolivia was not the only nation afflicted with a festering border dispute. Argentina seemed to be on the verge of enduring the same fate that befell La Paz. Chileans, many believing that the land belonged to Santiago, had filtered across the Argentine frontier into Patagonia and to the Strait of Magellan. Initially the Chilean intrusion did not appear to provoke Argentina. During the 1870s, Buenos Aires launched its War of the Desert, a struggle to domesticate, if not to eradicate, the Indian tribes that had periodically ravaged the nation's interior provinces. Having pacified the area, Buenos Aires was distressed to discover that Chileans had occupied large portions of the land that the Argentines considered theirs. The situation became increasingly acrimonious because Buenos Aires claimed not only Patagonia but also the eastern mouth of the Strait of Magellan.

Since most of Chile's political leadership considered the mineral riches in Peru and Bolivia as their country's principal area of economic interest, they evinced little enthusiasm about holding onto Patagonia. But because Argentina's claims to the Strait of Magellan threatened Chilean access to European markets, Santiago was prepared to go to war to protect its trade routes. Happily the situation did not reach that point. In 1878, the two capitals worked out a temporary solution to their dispute: Chile gave up Patagonia, and both nations would occupy the Strait of Magellan until they negotiated a permanent boundary. Faced with the loss of the once-disparaged pampa, Chilean nationalists belatedly discovered new beauty in the Patagonian wastelands, viciously denouncing the agreement—the Fierro Sarretea Treaty—as a violation of the nation's sacred interests. Despite this jingoistic bluster, the Chilean legislature approved the agreement. Unfortunately, the Moneda could not resolve its other diplomatic problems as easily.

The War

In February 1878, Bolivia's newest dictator, General Hilarión Daza, had increased the export tax on nitrates mined by the largely Chilean-owned Compañía de Salitres y Ferrocarril. The reason for Daza's actions seem quite clear. Chronically wracked by civil war, Bolivia desperately needed revenues. Seeing the Moneda embroiled in a bitter boundary dispute with Buenos Aires, Daza decided to fill his treasury at the expense of Santiago. Facing the possibility of war with Argentina, Chile, Daza reasoned, would have to accede to his demands as abjectly as it had renounced its claims to Patagonia. In January 1879, when the Chilean company refused to pay the tax, Daza ordered the seizure of the corporation's holdings.

Bolivia's action, following on the heels of what many perceived as a capitulation to the Argentines, infuriated Chileans. Santiago might tolerate the loss of Patagonia to "white" Buenos Aires, but the Chilean government proved less generous toward the Indian republic to the north. Public demonstrations in Santiago and Valparaíso, incited by a jingoistic press, demanded war. As one minister privately noted, either the Moneda could act to protect the economic interests of its nationals, or the mob would violently depose the government. Consequently, Chile's president, Aníbal Pinto, ordered his fleet to occupy Antofagasta in February 1879. Within days of the Chilean landing, Bolivia declared war on Santiago.

Fighting only Bolivia did not unduly trouble the Moneda, but the possible involvement of Peru, with its substantial navy, did alarm the Chilean government. Precisely this possibility became increasingly probable. In 1873, Lima and La Paz had signed a secret military alliance. The Moneda had long known of the treaty's existence but chose to ignore it because it appeared that neither Peru nor Bolivia would invoke its provisions. When Bolivia declared war, it became possible that Daza might demand that Peru fulfill its treaty obligations. Pinto had hoped to avoid a war that would devastate Chile's already weakened economy. Although Pinto tried to appease Lima by offering various concessions in return for a pledge of neutrality, it became clear that most Peruvians favored Bolivia. Faced with mounting domestic pressure and aware that Peru was arming, Pinto formally demanded to know if Lima intended to honor its treaty commitments. In April 1879, the Peruvian envoy admitted that his nation would support Bolivia. Pinto had little choice: Chile declared war on Peru and Bolivia.

Since enormous distances separated Chile from its adversaries, control of the sea-lanes seemed a prerequisite for victory. Santiago moved first. Operating out of Antofagasta, its squadron blockaded Iquique, depriving Lima of its principal source of income, the export tax on nitrates. Given the financial consequences of the blockade, the Chileans expected the Peruvian fleet to leave the fortified harbor of Callao and counterattack. In May, the Peruvian fleet lifted the quarantine on Iquique by attacking two Chilean naval vessels guarding that port. During the battle, an inept Peruvian naval commander ran the *Independencia* aground. While the loss of one of Peru's two ironclads substantially weakened Peru's navy, Chile did not win complete maritime supremacy until October, when it captured Peru's remaining ironclad.

With its navy in control of the sea, Chile landed troops at two points on the coast of the nitrate-rich province of Tarapacá. After consolidating his position, the Chilean commander ordered various units inland to reconnoiter. In the meantime, Daza had marched with his troops from the Altiplano to the coast, where he would rendezvous with a Peruvian army that was moving north from Iquique to attack the Chileans. The Bolivian expeditionary force, riddled by illness, poorly equipped, and wretchedly led, quickly became demoralized. Instead of linking up with the Peruvians, Daza, without informing his allies, lost his resolve and returned to his base. Unaware of Daza's defection, the Peruvians marched north, unexpectedly colliding with Chilean forces. This surprise encounter initiated a campaign in which the Chileans successfully pushed the Peruvians out of Tarapacá. In February 1880, Santiago's forces invaded the province of Tacna. After a period of inaction, the Moneda's troops drove south from the port of Ilo, capturing first the city of Tacna and then the strategic harbor of Arica. By October, the Moneda was poised to attack Lima.

U.S. Mediation

At this crucial point in the war, Washington became actively involved in the War of the Pacific, an involvement that, when finally terminated, infuriated Chile, alienated Peru and Bolivia, and humiliated the United States. Europe had not looked with indifference upon the War of the Pacific. French capitalists had lent large sums of money to the Peruvian government, and various French citizens held Peruvian bonds. Paris, therefore, was distressed upon learning that the Chileans had captured Tarapacá's *salitreras*, which constituted Peru's only means of repaying its international debt. Great Britain also seemed concerned because British citizens had purchased shares of nitrate mines located in Tarapacá. Consequently, England sought French and German help in trying to impose a peace settlement in order to protect their nationals' investments. Fearing Washington's response, the Germans instead proposed that the United States act in concert with Berlin and London. Invoking the Monroe Doctrine and George Washington's dictum against entangling alliances, the White House rejected the suggestion.

Initially, some Chileans also favored a diplomatic rather than a military resolution of the war. Setting the terms for peace, however, proved a problem. The most generous Chileans demanded that the allies disarm as well as pay reparations. Until Lima and La Paz liquidated their debts, Santiago's troops should occupy Tarapacá and the littoral. The less forgiving demanded the annexation of Tarapacá, in part to punish Lima for starting the war and in part to buffer Chile from a possible future wave of Peruvian revanche.

Prolonging the war cost Chile additional funds and lives, reinforcing the proannexationist sentiments. Chileans increasingly insisted that they must retain Tarapacá, not only for security reasons but also because they believed that ceding the property constituted Lima's only way of liquidating its debts. The bankrupt Peruvian state, they argued, simply did not have the assets to pay any war reparations that the Moneda might impose. Lima had no choice but to cede Tarapacá to Santiago in order to liquidate its indemnity. Although defeated on the battlefield, the allies refused to accept Chile's territorial demands.

Given the disparity between the two belligerents' stances, mediation seemed impossible. Yet this is precisely what the United States would so maladroitly try to accomplish when Washington eventually offered its good offices to settle the war. Secretary of State William Evarts initially did not wish for the United States to become involved in the struggle. The prospect of European intervention, however, convinced Evarts that Washington had to act. In July 1880, he ordered his envoys to Peru and Chile to offer American good offices to settle the war.

Evarts's ministers—Isaac Christiancy in Peru, the pro-Chilean Thomas Osborn in Santiago, and Newton Pettis in Bolivia—shared none of the secretary of state's reluctance. As early as May 1880, Osborn had suggested to Christiancy that they try to bring the warring nations to the peace table. Thus when Osborn and Christiancy received Evarts's authorization, the American envoys redoubled their efforts. Osborn convinced President Pinto to accept America's good offices; Christiancy traveled to Santiago to confer with his colleague as well as with Pinto. Eventually the two U.S. ministers arranged for the belligerents to meet to discuss terms for ending the war.

Unfortunately, the peace conference appeared preordained to fail. During his visit to Santiago, Christiancy learned that Pinto insisted on Tarapacá as the price for peace. Inexplicably, he refused to relay this unpleasant fact to Peru's dictator, Nicolás Pierola. The belligerents, consequently, completely misunderstood each other's intent: the Chileans believed that Peru accepted territorial concessions as a prerequisite for peace discussions, and the Peruvians thought that Santiago had entered into the talks with no preconditions. The Bolivians were equally intransigent, demanding a return to the antebellum status quo before even considering the more substantive issues. Chile, however, refused to return to the pre-1879 frontier; it insisted upon retaining the Atacama. In what became the trademark of Washington's diplomatic efforts, the various ministers failed to communicate their ideas accurately or completely. Not surprisingly, the American attempt miscarried.

Some Chilean newspapers considered the U.S. mediation effort as sincere but misguided. Others opposed treating with Lima, which they feared would utilize the peace talks to rearm, thereby prolonging the war. Chile's battlefield victories, they argued, conferred upon it the right to dictate peace terms. Peru must cede Tarapacá as well as disband its armed forces so that Santiago's "domination of the Pacific . . . [would] be complete."[1] When the warring parties met on the USS *Lackawanna* in October 1880, the Chilean envoys demanded the cession of Tarapacá and Atacama, the payment of twenty million pesos, the return of Chilean property and war prizes, the abrogation of the once-secret 1873 military alliance, a Peruvian pledge not to fortify Arica, and the right for Chile to occupy Tacna and Arica until Peru fulfilled its treaty obligations. Appalled at the draconian terms, the Peruvian envoys refused to negotiate, and the Chileans, infuriated by Lima's intransigence, quit the meeting.

Failure, of course, had been virtually assured. Christiancy's refusal to transmit accurately the Moneda's position incensed not only the Chileans but also Osborn. Following the collapse of the Arica peace conference, the Chileans returned to war, capturing Lima in January 1881. With Bolivian forces isolated in the Andes and Chilean troops occupying most of Peru, peace seemed at hand. Unfortunately, the Chilean army would have to fight two more years before settling the dispute.

The struggle continued for a simple reason: no single individual ruled Peru. Pierola established a government in the Altiplano, while other regional leaders, such as Admiral Lizardo Montero and General Andrés Cáceres, created enclaves of armed resistance in the interior. Either the Moneda treated with Pierola, who refused to cede Tarapacá, Tacna, and Arica, or it had to find someone willing to accept the onerous responsibility for entering into a very unpopular peace treaty.

It seemed that the Moneda had found such a person. A rump Peruvian legislature elected a lawyer, Francisco García Calderón, provisional president, granting him the power to negotiate with Santiago. The Moneda, anxious to speed the peace process, rushed to embrace García Calderón, giving him a seat of government in the provincial town of Magdalena, permission to form an army, and all the trappings of glory—but not the power of a chief of state.

Just as the Chileans seemed on the verge of settling with a demoralized Peru, the Americans resurrected their moribund effort to mediate the war. Newly elected president James Garfield selected James G. Blaine as his secretary of state. Except for a brief trip to Europe, the Plumed Knight of Maine possessed no diplomatic training. He had won his post not because of his international expertise but because of his domestic political skills. The new secretary of state was also an outspoken advocate of U.S. economic expansion, especially in Latin America. Before nations could trade, he reasoned, tranquility had to reign. Peace might not guarantee prosperity, but it would provide a nurturing economic environment. A Latin America at peace facilitated trade, benefiting both the United States and the other hemispheric nations.

Ensuring hemispheric stability, Blaine believed, was a suitable mission for the New World's oldest state and the government that had proclaimed the Monroe Doctrine. The Latin American republics were, after all, Washington's "younger sisters."[2] Hence, the United States had a moral obligation to prevent outside interference in hemispheric affairs and to protect Latin American nations from each other. Blaine, in short, amplified the Monroe Doctrine. Either the United States acted unilaterally to ensure domestic political order to Latin America, or it would "give way to foreign governments that are willing to accept the responsibility of the great trust and secure enhanced influence and numberless advantages resulting from such a philanthropic and beneficent course."[3]

Racism clearly influenced Blaine's attitudes. Like many of his contemporaries, the secretary of state firmly believed in the supremacy of the Anglo-Saxon people, whose presence, he was sure, invariably brought benefits in their wake. And since Latins were a "race . . . of hot temper, quick to take affront, ready to avenge a wrong whether real or fancied," they needed the United States to restrain their impulses.[4]

Chile's struggle with its neighbors provided Blaine an opportunity to implement his ideas. Regrettably, the American diplomat interpreted the War of the Pacific in almost Manichaean terms. The struggle was not a Latin American conflict, he argued, but "an English war on Peru, with Chili (sic) as the instrument. . . . Chili (sic) would never have gone into this war one inch but for the backing of English capital."[5] By intervening on behalf of Peru, the United States could repel British imperialism while simultaneously assuring the "peaceful maintenance of the status quo of the American Commonwealth . . . the very essence of their policy of harmonious alliance for self preservation."[6]

As the first step in accomplishing this goal, the secretary of state had to save Peru from dismemberment. Against the advice of Christiancy and Lima's diplomatic corps, Blaine recognized the García Calderón government in early 1881. While this act was unwise, his next step— appointing a man of questionable ability to serve as minister to Peru —proved disastrous. In truth, none of Washington's representatives to the belligerents seemed qualified to protect U.S. interests. Its envoy to Santiago was Judson Kilpatrick, a former Civil War general who had married into a Chilean family and whose ties to that country thereby clouded his judgment and perhaps compromised his objectivity. But Kilpatrick appeared to be a model of virtue in comparison with his colleague in Lima, the alcoholic and allegedly corrupt General Stephen J. Hurlburt. Blaine instructed the two emissaries to resolve the war as expeditiously as possible, a task complicated by Santiago's annexationist demands.

Ironically, Blaine never disputed the victorious Chileans' right to seize Tarapacá as compensation. Citing the recent Alsace-Lorraine dispute, he argued that territorial annexation, by fostering international tensions, created a poor environment for business. Hence, if Santiago would accept a monetary indemnity instead of land, it would contribute to a "more permanent peace." In that spirit, Blaine instructed

Hurlburt to try to persuade Santiago that "the cession of territory should be the subject of negotiation and not the condition precedent upon which alone negotiations will commence."[7]

Hurlburt played a crucial role in eroding Washington's prestige and in exacerbating strained diplomatic relations between Chile and the United States. Virtually from the onset of negotiations, he opposed Chilean demands for territorial concessions. Peru, he argued, possessed sufficient funds to pay a monetary indemnity. Hence, Chile should not seek to take Tarapacá. Hurlburt subsequently claimed that Blaine had verbally authorized him to tell Chile that Washington opposed its annexing property, a charge the secretary of state denied. Hurlburt apparently communicated his personal and unofficial views to Admiral Patricio Lynch, commander of the Chilean army occupying Peru, informing him that Chile would become an international pariah if it pressed its claims for land.[8] When Lynch informed his superiors of his dealings with Hurlburt, the Moneda was incensed. The U.S. minister managed to offend not merely Chileans but Peruvians as well. He became involved in the mare's nest of Peru's domestic politics by criticizing Pierola—whom he described as a despot—becoming García Calderón's booster, and urging all Peruvians to support the Magdalena government. He even encouraged the U.S. minister to Buenos Aires to urge the Argentines to recognize García Calderón as well.

Hurlburt committed a more egregious blunder when he negotiated an agreement with García Calderón granting the United States a coaling station in the port of Chimbote. Because the proposed deal called for the American minister to own a substantial interest in the local railroad, many Chileans believed that personal greed had influenced Hurlburt's actions. Kilpatrick valiantly tried to neutralize his colleague's gaffe by issuing a statement promising U.S. objectivity. The Chilean press seemed perplexed. They approvingly noted that Kilpatrick, as well as most of the American press, disavowed Hurlburt's actions, but his less than diplomatic dealings made it clear that he was hardly an honest broker. More than a few Chileans believed that Blaine would profit from Hurlburt's dealings. Others feared that the United States wanted to establish a protectorate over Peru. It became clear that American involvement, if improperly executed, might cost Washington friends as well as endanger its economic relations with Latin America.

Other factors, in addition to Hurlburt's activities, compromised, if not doomed, Washington's peace efforts. From his Andean redoubt, Pierola had organized a new government. Peru now possessed two presidents—Pierola and García Calderón. García Calderón, emboldened by Washington's opposition to Lima's territorial concessions, refused to allow Santiago to dismember Peru. To avoid ceding land, García Calderón hoped to borrow enough money so that Lima could pay Chile's war reparations. This process proved complicated. Given Lima's wretched credit rating and the fact that Chile occupied the nation's richest province, most international bankers seemed reluctant to invest in Peru. García Calderón, however, discovered some potential economic saviors. The Credit Industriel, a French corporation with powerful American contacts, offered to service Peru's international obligations, liquidate any indemnity that Chile might levy, and provide Lima an annual income. In return, the company demanded the right, under American protection, to exploit Tarapacá's mineral resources.

A few years before, Evarts had received similar proposals. While opposing the idea of an American protectorate, he nonetheless forwarded the proposal to Christiancy. Blaine had been apprised of the plan by the Credit Industriel's American agent, the brother of the speaker of the House of Representatives. The secretary had transmitted the news to Hurlburt, with the notation that the United States might, under certain circumstances, try to arrange an agreement between Lima and the French corporation if such an agreement preserved Peru's territorial integrity and pacified Chile. The Credit Industriel's prospects improved when the U.S. minister to France, Levi Morton, obtained the right for the company to market Peru's guano in the United States. Because of this concession, the French president, Jules Grevy, who had ties to the Credit Industriel, urged Morton to convince the United States to intervene on behalf of Peru in conjunction with other European powers. Morton refused.

Yet another claim was that of a French-born, naturalized American citizen, John Landreau, who contended that he had inherited his deceased brother's mineral rights to Tarapacá. Landreau had lost his case in Peru's courts. Rather than accept this judgment, Landreau assigned his claim to the newly formed Peruvian Company, headed by a notoriously unsavory speculator, Jacob Shipherd, who hoped to use his Washington political connections to advance the corporation's cause. Like the Credit Industriel, the Peruvian Company offered a way for Lima to avoid economic emasculation. In return for paying Lima's reparations, the Peruvian Company would acquire the right to mine Tarapacá's guano and nitrates. Peru might be indentured for decades, but it would, at least, preserve its territorial integrity.

These potential sources of financing delighted Hurlburt as well as Blaine. García Calderón became so heartened that he refused to cede Tarapacá to Santiago. Faced with this unexpected resistance, Admiral Patricio Lynch moved against the suddenly recalcitrant Peruvian. First, the Chilean confiscated García Calderón's treasury; then he reduced García Calderón's control over his largely ceremonial army. Painfully aware that his days were numbered, García Calderón requested that his legislature approve Admiral Lizardo Montero as his successor and issued a statement reaffirming his opposition to ceding any territory to Chile. Lynch responded by arresting García Calderón in November, exiling him to Chile's south.

Removing García Calderón did not solve the Moneda's political dilemma. Henceforth, the Chilean government had to face a legion of pretenders to power: Pierola, Admiral Montero—still entrenched in his mountain redoubt in Arequipa—and General Andrés Cáceres. Although victorious on the battlefield, Chile seemed on the verge of losing the peace. The situation became so vexing that the Moneda considered negotiating with the once-despised Pierola. As Santiago pondered what policy to adopt, resistance to Chile's occupation spread. Guerrilla bands, *montoneros,* began ambushing Chilean units in the Peruvian countryside and even murdering soldiers on Lima's streets.

Santiago's relations with Washington worsened. Hurlburt, who considered the arrest of García Calderón as an insult to the United States, redoubled his efforts on behalf of Lima. The American envoy continued meddling in Peru's domestic politics, first recognizing Montero as president and then urging Cáceres to support the admiral in his attempt to stop Santiago from disfiguring Peru. The American envoy even informed Peru's legislature that the United States opposed Chile's territorial aspirations.

Angered by Hurlburt's unauthorized negotiation of the Chimbote coaling station concession, Blaine realized that he could no longer trust his envoy in Peru. He had also lost confidence in Kilpatrick because of the minister's ill health. (Some claimed that the U.S. minister became so infirm that his Chilean wife was running the American legation. Kilpatrick died in December 1881, receiving a state funeral, presumably as a mark of respect to the deceased envoy and to his nation.) The combination of Kilpatrick's demise and Hurlburt's bombast forced Blaine to act. As a temporary solution, and in order to obtain a more objective reading of the situation, Blaine dispatched two new envoys to Chile: William Trescot, a career diplomat with limited experience in Latin America, and Blaine's son Walker. Among his tasks, Trescot had to determine if Chile had arrested García Calderón in order to demonstrate its disdain of Washington and U.S. mediation efforts. If so, then Blaine had an excuse to intervene. Preserving Peru's territorial integrity, however, was the American diplomat's most important mission. Blaine, therefore, ordered Trescot to offer Washington's good offices to Santiago. If Chile spurned U.S. efforts, Blaine warned, the United States would convoke an inter-American congress to pressure the Moneda to change its policies. Chile's persistent rejection of Washington's good offices, the secretary of state intimated, could mean war.

Blaine's aggressive diplomatic effort first mystified and then infuriated Santiago. Most Chileans considered their annexation of Tarapacá to be eminently reasonable: since the *salitreras* could not have been developed without Chilean labor and capital, Santiago had a moral right to the territory. Chilean occupation, moreover, had brought good government and economic progress to the former Peruvian province. Thus, if the Moneda capitulated to U.S. pressure, then it was abandoning an almost sacred duty. Finally, Chile's defeat of the Peruvian army conferred upon the victors the right to annex the land. Surely the United States, which had feasted upon the territory of its neighbors, particularly Mexico, should understand and sympathize with the Moneda's reasoning.

Seeking an explanation for Blaine's actions, Chilean newspapers accused the secretary of state of acting on behalf of financial interests by subordinating U.S. foreign policy to his "sordid cupidity [and] the mean wish for personal wealth." Certainly Chileans did not believe that the White House enjoyed any mandate to intervene. The boundary problem was a local affair, and Chile should be respected as the "master of its own house." Indeed, Washington's policies seemed calculated to provoke rather than prevent European intervention. Some feared that the United States wished to establish a protectorate over Peru in order to convert it into a base "of Northamerican power and wealth" from which the United States would expand outward to envelop all of Latin America. By opposing Washington's meddling, Chile reasoned, it was safeguarding the entire continent.[9]

The Trescot mission never fulfilled its original purpose. A disgruntled office-seeker mortally wounded President Garfield. His successor, Chester Alan Arthur, replaced Blaine with a new secretary of state, Frederick Frelinghuysen. Although he was not reluctant to protect American interests, Frelinghuysen's vision of the U.S. role in Latin America seemed less ambitious than that of his predecessor. He was certainly less energetic than Blaine. The new secretary of state, for example, waited a month after receiving Senate confirmation before assuming the duties of his office. Then, perhaps fatigued by this effort, he went on vacation. Happily, Frelinghuysen's second in command, Bancroft Davis, acted more dynamically. Examining Blaine's policies, Davis concluded that "we are on the highway to war for the benefit of about as nasty a set of people as ever gathered about a Washington department."[10] Prompted by his subordinate, Frelinghuysen charged Trescot to ignore Blaine's confrontational instructions: Washington should not break diplomatic ties with Santiago, attempt to dictate a peace settlement, or convoke an inter-American congress to arrange a peaceful end to the War of the Pacific.

Not surprisingly, Frelinghuysen's appointment pleased many Chileans who considered Blaine's actions as atypical of Washington's traditional policies. Greed, not principle, they claimed, had motivated the former secretary of state. Blaine's dismissal by Arthur indicated that the White House had adopted a more balanced policy. One newspaper urged the president to discharge Hurlburt and Charles Adams, the envoy to Bolivia who, by misleading the allies with false promises of U.S. intervention, had unnecessarily prolonged the war.

Regrettably, Trescot and the younger Blaine were the last to hear of Washington's policy shift. The State Department had sent new instructions via ordinary mail. Chile's minister to the United States, Marcial Martínez, learning of the White House's diplomatic about-face, immediately wired the news to Foreign Minister José Manuel Balmaceda. Consequently the Moneda knew that the State Department had changed its policies two weeks before the envoys received official notification.

The American diplomatic mission was fatally compromised. Kilpatrick's death left the American legation without a minister and Trescot and Blaine without any information about Chile. Worse, the two envoys had to suffer the indignity of learning from Balmaceda of Washington's abrupt shift in their instructions. Trescot met with the Chilean foreign minister, manfully trying to resolve the outstanding issues. Balmaceda assured the American that the Moneda had intended no insult to Washington when it jailed García Calderón. He also explained that Chile deserved Tarapacá because its nationals had developed the area and because its army had captured the land in the war. But Tarapacá alone, the minister warned, would no longer satisfy Santiago's appetite. To defray the cost of an additional year of war, the Moneda demanded not only Tarapacá but also the right to occupy Tacna and Arica for ten years and to exploit the guano deposits of the Lobos Islands until Peru paid an indemnity of twenty million pesos. In delivering what was tantamount to an ultimatum, Balmaceda intimated to the befuddled American diplomat that the Moneda was prepared to be flexible.

The result of the diplomatic meeting was the Viña del Mar Protocol, a communiqué in which Chile disavowed any intention to insult the United States when it arrested García Calderón. In return, the White House formally abjured any idea of armed intervention in Santiago's dispute with Lima. Chile graciously stated its willingness to accept U.S. mediation, but only under the condition that Peru cede Tarapacá. While Chile would occupy the Lobos Islands, it promised to share with Peru the revenues generated by the exploitation of the local guano deposits. Trescot did extract one concession: Chile could occupy Tacna and Arica for ten years, but the Moneda agreed to reduce, from twenty to between five and nine million pesos, the monetary indemnity it demanded from Peru. The U.S. position, largely the result of Blaine's mishandling, had deteriorated because Washington lacked the ability to force the Moneda to moderate its draconian demands. Chile's navy, the local American naval commander dolefully communicated to Washington, could easily overpower the U.S. fleet. If Washington wished to influence the diplomatic situation, it would have to do so by cajoling, not threatening, the Moneda.

Within these limitations, Trescot still attempted to settle the war. In March 1882, he traveled to Lima to convince the Peruvians to be more amenable. By the time Trescot reached Peru's capital, Hurlburt had died. His demise removed one obstacle to a settlement, but another remained: no one had emerged in Peru who would negotiate a peace treaty. So Trescot trekked into the Altiplano to parley with Montero, who informed him that, while he would accept the loss of Tarapacá, he would not cede Tacna or Arica. After relaying the admiral's reply, Trescot tried to convince the Moneda to recognize Montero's government. Perhaps remembering the García Calderón fiasco, Santiago refused to accept Montero's demands, denouncing Trescot for acting as Montero's messenger and for suggesting that Santiago sign an armistice. Essentially Lima's credibility remained a problem: the Moneda did not believe that Peru would surrender Tarapacá. The war of words continued.

Two enormous diplomatic hurdles confronted Washington: after helping form a government in Peru, it would have to convince Lima's new leader to cede land to Chile. Ironically, the only way for Washington to achieve this goal would be by making it clear to Lima that the United States no longer would defend Peru against the Moneda's demands for territory. As part of his new policy, Frelinghuysen replaced his diplomatic representatives to the belligerents. This time he chose wisely: Dr. Cornelius Logan, who had earlier served as minister to Chile, returned to Santiago. His colleague in Peru was another former minister with experience in Latin America, James R. Partridge. George Maney, who had also served in South America, held the post in La Paz.

Frelinghuysen tried to cover both sides of the dispute. He instructed Logan to convince Santiago to moderate its territorial demands and ordered Partridge to encourage Lima to prepare itself to cede more land than just Tarapacá. Both envoys received identical briefs: to inform their respective governments that Washington would not attempt to curb Chile's appetite for Peruvian land. These instructions pleased neither minister. Partridge, believing that no Peruvian leader would accept the Moneda's demands, feared that European nations would intervene. Meanwhile Logan futilely attempted to convince García Calderón to accept the Moneda's conditions. While the former president appeared prepared to tolerate the loss of Tarapacá, he refused to yield on the demand for Tacna and Arica. He also insisted that if Chile annexed Tarapacá it must do so subject to settlement of any outstanding economic claims.

Another complication developed: Partridge, like his predecessor Hurlburt, moved from being an envoy to Lima to becoming its partisan. Thus, instead of cooperating with Logan, Partridge began to quarrel with his colleague. He wrote to García Calderón, suggesting that the Peruvian ignore Logan. Meanwhile, the desperate Logan beseeched Admiral Montero to convince García Calderón to accept Chile's terms. When Logan's letter became public, it seemed as if Washington's minister to Chile had become the Moneda's paladin. As the situation became more convoluted, Washington became less sure about what it should do. In late 1882, President Arthur reiterated that the United States would not exert itself to resolve the Chilean-Peruvian dispute. Lima should not expect Washington's protection.

Always the diehard, Partridge refused to abandon his pro-Peruvian policy. Working in consort with various European diplomats, he fashioned a new solution: they would issue a statement opposing Chile's dismembering of Peru and calling for a joint U.S. and European intervention. By inviting European nations to become involved in the affairs of the Western Hemisphere, Partridge's proposal simultaneously violated Arthur's stated policies and also the Monroe Doctrine. Frelinghuysen, therefore, immediately relieved Partridge of his post. His dismissal finally convinced Lima that it had no alternative. Their champion had gone. Maney subsequently lost his posting to La Paz, apparently for financial misconduct. The implacable Logan had won the game of diplomatic musical chairs.

Peru ended the war when General Miguel Iglesias, who indicated that he opposed continued resistance to Santiago, came to power. The Chileans responded by helping Iglesias create a government and by providing him with the facade, although not the substance, of power. Various European nations recognized the new regime. Seeing that the general constituted the only viable alternative, Logan urged Washington to abandon García Calderón and recognize Iglesias.

By late 1883, the situation seemed to be moving toward closure. Peru had managed to patch together a government. Weary of the bloody war, Chile moderated its demands: if Peru ceded Tarapacá, then Chile would control Tacna and Arica for only ten years. After a decade of Chilean occupation, the two nations would conduct a plebiscite to determine the status of the disputed lands. The winner would receive title to the territory and pay the loser ten million silver pesos.

In October 1883, Chilean troops defeated the army of Andrés Cáceres. Finally free of internal opposition, Iglesias quickly signed the Treaty of Ancón, terminating the war. Peru's surrender placed Bolivia in the uncomfortable position of being Chile's only belligerent. Initially, Santiago tried to woo La Paz. When this tactic failed, it prepared to launch an invasion. Bolivia's leaders finally saw the light: they signed an armistice in 1884. The War of the Pacific had ended.

Santiago's triumph in the War of the Pacific marked a new threshold of its grandeur. For a second time, Chile had defeated the Peruvians and Bolivians. With the strongest fleet in the Pacific and a veteran army, Chile emerged as the Southern Cone's premier power. In triumph, Chileans fabricated a myth that they were, if not racially pure, then at least genetically superior to Peruvians and Bolivians. While the nation's elites were undeniably white, the mass of Chileans was not. Faced with the uncomfortable reality of being a mestizo, if not an Indian, nation, Chileans took consolation in the fact that they were a fusion of the European and the heroic Araucanian Indians. Although Chile's Indians had been denigrated when they opposed the central government's pacification of the south, their ferocity suddenly became an important element in forging the nation's cultural self-identity.

Many Chileans considered Peruvians and Bolivians racially inferior to themselves. Not only did black and even Asian blood taint their collective gene pool, but their Indians simply could not match the heroic Araucanians. The product of promiscuous interbreeding, the result was not the fierce Chilean *roto* but the Andean *cholo*—a weak, effeminate, almost subhuman creature of diminished intellect and questionable sexual preference.[11] Such nations were clearly incapable of absorbing the benefits of Western society. Peru, as one newspaper noted, was a "savage dressed like a European. Civilization, culture, progress of the century are phrases found on their lips but not in their spirit."[12]

Genetic inferiority simultaneously doomed Peru and Bolivia and justified Chile's civilizing mission. Its army of occupation had established a stable government of "probity, work, and liberty" that had regenerated Peru.[13] Since Lima prospered under Santiago's rule, many Chileans sincerely believed that the former viceroyalty's citizens preferred that the Moneda regulate their affairs rather than endure the uncertainty of home rule. Others suggested that Santiago annex the vanquished country. If by invading Peru Chile had introduced the benefits of Western culture, then its continued occupation "guarantee[d] order, tranquility, and a powerful impulse for progress and welfare of the sister republics of the Pacific." The war, moreover, demonstrated Santiago's moral superiority to the United States. Having imposed peace on its neighbors in defiance of Washington, the Moneda had proved that Chile merited the title Empress of the Pacific.[14]

3 Chile Confronts the United States, 1884–1891

After the War of the Pacific, a hostile ambivalence characterized American attitudes toward Santiago. If U.S. writers described post-1881 Chile as a predominantly mestizo nation, they acknowledged that its oligarchy, at least, was composed of "pure blooded descendents of the Spanish."[1] Although racially tainted—and hence, by implication, inferior to the United States—Chile nonetheless seemed superior to its neighbors. Santiago, at least, had avoided black slavery with its presumably adverse impact on the nation's gene pool. The absence of Negroes provided only partial relief because Chile's Indian heritage still condemned its citizens to a life of immorality, sexual license, recklessness, gambling, and profligate spending. As one American noted, most Chileans lived "as though they had never emerged from the savage state."[2]

But America's supposed racial purity provided little solace because the Moneda clearly had bested Washington in the diplomatic conflict over the War of the Pacific. Some Americans believed that Santiago would have retreated if the White House had not abandoned Blaine's policies.[3] Instead a supposedly "craven" President Arthur had permitted the Moneda to administer "to the United States a snub as complete and successful as was ever given by one state to another."[4]

Hence Chile emerged from the War of the Pacific as a potential threat to the United States. Congressmen periodically spun tales of horror, predicting that, with its stronger navy, Chile "can, if she pleases, at this moment, command the Pacific Coast of the United States," holding hostage California and Oregon. "Any one of her three ironclads," noted Albert Browne, "can sink every wooden vessel in our wretched navy, and the contrast between her ability and our impotence is a daily source of shame to every citizen in our country who resides or travels between Panama and Cape Horn."[5] Worse, working in conjunction with the British and French, Chile could frustrate Washington's attempt to control the isthmus, thereby threatening to eclipse the United States as the Pacific's preeminent power.

Chile also viewed the United States as a rival. But unlike the White House, Santiago possessed a strong navy. Following the War of the Pacific, the Moneda modernized its fleet, purchasing additional vessels, including the battleship *Esmeralda*, which the American *Army and Navy Journal* stated "could destroy our entire Navy, ship by ship, and never be touched." Clearly the Chilean navy planned to go in harm's way. As President José Manuel Balmaceda stated, "Chile should be able to resist on its own territory any possible coalition, and if it cannot succeed in attaining the naval power of the great powers, it should at least prove, on the base of a secure port and a fleet proportionate to its resources, that there is no possible profit in starting a war against the Republic of Chile."[6]

An 1885 isthmian crisis clearly illustrated Chile's aggressiveness. When unrest in the province of Panama threatened Colombia's stability, units of the U.S. navy occupied Colón. The Moneda believed that Washington planned to capitalize on the political turmoil in order to seize land for its proposed canal across Panama and, perhaps, to move against Ecuador if Quito opposed American expansion. Chile dispatched the *Esmeralda* to Panama to restore order. Publicly the Moneda claimed that it was acting in the name of Latin American solidarity. Privately, the Chilean government secretly commanded Captain Juan López, the *Esmeralda*'s captain, to take any action he deemed necessary in order to stop the U.S. fleet from annexing the Colombian province. López occupied Panama, refusing to leave until after the Americans evacuated Colón. When the United States withdrew from the Colombian city, the *Esmeralda* sailed to Guayaquil in order to prevent the U.S. fleet from attempting to cow the Ecuadorean government. While Benjamín Vicuña Mackenna may have exaggerated when he crowed that the Moneda had forced the Americans to retreat, the Panamanian incident indicated the extent to which Santiago would go in order to ensure its Pacific hegemony.[7]

Three years later, Chile annexed Easter Island, a dot of land located some two thousand miles west of Valparaíso. Various Chileans had advocated seizing the isle, believing that it would facilitate Chile's trade with Australasia as well as serve as an advance sentinel to warn the mainland of an impending attack. By occupying the island, Santiago joined the imperial nations. It also stopped the slow penetration of American imperialism. Vicuña Mackenna, whose florid prose once excoriated American materialism, rhetorically inquired if "our nation . . . a comparatively small republic but one which with great sacrifices maintains a fleet sufficiently powerful to inspire fear in the defenseless coasts, should . . . remain without a piece of stone in the continual and inequitable division of the Pacific?"[8]

Chile's newfound sense of self galled those Americans who saw their nation's destiny inextricably linked to the economic penetration of the Pacific Basin. Alfred Thayer Mahan's new naval doctrine reinforced the lesson of the War of the Pacific: the United States needed a powerful fleet to repulse potential enemies, such as Chile, and to safeguard its commercial interests in Asia and the Pacific. Perhaps inspired by the Chilean example, the United States built a large fleet. Consequently, the next time Santiago and Washington clashed, it would be the Chileans, not the Americans, who retreated.

The 1891 Civil War

Between January and September 1891, a civil war convulsed Chile. When the struggle ended, the victorious rebels—called either Congressionalists or Constitutionalists—had driven President José Manuel Balmaceda from the Moneda. Justifiably fearful for his life, the luckless former leader fled to the uncertain hospitality of the Argentine embassy, where he remained until 18 September. The following day, when his term of office expired officially, he committed suicide. In October the *Baltimore* incident occurred, Chile's second diplomatic confrontation with the United States in less than a decade.

The 1891 civil war marked the end of an regime that, at its inception, appeared promising. Balmaceda had assumed control of a nation whose coffers bulged with the newly acquired wealth of the *salitreras* and whose armed forces made it the Pacific's premier power. Within a few years, the Balmaceda government first degenerated into partisan squabbling and then stumbled into a savage domestic conflict. The historical judgment on Balmaceda still remains divided: his admirers revere him as an economic nationalist, a man who planned to return the control of Chile's nitrate mines to the nation; his critics depict him as a scheming, self-serving politician, a loose political cannon.

Balmaceda possessed both vision and energy. He planned to re-structure Chile by launching various public works projects in order to diversify the nation's economy. Completion of these enterprises, however, required a constant flow of revenue from the nitrate mines. Although Chile's *salitreros* controlled the world's nitrate market, they did not enjoy complete economic security. Periodically the world econ-omy slowed, reducing demand for raw materials. The nitrate indus-try could not escape world market forces. During bad times, *salitre* prices, like those of other commodities, declined. Producers generally responded by forming cartels that increased the value of nitrates by restricting production. While this policy benefited the *salitreros,* it ad-versely affected the government, because lowered output diminished the export taxes the Moneda collected.

Such a situation developed during the Balmaceda regime. The world depression of 1890 savaged world commodity prices, effectively undermining the president's economic program. When the Nitrate Combination—a cartel composed of various *salitreros*—reduced out-put, it endangered the president's public works projects and limited his ability to appease his political cronies by dispensing patronage. Balmaceda became fixated upon one English capitalist, John Thomas North, for exercising so much control of the nitrate industry. The president bitterly denounced the foreign owner of Chile's *salitreras* for taking "the profit of native wealth . . . to give to other lands and un-known people the treasures of our soil, our own property, and the riches we require."[9]

Balmaceda's complaints were not without merit. Foreigners did

dominate the nitrate trade, the British alone owning more than 50 percent of Chile's *salitreras*. Balmaceda objected to this situation, arguing that Chilean capitalists should control the country's crucial mining sector. But Balmaceda erred in believing that all Chileans supported his policies. The northern mining interests and their economic allies in the central valley shared congruent, albeit not identical, goals with the British *salitreros* and businessmen. Both groups were too enmeshed in the North Atlantic economy to change the system. The *salitreros* and the economic groups tied to the north, fearing that the president might turn on them, became alienated from the Moneda. In January 1891, their support proved crucial to Balmaceda's political enemies.

It would be simplistic to presume that only economic grievances precipitated the 1891 revolution. Balmaceda's political policies had become so heavy-handed that the president first disillusioned and then antagonized many of his supporters. For example, Balmaceda attempted to rule without seeking the legislature's advice or consent. When he recognized that he could not muzzle his congressional critics, he shamelessly manipulated the 1888 congressional elections. Balmaceda often authorized public works projects or created civil service positions without seeking congressional approval. Finally, it became clear that he would install a crony as president. Eventually the disenchanted legislators demanded that Balmaceda permit the congress to share in the decision-making process.

By 1890, the hostility between the president and his congress became palpable. In October, Balmaceda submitted his budget for the legislature's approval. The opposition withheld its consent until the president promised to institute political reforms and cease meddling in the electoral process. When Balmaceda demurred, the congress, as the 1833 constitution provided, refused to authorize his budget for 1891. Faced with what he perceived as legislative obdurateness, Balmaceda unilaterally declared that he would simply use the 1890 budget for 1891. While cutting the economic Gordian knot, the president's decree was clearly illegal. Furious that Balmaceda had both flaunted established political custom and violated the constitution, his opposition rebelled in January 1891.

The revolt divided the nation as well as the as the armed forces. The army's officer corps, with a few exceptions, remained loyal to the Moneda, but the navy, under the leadership of Captain Jorge Montt, joined the Congressionalist cause. On 7 January, many of Balmaceda's legislative enemies escaped aboard the rebels' naval vessels, sailing to the nitrate enclave of Iquique, where the insurgents established a temporary capital. By controlling Iquique, the insurgents could simultaneously deprive the Moneda of the revenue generated by the sale of *salitre* and guarantee themselves enough income to finance the uprising.

Maritime supremacy proved as decisive to winning the 1891 civil war as it had the War of the Pacific. Dominating the sea-lanes would provide access to weapons and expose the central valley to invasion. Thus, Balmaceda's navy, which consisted of only a few vessels, futilely tried to gain possession of two cruisers under construction in French shipyards. While these ships could not equal the combined strength of the Congressionalist fleet, they would nonetheless give the Moneda some naval clout. Conversely, the Congressionalists did not need ironclads, but more mundane weapons: rifles, artillery, and ammunition. Consequently, both belligerents tried simultaneously to obtain weapons while denying their enemies access to armaments.

Inevitably this competition, as well as the fighting, involved the United States in Chile's civil war. In their quest for arms, the Congressionalists sent representatives, including the Yale-educated Ricardo Trumbull, to the United States. State Department officials refused to parley with these men. Although spurned by the government, Trumbull used the good offices of the W. R. Grace Company to purchase a large quantity of rifles and small arms ammunition, which he shipped to California for transport to Chile.

When Balmaceda's envoy to Washington, Prudencio Lazcano, learned of this transaction, he asked the State Department to prevent the export of Trumbull's weapons. James G. Blaine, secretary of state for the second time, refused to intervene on the grounds that American law did not prohibit the sale of weapons. Lazcano persevered, hiring the services of a prominent lawyer, John W. Foster, to argue

Balmaceda's cause. Foster warned Washington that its failure to act might subject the United States to the same legal liabilities that befell Britain when it failed to stop the sailing of a Confederate raider, the *Alabama*. This argument proved persuasive. Fearful of problems, the government embargoed the weapons until it could investigate the situation.

As the lawyers wrangled, the weapons arrived in San Diego, where local agents loaded them onto a coastal steamer, the *Robert and Minnie*, for transfer to the *Itata*. This vessel, falsely described as belonging to the Grace Company, was in fact a Chilean ship. It had sailed under naval escort from a rebel port to San Diego in order to bring the weapons back for the Congressionalist army. Anxious to delay the transfer of the arms, U.S. authorities sent a marshal to board the *Itata* and made preparations to seize the *Robert and Minnie*, whose captain cleverly retreated to the safety of Mexico's territorial waters. Capitalizing on the confusion, the *Itata*'s captain took the U.S. marshal hostage and sailed out of San Diego. The two vessels later rendezvoused off San Clemente, where the *Robert and Minnie* off-loaded its cargo onto the *Itata*, which sailed for Chile.

Washington had ample cause for anger: not only had the *Itata*'s captain kidnapped a government official—who was put ashore once the vessel had cleared the harbor—but he had mocked U.S. courts by sailing in violation of a court injunction. Worse, the Balmaceda government could still hold the United States liable for any damages caused should the weapons reach the Congressionalists. Consequently, the State Department ordered the USS *Charleston* to force the *Itata* and its cargo to return to the United States.

The ensuing chase proved futile, because the *Itata* reached Iquique before the *Charleston*. The Chilean captain might as well have remained in San Diego. Fearful of antagonizing Washington, the Congressionalist foreign minister, Isidoro Errázuriz, ordered the *Itata* to return to San Diego to face outstanding charges. (Federal courts subsequently exonerated the Chileans, allowing the ship to return to its home port.) But the incident inflamed Chilean public opinion. Congressionalist critics described Washington's attempt to intercept the arms ship as behavior worthy of the Barbary pirates. One observer argued that by preventing the timely arrival of the weapons, the Americans had delayed the rebel offensive.[10]

Regrettably, the *Itata* affair was but one of many incidents that tainted American-Chilean relations. As Balmaceda's troops prepared for an expected rebel landing at Valparaíso, the commander of the U.S. fleet, Admiral George Brown, unwittingly precipitated another diplomatic dispute. Anxious to provide Washington with the latest intelligence on the progress of the war, Brown ordered his ship, the USS *San Francisco*, to sea. After confirming that rebel units had gone ashore near Valparaíso, Brown returned to port, where he sent a coded message informing Washington of the insurgent's troop movements. The Congressionalists subsequently alleged that Brown had warned Balmaceda about the invasion and that the president, capitalizing on the admiral's information, reinforced the units defending Valparaíso. Thus Brown's duplicity, they believed, caused the rebel forces to suffer greater casualties than expected. In fact, Balmaceda's officers had learned of the landing almost twelve hours before the *San Francisco* docked in Valparaíso. The U.S. minister considered the attacks insulting "to the navy and the flag of the United States."[11] But nothing the admiral said could dispel the image of the United States as troublemaker.

Unfortunately the Brown affair was not the last American faux pas of the 1891 civil war. Before the rebellion, a U.S. corporation, the Central and South American Cable Company, had laid a submarine cable connecting Santiago with Lima. When the war began, the Congressionalists severed the line at Iquique, cutting Santiago's communications with the north. Anxious to restore service, Balmaceda promised to allow the company to string a telegraph line connecting Chile and Argentina, with the proviso that the corporation restore service between Callao, Peru, and Chile. Tantalized by the prospect of winning a new concession, the U.S. concern complied. Operating in international waters, under the protection of U.S. naval vessels and with the authorization of the Balmaceda government, the cable company cut the line at Iquique, splicing in a new section. Consequently, while linking Santiago with Peru, it sundered the cable connection to the Congressionalist headquarters. Although legal, and carried out at the behest of the Moneda, this act merely aggravated the rebels, who saw it as yet another example of American favoritism.

Obviously, many of these vexing issues would not have emerged if Balmaceda had triumphed. Precisely because his cause failed, however, each incident constituted a provocation, if not an insult, to the victorious Congressionalists, who interpreted Washington's behavior as part of a concerted U.S. plan to thwart Chile.

Perhaps an able diplomat could have neutralized the damage. Lamentably, the U.S. minister proved to be a singularly maladroit defender of American interests. Patrick Egan, an Irish-born, naturalized U.S. citizen, had served as minister to Santiago for three years. Egan did not enjoy high regard in his adopted homeland. Numerous American newspapers, including the *Nation* and *Harper's*, described the envoy as a thief and a Tammany Hall hack. Despite his poor reputation, Egan had done some good work in Chile. He was a specialist in flour milling, and he shared some of his knowledge with local Chilean millers. Egan also developed close ties to the Balmaceda regime. Indeed, some have argued that his proximity to Balmaceda clouded the U.S. envoy's judgment, leading him to side with the Moneda. In fact, as perhaps befits a former Irish nationalist, Egan saw everything through the prism of Anglophobia. Convinced that the Congressionalists favored Great Britain, Egan threw in his lot with the president, predicting that Balmaceda's forces would defeat the insurgents if the Moneda's army remained loyal.[12]

Despite Egan's enthusiasm for Balmaceda, the U.S. minister offered diplomatic asylum to various Congressionalist leaders. When the Moneda demanded that Egan surrender these individuals and even threatened to search the embassy, the American envoy refused. The Congressionalists remained Egan's guests until he arranged their safe conduct out of the country. Curiously, the triumphant Congressionalists later proved ungrateful for Egan's hospitality.

Although Santiago was declared an open city, the victorious Congressionalist mobs roamed the Chilean capital, surgically looting and sometimes destroying the homes of prominent Balmacedistas. Regrettably, more than property suffered. Just as the triumphant Congressionalist troops had savagely murdered and mutilated the bodies of Balmaceda's unfortunate generals, so they turned on those politicians and officers who remained loyal to the fallen regime. Many were ordered shot by rump court martials; others were less ceremoniously murdered on the streets. Those who eluded the mob sought refuge in various foreign embassies, including that of the United States. Ironically, Congressionalists who had earlier enjoyed American sanctuary now called upon Egan to surrender the newest refugees to the authorities. Egan again refused. The furious Congressionalists put the American legation under surveillance, stationed police in the area, and threatened visitors as well as the embassy's staff. Thus, the American minister's humane policies made him the Congressionalist bête noire.

Diplomatic relations between Washington and Santiago became dangerously frayed. The United States resented Chile's threats against its diplomats, hinting that it might use force to defend the legation's integrity.[13] Still smarting over the White House's clumsy interference in the War of the Pacific, Chileans compiled their own list of complaints. Americans, they claimed, had tried to stop the Congressionalists from purchasing weapons, denied the rebels access to international telegraph traffic, spied on the insurgent troops, and refused to surrender war criminals. Little that Washington did, including recognizing the Congressionalist regime, could smooth the troubled past. As one American diplomat noted, the "feeling of animosity against Americans is very decided . . . in social gatherings and in groups of Chileans on the street corners, when I have passed, I have heard chants of 'abajo los Yankees (down with the Yankees).'"[14] Given this malign climate, the American naval commanders should have thought twice before unleashing a crew of uniformed, lusty mariners on the streets of Valparaíso.

The *Baltimore* Incident

On 16 October 1891, the liberty boats of the USS *Baltimore* docked at Valparaíso's wharfs. Because the sailors had been cooped up on the cruiser for approximately five months, they doubtless alighted with a certain urgency. The blue jackets quickly fanned out, anxious to savor the seamy delights of Valparaíso's infamous cabarets and bordellos.

A small group of men, including Charles Riggin and John Talbot, visited a series of bars before arriving at the True Blue Saloon. As they were leaving, Riggin began to argue with a Chilean sailor. A fight erupted, and within minutes a mob began chasing the two American sailors. During the melee, Riggin was stabbed and then shot. The unfortunate sailor was not the only American casualty. In separate incidents, Chileans set upon other sailors. When the day ended, another American had been fatally wounded, seventeen were beaten, and approximately thirty more were residing in Valparaíso's squalid jails. This brawl, which almost precipitated a war between Chile and the United States, might have been averted had the American commander acted with more foresight and the Chilean authorities with more alacrity.

Admiral Winfield Scott Schley, commander of the *Baltimore*, convened a board of inquiry, which, after investigating the incident, blamed the riot and the sailors' maltreatment on Valparaíso's unruly populace. The American investigators also criticized the port's police, alleging not only that they had permitted the mob to mistreat the U.S. sailors but also that they joined in beating the men and that they had abused them when they were in custody. When Schley's report reached Washington, the White House demanded that Chile apologize for the incident and pay reparations to the injured sailors and to the relatives of the deceased.

Predictably, the Chilean authorities insisted upon making their own investigation. Pressed by Washington for a quick response, the minister of foreign relations, Manuel Matta, refused to rush to judgment. The Chilean legal system, he noted, worked well but sometimes slowly; the Americans must wait. This process proved time-consuming and involved legal customs that were totally alien to American jurisprudence. The proceedings, for example, were held in camera; a witness did not enjoy legal counsel. Other problems complicated the investigation. Enrique Foster, the presiding magistrate who zealously guarded his judicial prerogatives, considered the incident a simple drunken brawl. Consequently, he refused to respond to the American charge of police brutality. The U.S. authorities also contributed to the slow pace of the proceedings by not allowing members of the crew to testify. Egan, moreover, may have withheld vital evidence. Thus, due to the American and Chilean authorities, the hearing dragged on for weeks.

Initially the United States endured the delay. Even the U.S. press, while angry, did not lapse into crass jingoism. Eventually, however, what many considered Chilean indifference, if not sloth, eroded American tolerance. The American financier William Grace, who had substantial investments in Chile, privately warned Pedro Montt, Santiago's minister to the United States, that Americans were furious and that the Moneda should apologize and offer compensation.[15] Even the normally phlegmatic Benjamin Harrison became impatient. In December 1891, he issued a statement on the *Baltimore* incident, blaming the Chileans for what had occurred and demanding that Santiago apologize as well as pay reparations.

Matta telegraphed Montt, injudiciously describing the American president's report as biased, "erroneous or deliberately incorrect." Harrison, in other words, was either stupid or a liar. Not content with simply insulting the American president, Matta used his cable to complain about a variety of offenses that the United States had perpetrated during the recent Chilean civil war. Wisely Montt refrained from passing on his superior's statements, but Matta, who possessed almost no diplomatic experience and who apparently disliked Americans in general and Egan in particular, proved less discreet. Instead of keeping his correspondence secret, Matta read the abusive telegram to the Chilean Chamber of Deputies, and, the next day, the full text appeared in *El Ferrocarril*, a Santiago daily. After verifying the newspaper's story, Egan, who reciprocated Matta's ill feelings, forwarded a copy to Washington.

What began as a barroom brawl evolved into a dangerous political confrontation. American sailors in Chile became the targets of scorn, obscenities, and the occasional rock. Chilean naval authorities also acted in a provocative manner, using the USS *Yorktown* as a target for mock torpedo attacks and, on another occasion, almost hitting it with a rocket. Initially the U.S. government did not react to these provocations. In January 1892, Chilean authorities released a report that blamed the American sailors for precipitating the riot and not only exonerated Valparaíso's police for Riggin's death but praised them for acting in an exemplary manner. While the court sentenced three Chileans to brief terms in jail, it also sought to indict several American sailors for their roles in the disturbance. Matta forwarded the authorities' conclusions to Washington along with a tepid expression of regret for an incident that he continued to describe as a saloon fight.

Matta's endorsement of his government's report, which criticized the American sailors, and his earlier injudicious telegram infuriated Harrison. The U.S. president demanded that the minister of foreign relations repudiate his report and apologize for his inflammatory remarks. It momentarily appeared that the two nations might avoid a crisis when Santiago replaced Matta with Luis Pereira. Initially the new foreign minister seemed more affable, indicating that he would be willing to take some of the sting out of Matta's earlier statements. Domingo Gana, who took Montt's place in Washington, urged Pereira to apologize for the incident. Such a step, he claimed, "enhances, not dishonors a nation which recognized its errors completely and honestly."[16] In the meantime, Blaine, although ill, had not been idle. After some discussions, he and Montt worked out some unofficial compromises: if the two countries reached an impasse on the *Baltimore* issue, both sides accepted the idea of a third nation arbitrating the dispute. The Chileans also agreed to repudiate the more truculent sections of Matta's telegram. Finally, the United States would accede to a Chilean demand calling for Egan's recall.

If Blaine and Montt's unofficial efforts prospered, then Pereira's official attempts appeared mired in the Chilean bureaucracy. This problem may not have been the minister's fault; it was January, and the government officials, like all affluent Chileans including the president, had decamped for either the seashore or some bucolic rural resort. Harrison, unaware of the Chilean government's migratory habits, seethed in Washington's frigid winter, impatiently waiting for a response to his demands. While he fumed, Harrison reviewed the documents, including a second report, prepared by another naval board of inquiry, that essentially confirmed Admiral Schley's judgment that the *Baltimore's* crew had been the victims of a cowardly and brutal attack. Consequently, the new study reinforced the president's hostility toward Chile. He would soon have additional cause for anger.

Harrison became livid when he learned that the Moneda, in addition to refusing to apologize for Matta's telegram, had requested Egan's recall. Consequently, the president threatened to break diplomatic relations unless the Moneda disowned Matta's offensive remarks, apologized for the Valparaíso riot, and paid reparations. Obviously Egan would continue to serve as minister to Chile until the Moneda addressed Washington's demands. After waiting two days without receiving a response, Harrison went to the U.S. Congress, where he recounted the events that precipitated the crisis, the failure of the Chilean authorities to react in a timely and appropriate fashion, and the grotesque nature of Matta's telegram. It became clear that Harrison saw the issue as a matter of American prestige: "We must protect those who, in foreign ports, display the flag or wear the colors of this Government against insult, brutality, and death, inflicted in resentment of the acts of their Government, and not for any fault of their own." [17] The president, therefore, requested that Congress be prepared to take appropriate action.

Many interpreted Harrison's speech as an ultimatum that, if ignored, would lead to war. Certainly the American military responded in that fashion, preparing its ships, purchasing additional weapons and ammunition, and planning to blockade most of Chile's important ports. The possibility of an American-Chilean conflict gave Washington pause. If the American navy had improved dramatically since the 1882 fiasco, then so had the Chilean fleet. The Moneda had recently taken delivery of two new cruisers, the *Pinto* and *Errázuriz*, and would soon commission another battleship, the *Prat*. Thus Chile's navy, although perhaps smaller than the U.S. squadron, remained "a foe worthy of any maritime people."[18]

Even with its recent naval acquisitions, the Moneda's situation did not appear particularly enviable. Barely recovered from a brutal and costly civil war, Chile confronted the larger and stronger United States. More crucially, Santiago could not count on any support in the international community: Britain tended to side with Washington; Germany, the Moneda's other possible ally, appeared lukewarm, if not cool, to Chile's dilemma. Nor did Santiago's immediate neighbors evince sympathy. On the contrary, some Chileans feared that Peru and Bolivia might use the Moneda's dispute with the United States to launch a revanchist war. Buenos Aires demonstrated an unfraternal duplicity by generously offering the Americans the use of Argentine bases should Washington wish to attack Chile overland. Santiago, in short, was alone, confronting a larger and more powerful nation, which, it learned, was ready to occupy the northern nitrate provinces. Faced with enormously unpleasant choices, the Moneda decided to compromise.

Twelve hours passed before Chile's reply to Harrison's ultimatum arrived in Washington. The response constituted a nimble solution to a difficult situation. The Moneda's telegram began by reaffirming its continuing friendship with the United States, a friendship, it noted, which dated to the days of Chile's war for independence. In this spirit, Chile belatedly recognized that the *Baltimore* incident had somehow inadvertently mushroomed into a serious dispute. Not only did Santiago offer to pay reparations, but it would even permit the U.S. Supreme Court to set the amount of compensation. The Moneda also admitted that Matta's telegram contained some serious errors. Consequently, the Chilean government happily disassociated itself from the former minister's remarks, hoping that such a matter would not poison a long-term friendship. Fortunately, the chairmen of the foreign affairs committees of the House and Senate indicated that they considered the Moneda's telegram a full apology. Apparently Harrison would have preferred to reject the cable, but realizing that he lacked congressional support, he agreed to submit the outstanding issues to arbitration. The *Baltimore* crisis had ended.

A fight in a sleazy Valparaíso bar almost precipitated a war. In part the crisis developed as a result of a series of misperceptions. Apparently Chile's leaders regarded American anger with a certain nonchalance, if not disdain. Their reaction, ironically, did not lack logic. The Moneda had twice seen Washington back down from a confrontation: in 1866, when Seward refused to stop the Spaniards, and in 1882, when President Arthur avoided a clash with Chilean president Domingo Santa María. Why, in 1891, should Washington suddenly adopt a new, more aggressive policy?

In part, of course, the equation of power had changed. The United States possessed more naval power in 1891 than it had a decade earlier. More significantly, elements in the United States government—particularly Alfred Thayer Mahan's blue water boys—bristled with joy at the prospect of unleashing their recently acquired naval weapons against Santiago. The Chileans also failed to understand American sensitivities. Harrison had a highly developed sense of patriotism. He had served with great distinction in the Civil War: the Union meant more to him than the G.A.R.'s "bloody shirt" rhetoric of the Fourth of July picnic and the Republican party convention. Even if the Chileans did not understand Harrison's personality, they should not have discounted American *amour prope*. In 1866, the Moneda had endured a cruel bombardment rather than fire the first shot of a salute. In the 1870s, Santiago had vigorously protested when Bolivian authorities maltreated its citizens working the Caracoles mines. Less than a decade later, it had gone to war to protect its nationals' economic rights. Chilean officials grievously miscalculated when they presumed that the United States would not respond similarly to Chilean provocation.

Racial mythology may have clouded the Chilean authorities' judgment. Santiago still believed that Americans, as members of some primitive German tribe, lacked a sense of honor. Chile's presumption that only Latins would endure sacrifice before betraying their principles—and that Anglo-Saxons would not—proved false. If racism influenced Chile's perception of the United States, then it also warped Washington's vision of Chile. Increasingly, some Americans regarded Chileans as biological inferiors, individuals who, because of their color and mixed ancestry, merited little courtesy and less respect. Chile might be South America's dominant power, but it nonetheless remained an inferior nation, unworthy of consideration. Even the "whitest Chilian (sic) resembles the sallow Spaniard. . . . the Chilian (sic) of today is a sad amalgamation of Spanish, Indian, and negro blood, and combines the bad qualities of those three races."[19] A *Puck* cartoon perhaps best epitomized prevailing American attitudes in a caricature of a benign Uncle Sam trying to discipline a small, swarthy, delicately dressed, petulant child called Chile. The United States, in short, would not be pushed around by racially inferior and immature nations.

The *Baltimore* incident, as one British diplomat noted, created a "passionate sense of hatred toward the United States, which will take a long time to remove."[20] Americans, observed one Chilean statesman, "are very dangerous and it is necessary to treat them with formality and care. . . . My cheeks still burn when I remember the unfortunate *Baltimore* incident. For that reason, I believe the best policy toward them is to have the best possible relations, but always, with the strictest formality and maintaining possible cordiality."[21] Anti-American elements so exaggerated Washington's actions that they even fabricated the myth of Lieutenant Carlos Peña. Supposedly the United States demanded that a Chilean warship apologize for the *Baltimore* incident by striking its colors. No one would perform this humiliating task until a Lieutenant Peña voluntarily lowered his nation's flag and then, as an act of expiation, shot himself. Peña never existed, and the event never occurred, but the story became a metaphor for Chile's attitudes toward the United States.

In time Chilean bitterness subsided. A prominent Chilean diplomat recently noted, "The conduct of Washington was not so rude as was then said, and behind the habitual peculiarities of its [system of] justice, function a diplomatic technique sufficiently courteous and tolerant—above all [when dealing] with the expressions of Matta—than it used in dealing with any other South American nation."[22] But because it marked a dramatic shift in United States–Chilean relations, the *Baltimore* incident remains a nodal event. Santiago has chosen to describe the episode as an example of American bullying. In fact, the Moneda had badly miscalculated. Perhaps, having bested Washington in 1882 and 1885, it presumed that its luck would hold. But weakened by a civil war, surrounded by enemies, and deserted by its former allies, Santiago had blundered into a confrontation that it could not win.

4 Chile's Long Descent, 1892–1920

Chile's 1891 revolution shifted the political balance of power from the chief executive to the legislature. Thereafter, a hybrid political system known as the parliamentary regime ruled the nation. Through a combination of vote fraud, bribery (*cohecho*), and intimidation, only the wealthy or politically well connected won congressional seats. The widespread purchasing of votes virtually guaranteed that no party could achieve a parliamentary majority. Thus, governments became revolving doors, incapable of formulating or implementing policies. Worse, these legislatures, insulated from the well-deserved wrath of the electorate, blithely ignored the needs of the nation—widespread malnutrition, wretched housing, inadequate health and educational facilities—in order to advance their own interests or those of their friends. The congress, for example, replaced most of the direct levies with an export tax on nitrates, thereby shifting the burden of taxation from the wealthy to the foreign consumer. When the impost on *salitre* did not yield enough revenue, the Moneda borrowed from international bankers.

Only a few years passed before the more observant realized that the parliamentary regime had miscarried. With the easy nitrate money, the wealthy indulged their wish for conspicuous consumption, while the rural and urban poor lived in squalor. The state did little to improve the condition of the poor because, as one of Chile's presidents announced, the nation suffered from two types of problems: those that could not be solved and those that solved themselves. Some Chileans fondly remembered the days when men of honor and probity had ruled; when materialism had not corrupted the country; when politics had not become an obsession or an invitation to rob; and when the

69

government, like private individuals, lived within its means. Modern Chile, complained one venerable social critic, "is a victim of an economic, as much as a moral crisis, that stops its old progressive march forward."[1]

The Foreign Problems

Unfortunately for Chile, its political system began to atrophy at precisely that moment when the nation faced a host of foreign enemies, real and imagined. Thanks to a flood of European immigrants and the development of its agricultural sector, Argentina became the Southern Cone's most populated and wealthiest nation. Eventually the newly rearmed and assertive Buenos Aires decided to use its power to force Chile to accept Argentina's terms for establishing their common border.

An earlier treaty, though stipulating that both nations nominate delegates to define the frontier, contained such ambiguous language that neither signatory could agree on the agreement's intent. Argentina, for example, claimed that the frontier should run along the peaks of the Andes Mountains; Chile argued that the border should follow a line "between the highest peaks." If Buenos Aires prevailed, then it gained access to the Pacific Ocean. Conversely, a Chilean triumph would allow the Moneda to control a portion of Patagonia. The boundary issue, which twice almost precipitated a war, was not Chile's only foreign policy dilemma. The Moneda feared that Bolivia and Peru might capitalize on Santiago's preoccupation with Argentina to launch a war to recover their lost provinces. In such a conflict, a Peruvian-Bolivian army, reinforced by the Argentine navy, could crush Chile like a nut between the jaws of a nutcracker.

Initially, the Moneda attempted to ensure its dominance by expanding and rearming both its fleet and its army. But each time Santiago acquired a warship, Buenos Aires bought one. Chile's economy could not endure a costly naval arms race. In order to purchase two battleships, the Moneda not only consumed the money set aside for returning the nation to the gold standard, but it had to borrow from European bankers.

Faced with bankruptcy, the Moneda agreed to a negotiated compromise. Prodded by the British, Chile and Argentina signed in 1902 the Pactos de Mayo, which, by limiting the size of the Chilean and Argentine fleets, ended the naval arms race. The agreement also stipulated that Great Britain would fix the boundary between the two nations. More significantly, the pacts divided Latin America into two spheres of influence: henceforth Argentina would not threaten Chile's Pacific Coast hegemony, and Santiago promised not to intrude beyond the Andes.

The Pactos de Mayo, by freezing the arms race when Argentina enjoyed naval supremacy, marked the beginning of Chile's descent as a South American power. Prior to 1902, Santiago had aggressively pursued its goals through a combination of diplomacy and military intimidation. As Peru and Bolivia twice learned, Chile had succeeded because it was stronger, wealthier, and better organized. Now, without having to defeat Chile militarily, Argentina had demonstrated the limits of the Moneda's power. Although dispelling the Moneda's imperial fantasies, the Pactos, by extricating Chile from a costly arms race and removing the Argentine threat, allowed the nation to concentrate on consolidating its control of the Pacific.

The Pactos de Mayo benefited Chile, but they hurt Bolivia. The 1884 armistice had subordinated La Paz's economy to that of Santiago. Chilean wheat and manufactured goods entered Bolivia duty free. The Moneda also received approximately half the duties collected on imports arriving in Bolivia through Antofagasta. In an attempt to woo La Paz, Buenos Aires offered a variety of economic concessions, including the right to use Argentina's railroads and ports. Bolivia decided to accept Argentine generosity in order to reduce its dependence upon Chile. The 1902 agreements, by limiting Argentina to the Atlantic Coast, ended La Paz's flirtation with independence. Although Bolivia formally ceded Antofagasta to Chile in 1904, La Paz extracted financial concessions that the Moneda would never have granted decades earlier.

The American Menace Grows

American support for Balmaceda and the *Baltimore* incident left an aftertaste that soured Santiago's already acid relationship with Washington. Lamentably, diplomatic relations continued to fester during the remainder of the nineteenth century. In 1893, diehard Balmacedistas tried to topple the government by kidnapping President Jorge Montt. When the authorities discovered the cabal, the conspirators scattered, but two of the plotters sought and received political asylum from the ubiquitous Egan. The diplomat's action infuriated the Chilean government, which claimed that the rebels were not entitled to safe conduct out of Chile. The U.S. State Department concurred, withdrawing the sanctuary and ordering Egan home. But although the White House had sided with Montt, the incident did not encourage closer ties between the two countries. American citizens claimed that the Chilean government owed them approximately twenty-six million dollars in damages for destroyed property. Only some of these claims could be traced to the 1891 civil war; a substantial portion were the remnants of earlier complaints, some dating as far back as the 1850s. One of these issues, the Lord Claims, involved a dispute arising out of a contract that Balmaceda had signed with a coterie of unsavory American railroad speculators who, although not laying a single track, nonetheless demanded approximately six million dollars. Thanks to State Department pressure, the Americans received a settlement of $150,000.

More complicated and divisive was the claim of the Alsop Corporation. A Brazilian averred that the Bolivian government owed him damages for nitrate mined in the Atacama Desert. By the time La Paz recognized his interest, he had assigned it to the Alsop Corporation, which in turn argued that Chile assumed the financial liability when it annexed the Atacama Desert. The private company was correct: the 1904 peace treaty stipulated that Santiago became responsible for certain outstanding debts when it took the Bolivian littoral. Because the Moneda offered too little in compensation, the prolonged dispute became increasingly bitter. In desperation, the claimants appealed to the United States. Claiming that the Alsop Corporation was a Chilean company, the Moneda argued that Washington had no standing in the case. The State Department nonetheless issued an ultimatum: Chile must pay the Alsop claimants one million dollars, a sum three times greater than what Santiago had originally offered, or the United States would sever diplomatic relations. At Santiago's suggestion, the two nations submitted their dispute to the arbitration of the king of England, who eventually ordered Chile to pay some compensation, albeit far less than the United States had originally demanded. Although both nations compromised, Chileans believed that the Americans had badgered Santiago.[2]

Apparently as a protest for the *Baltimore* incident, Chile boycotted the 1893 Chicago World's Fair. This snub did not pass unnoticed in Washington. In 1895, the American secretary of state privately confided to a group of diplomats that he considered Chile to be the only Latin American nation in which he had no confidence.[3] Chile responded in kind. Washington's policy of intruding into hemispheric affairs increasingly disturbed Chileans, who cited U.S. mediation of Britain's boundary dispute with Venezuela over British Guiana as proof that "today we have more to fear from United States' 'protection' than from European aggression."[4] Predictably, the 1898 Spanish-American War further besmirched Washington's already tarnished image in Chile. *El Ferrocarril*, an important Santiago newspaper, described the conflict as merely the latest stage in a war, which began with the conquest of Florida, between the "Anglo-Saxon and Latin Races." Clearly, the United States sought "the absorption or conquest of Latin America," which appeared unable "to stop it."[5]

Washington's crass intervention in the 1903 Panamanian revolution fueled Santiago's anger. As one Chilean diplomat noted, the White House's intrusion, which allowed the secessionists to succeed, epitomized "the right of the United States to take from America whatever suits its interests and needs." Distressed by the increasing U.S. economic presence, some critics feared that Chile might suffer the same fate as Panama. Consequently, Santiago tried to frustrate the White House's plans. Acting in consort with other Latin American nations,

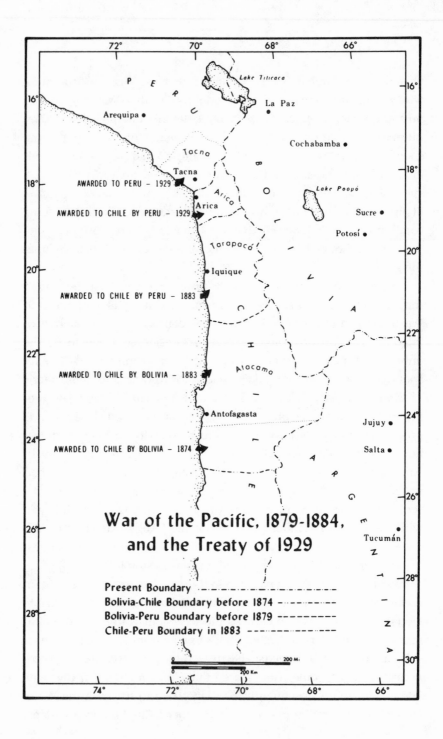

War of the Pacific, 1879-1884,
and the Treaty of 1929

Present Boundary
Bolivia-Chile Boundary before 1874
Bolivia-Peru Boundary before 1879
Chile-Peru Boundary in 1883

Chile unsuccessfully tried to withhold diplomatic recognition from the new republic.[6]

The following year, President Theodore Roosevelt asserted the unilateral right of the United States to intervene in Latin American nations in order to protect them from their European creditors. The Monroe Doctrine, one Chilean critic noted, had buffered Latin America from European intervention; the Roosevelt Corollary, however, indicated that the United States had moved from hemispheric protector to aggressor. Jorge Montt, Chile's former president, informed the British minister that the Monroe Doctrine threatened "the eventual subjugation of the entire American continent to the United States." Santiago, he observed, should view skeptically the protestations of friendship from an "unscrupulous and corrupt" American government. As part of this policy, Montt hoped to forge an alliance with Great Britain to prevent the "intromission of the United States into the South Pacific."[7]

Although Washington posed less of an objective threat to Santiago than to Peru, Bolivia, or Argentina, the Moneda seemed to dislike the United States not for what it had done but because it might become "an offensive weapon for those who conspire against Chile."[8] At no time did this sentiment become more apparent than when the Moneda confronted the inter-American movement and the Tacna and Arica issue.

Although the Treaty of Ancón granted Tarapacá to Santiago, the Moneda did not possess legal title to the two northern states of Tacna and Arica. The 1884 agreement stipulated that a plebiscite, to be conducted in 1894, would settle the issue of ownership. In fact, Santiago apparently never intended that Lima should regain its former provinces. When negotiating an end to the War of the Pacific, President Domingo Santa María realized that the Iglesias government could not survive the political consequences of ceding to Santiago not only Tarapacá but also Tacna and Arica. Hence, the Chilean president suggested a ruse: although the Moneda would annex Tarapacá, it would only govern Tacna and Arica. Then, after a decade of occupation, during which Peru would become adjusted to Chile's de facto rule, the

Moneda would formally incorporate the two provinces, paying Lima ten million silver pesos.

But Santa María's tactic failed because Peru obdurately insisted that Santiago abide by the Treaty of Ancón. Chile, of course, could have obtained permanent control of the area by winning the plebiscite. Since the Peruvian population outnumbered the Chileans by approximately two to one, however, this result seemed unlikely. Thus, the Moneda tried to postpone an election that it clearly could not win. The Peruvian government persisted, offering to conduct the plebiscite once Chile withdrew from the occupied territories in 1894. Lima even suggested that it oversee the election in Tacna while the Chileans conducted the plebiscite in Arica. The Peruvians clearly expected that the nation supervising the election would win, in effect allowing Chile to keep Arica but permitting Peru to regain Tacna. When Santiago rejected this solution, the Peruvians recommended that Peru, Chile, and a third nation conduct the proposed election. Chile spurned this proposal as well but offered to buy the two provinces for more than the ten million pesos specified in the Treaty of Ancón.

When Peru rejected this suggestion, Santiago launched a program to woo the population of Tacna and Arica into voting for Chile in the forthcoming plebiscite. Santiago revamped the educational system to inculcate Chilean nationalism; it prohibited Peruvians from celebrating their national holidays or from displaying any Peruvian national symbol. The Chilean authorities also closed the Peruvian press and social clubs, deported Peruvian priests, replacing them with Chileans, and assigned the two provinces to the ecclesiastical control of Chilean episcopal authorities. Finally, the Moneda settled Chileans, many of them veterans, in the contested area. Some of these ploys worked. The Chilean population, particularly after Santiago began to build the Arica–La Paz rail line, increased substantially. When subtle tactics failed, the local government apparently encouraged gangs of thugs to terrorize Peruvians. Lima objected to Santiago's efforts to convert its territory into Chilean satrapies. Consequently, Chilean-Peruvian relations alternated between avoidance and frigid civility. Periodically, the nations ceased talking to each other. In 1901, when the Peruvian press published stolen papers documenting Santiago's plan to "Chileanize" the two provinces, Lima broke diplomatic relations. Although the two countries renewed ties between 1905 and 1909, relations were again severed in 1910, the hundredth anniversary of Chile's independence.

Unfortunately for Washington, it inadvertently stumbled into the Chilean-Peruvian dispute. In 1889, the U.S. secretary of state, James G. Blaine, proposed creating the Pan-American movement. Chileans feared that their old nemesis, the Plumed Knight of Maine, having unsuccessfully tried to stop Santiago from annexing Tarapacá in 1881, would now attempt to prevent it from retaining Tacna and Arica. Blaine never intended to meddle in the Tacna-Arica dispute; he even promised that the conference would not discuss any ongoing territorial disputes. Santiago remained skeptical. It stipulated that it would not attend the conference unless the agenda was confined solely to economic and commercial issues. As if to reinforce this point, the Moneda instructed its delegates to abstain from any discussion involving arbitration of disputes.

The Chileans discovered that they had diplomatic adversaries other than Blaine. Argentina and Brazil, having annexed large portions of Paraguay in 1870, suddenly became the champions of the rights of small countries. Apparently intent upon humiliating Washington and Santiago, they introduced a motion calling for compulsory arbitration of any border dispute and condemning any nation that had used force to acquire territory. Since this provision simultaneously called into question the treaties of Guadalupe Hidalgo and Ancón, it made Chile and the United States diplomatic allies. Santiago adamantly refused to discuss the proposal. The ever-enthusiastic Blaine, and several other delegates, drafted a compromise providing that the arbitration agreement would not apply retroactively to disputes already resolved by treaties. Since this amendment excluded the Treaty of Ancón, it calmed Santiago's fears. Ironically, since none of the participants ratified the agreement, the Washington conference warned Santiago that its enemies would resurrect the arbitration issue to attack it at each Pan-American meeting. At the second, third, and fourth Pan-American conferences, held respectively in Mexico City in 1902, Rio de Janeiro in 1906, and Buenos Aires in 1910, the Chilean delegates, abetted by delegates from the United States, successfully fended off proposals for compulsory arbitration of the Tacna-Arica dispute.

In 1900, Lima, perhaps recognizing that the Pan-American Movement could not provide a forum, sought American intercession to resolve the Tacna-Arica affair. One group even suggested that Washington establish a protectorate over Peru. A year later, Lima offered the U.S. navy a coaling station. In return it demanded certain economic concessions, naval equipment and training, and U.S. help in settling the Tacna-Arica dispute, as well as its guarantee of Peru's territorial integrity. Although Washington balked at these proposals, it still pursued the idea of acquiring a coaling station in Chimbote.

The prospect of an American naval base located in Peru disturbed Santiago. This anxiety increased when the Moneda learned that U.S. naval authorities were reconnoitering the bay and drawing up contingency plans. The fact that earlier both nations had attempted to obtain a naval base on Ecuador's Galápagos Islands only exacerbated the rivalry. In 1905, Chilean hostility toward the United States, fanned by rumors that Washington had lent Peru money to buy arms, almost flared into another *Baltimore* incident. The U.S. fleet had paid a courtesy call on Valparaíso. This time, when fighting erupted between U.S. sailors and the local populace, the American admiral wisely ordered his men to return to their ships. Five years later, in the midst of yet another war scare, the Peruvian president, Augusto Leguía, again tried to win the White House's support by promising to purchase U.S.-built submarines as well as to allow Washington to use Chimbote as a naval base. Ultimately the Peruvian legislature's refusal to ratify the agreement aborted the exchange, but the suspicious Chileans appeared ready to go to war in order to prevent Peru from acquiring the naval vessels. Since Santiago, as the American minister warned, regarded the United States "almost . . . as an ally" of Peru, Washington had to act prudently.[9] (When Chile and Peru severed diplomatic relations in 1910, Lima requested that the United States take responsibility for the Peruvian legation in Santiago and assist any of Peru's citizens residing in Chile. The Peruvian petition conformed to established diplomatic practices. Still Santiago protested, warning the United States that such an action would damage American-Chilean relations.)

Resolving the status of Tacna and Arica, an issue which had once made Washington and Santiago allies, became a perpetual source of conflict between the two nations. Indeed, the one lesson that the White House learned was that it should try to avoid becoming enmeshed in Santiago's ongoing disputes with La Paz or Lima. "We have," as the U.S. minister to Chile noted in 1913, "everything to lose and nothing to gain by interfering." [10] The ownership of the two provinces, however, became less controversial when another issue, Chile's neutrality during World War I, became the principal cause of dispute between Santiago and Washington.

Chile and Wilson's Pan-American Vision

During the late nineteenth century, the United States and Chile did not trade extensively with each other. The expansion of America's agricultural and industrial capacity, however, altered this imbalance, and by 1913 the United States had overcome its historical trade deficit with Chile. Although substantially fewer than those of Great Britain or Germany, U.S. economic investments in Chile also increased, particularly in what became known as Gran Minería, the vast copper mining complex located in Chile's north, where Americans had invested fifteen million dollars. This U.S. participation in Chile's mining sector marked a watershed in Santiago's economic development.

An important copper producer during the nineteenth century, Chile's share of the world market eroded after the 1870s. Rather than invest in order to develop the less profitable copper ore, Chilean capitalists preferred to purchase shares in the *salitreras*, which returned a higher yield. Thus, while the Chileans happily collected their dividends, Americans led by William Braden and the Guggenheims acquired control of the nation's copper mines, and Bethlehem Steel bought its iron ore deposits located in El Tofo. Chilean nationalists have repeatedly bemoaned the loss of the copper and iron mines that the Yankees acquired, not through guile, but by default. Braden had repeatedly begged Chileans to invest in the copper industry, but they had refused. Consequently, American capitalists gained a foothold in what decades later became the principal resource of the Chilean economy.

Additional factors accelerated America's economic penetration of Chile. In 1913, the U.S. Congress permitted American banks to establish branches in foreign countries. Within three years the First National City Bank of New York opened an office in Valparaíso and, two years later, another in Santiago. The 1914 opening of the Panama Canal, moreover, dramatically shortened the trade lanes between the United States and Chile. "No longer," rhapsodized the *Bulletin* of the Pan-American Union, was Chile on "the wrong side of the world"—not a particularly consoling thought given Washington's often-truculent policies.[11]

Chilean-American diplomatic relations mirrored the countries' closer economic ties. In 1914 Washington and Santiago agreed to submit future diplomatic issues to an international arbitration board composed of two Americans, two Chileans, and one neutral. Both nations, however, retained the right to appeal the board's decision to the Permanent Court of Arbitration. While apparently establishing a mechanism to defuse potential problems, the treaty still contained a loophole: the signatories could refuse to arbitrate any issue that they believed compromised their vital interests or security. Despite this stipulation, the 1914 arbitration agreement nonetheless provided the two nations a means of averting future conflicts. Washington's decision to elevate its envoy to Chile to ambassadorial rank indicated that the U.S. government, despite the disputes, considered Chile an important nation.

The 1912 election of Woodrow Wilson presumably heralded a change in Washington's Latin American policy. Since the turn of the century, some Progressives had argued that all the hemispheric nations, not just the United States, should become involved in resolving the continent's political and international problems. Ideally,

Pan-Americanism then would replace the Monroe Doctrine, which, as its name indicated, represented a purely American vision for the Western Hemisphere, with a more broadly based movement.

While Wilson sought the friendship and respect of "our sister republics," he did not share this goal. The United States, he argued, would never treat a hemispheric nation as an equal unless its ruler had achieved power legally, respected its citizens' individual liberties, and adhered to constitutional principles. Regimes lacking these virtues, Wilson reasoned, simply did not deserve a place in the family of nations. Washington's new leader failed to explain who would assess the respectability of the "sister republics" that he so ardently courted. Obsessed with the political legitimacy of the hemisphere's nations, Wilson remained equally alert to the dangers from abroad. In a famous speech at Mobile, Alabama, in October 1913, he warned that Europe would use economic, not political, artifices to dominate Latin America. To contain the European economic menace, Wilson reaffirmed America's commitment to help Latin America repel intervention and vowed that the United States would never use force to seize Latin American territory. As Wilson's policy toward Mexico soon demonstrated, forswearing imperialism did not mean that Washington would cease meddling in Latin America's internal affairs.

Chile, the United States, and the Mexican Revolution

The Mexican revolution quickly demonstrated the shallow quality of Wilson's new Latin American policy. In 1911, Francisco Madero had led a revolution deposing Mexico's aged dictator, Porfirio Díaz. The collapse of the *Porfiriato* unleashed widespread unrest and plotting that the benign Madero could not contain. A few weeks before Wilson's inauguration, General Victoriano Huerta, with the connivance of the U.S. ambassador, ordered the arrest of Madero and his vice president, Jesús María Pino Suárez, who were both subsequently assassinated. Regarding Huerta as the personification of predatory militarism, Wilson refused to recognize the general's government, hoping that diplomatic isolation might speed the dictator's removal. When it became clear that denying recognition would not topple Huerta, Wilson, pressured by U.S. economic magnates with large investments in Mexico, considered an invasion as one way to protect U.S. interests from revolutionary turmoil. Realizing that using force would alienate other hemispheric nations, Wilson abandoned intervention in favor of diplomatic pressure and "watchful waiting." In the meantime, the U.S. navy patrolled the Mexican Gulf coast.

In April 1914, Huerta's soldiers arrested a group of American sailors from a U.S. warship who had inadvertently entered a prohibited area in Tampico. Wishing to avoid confrontation, the local Mexican authorities profusely apologized for detaining the U.S. servicemen, but their commander demanded a salute to the American flag. Clearly spoiling for a fight, Wilson ordered American sailors and marines to land in Vera Cruz on the questionable grounds that the occupation was necessary to intercept an arms ship en route to Huerta. Seizing the port would also deprive the general of the revenues of the Vera Cruz Customs House. The cutting off of Huerta's military and economic resources, the American president reasoned, would drive the general from power. Paradoxically, the U.S. occupation, instead of upending the dictator, fused the heretofore warring Mexican factions into a solid front opposing Washington.

Most Latin American governments considered Wilson's acts as brazen intervention. Anti-American demonstrations erupted throughout Latin America, including Chile. One Santiago newspaper feared that the president's move against Huerta constituted only the first step in a campaign to occupy Mexico.[12] Wilson, of course, believed that replacing Huerta with a popularly elected government was morally right. It appeared, therefore, that the president's principled intervention might push the United States and Mexico into war. Fortunately, the Chilean ambassador to the United States persuaded his Argentine and Brazilian colleagues to offer to mediate the Mexican-American dispute. Both nations stood to benefit from the mediation: Wilson could avoid a Mexican fiasco, and Huerta gained time to consolidate his position. For Chileans, their nation's mediation effort not only

averted a war but also marked the emergence of the ABC nations
—Argentina, Brazil, and Chile—as a regional power bloc that might
limit Washington's imperialist urges.

The U.S. delegates, the diplomatic envoys of the ABC powers, and
the Mexican representatives assembled on the Canadian side of Niagara Falls in May 1914. Washington adamantly insisted upon replacing
the general with a democratically elected leader, but Huerta, abetted
by his political foe Venustiano Carranza, argued that Wilson's proposals constituted an unwarranted intervention into Mexico's internal affairs, an opinion that some Chileans shared. After prolonged
debate, in late June 1914, the Mexican participants accepted a vaguely
worded proposal calling for the establishment of a provisional government. The United States, in return, promised to recognize this
as-yet-unformed regime. The conference restored Chile's diplomatic
status in South America. The ABC powers had neutralized the United
States, "one of the most powerful forces of the world, [and] frequently
inclined to use the supreme argument of force," thus marking "the
triumph of the Pan American idea and for the significant constitution
of a new moral force in American politics." [13] In truth, other than preventing a war—not an inconsiderable feat—the meeting did not mark
the dawning of a new diplomatic era. Wilson still refused to relinquish
his right to intervene unilaterally in Latin America.

While the Mexican episode indicated the dangers inherent in Wilson's willful idealism, Washington, at least, had not directly threatened Santiago. But in December 1914, when Wilson suggested that
Latin America adopt a Pan-American treaty, his proposal caused con-
sternation, if not fear, in the Moneda. The president's proposed agreement called for "mutual guaranties of political independence under
Republican forms of government and mutual guaranties of territorial
integrity." [14] An additional clause insisted that nations must resolve
their ongoing territorial or boundary disputes within one year. If they
could not accomplish this goal within that time, then they would have
to submit the dispute to compulsory arbitration. The treaty also stipulated that no nation could use violence against a neighbor until it first
submitted its dispute to arbitration.

Because a prompt settlement with Peru over Tacna and Arica was unlikely, Wilson's treaty threatened Chile's interests. Santiago's foreign minister, Enrique Villegas, quite properly considered the U.S. measure as jeopardizing Chile's occupation of the two provinces. Since Chilean diplomats wanted no foreign power questioning Santiago's right to control the nation's northern territories, they exhorted their Latin colleagues to launch a crusade against the treaty. To enlist support, Villegas began to play on the hemisphere's latent fears of American imperialism. The Chilean diplomat warned, for example, that Wilson's insistence that all New World nations adopt a republican form of government permitted the United States to intervene in the rest of Latin America as cavalierly as it had so recently done in Mexico.

Wilson's new secretary of state, Robert Lansing, launched a campaign of his own. Unlike either his predecessor, William Jennings Bryan, or the president, Lansing was a trained diplomat who tried to appease Santiago by modifying the language requiring compulsory arbitration and mandating the establishment of republican government. Even Wilson began to sound conciliatory. In an address to the U.S. Congress, the president renounced America's role as "some sort of guardian of the republics to the south." [15] Instead of acting unilaterally, the United States promised to work as a disinterested partner with the nations of Latin America. Addressing the Pan-American Scientific Congress, Wilson reaffirmed his support for a new partnership based upon equality, suggesting that disputing parties would not be under any time constraints to resolve their diplomatic differences. But if these nations could not settle their differences, then he insisted that they accept arbitration.

Chile again successfully foiled the U.S. plan. Eduardo Suárez Mujica, the Moneda's ambassador to the United States, warned, for example, that the American treaty gave Washington carte blanche to intervene in the domestic affairs of the member states. Santiago insisted that the United States must exempt from the treaty's purview such questions as the status of Tacna and Arica, which involved a nation's national pride, and that it must also abandon the notion that Latin American nations had to adopt the republican form of government. In March 1916, the Chilean ambassador added yet another demand: the United States must delete the provision requiring compulsory arbitration. Obviously these suggested changes emasculated the White House's proposal.

In the end, the Pan-American pact fell victim to Wilson's intervention in Mexico and the Caribbean, thus ending the Moneda–White House squabble. In June 1916, Washington ordered General John Pershing to lead an expeditionary force into Mexico. Initially, the United States claimed that it had acted in self-defense. But when the Latin American nations offered to arbitrate the outstanding issues between the White House and Carranza, Wilson refused. Washington preferred to act unilaterally rather than work through the good offices of the Latin American states.

The episode embarrassed Wilson's government. American intervention in Mexico clearly demonstrated that, while Washington advocated arbitration for other nations, it had not renounced the use of force. Certainly Wilson's intrusion into Mexico reinforced Chile's already strong fears about the United States. Apparently the Mexican expedition also convinced the other Latin American nations not to support the proposed Pan-American pact. Thus, Chilean opposition foiled Washington's attempt at establishing a new Pan-American order. Although Chile and the United States clashed on the issue of Mexico and the Pan-American movement, they avoided a direct confrontation. World War I, however, would strain relations between the Moneda and the White House more dangerously than any hemispheric issue.

World War I

Both Chile and the United States had hoped to avoid involvement in World War I. Both nations contained large numbers of immigrants who still entertained residual loyalties, if not close ties, to the belligerents. Such feelings seemed stronger in Chile than in the United States, where many immigrants had apparently accepted the domi-

nant American culture. Chile's south, for example, remained a Teu-
tonic enclave, where Indian nannies coaxed their charges to eat, not
puré de manzana, but *Apfelmus.* Prussian military missions had taught
the Chilean army to goose step, and its officers wore German-style
uniforms, complete with *Pickelhauben,* and sported Kaiser Wilhelm
mustaches. German pedagogues had reorganized the country's educational system.[16] German economic influence was also strong. The
Prussian empire consumed a quarter of Chile's exports while providing 22 percent of its imports.[17] German-owned banks, with a capital
of approximately one million pounds sterling, operated throughout
Chile. Although Germans owned only 15 percent of the nation's *salitreras,* they dominated the chemical and pharmaceutical industries and
controlled the Kosmos Line, which carried a quarter of the nation's
maritime traffic.

British citizens, who had invested some seventy-five million pounds
in Chile, exercised even more economic clout than the Germans. The
English controlled the northern *salitreras* and owned 25 percent of
Chile's southern sheep-raising lands. Since London dominated Santiago's foreign trade, English merchants played an important role in
the commercial life of Chile's ports. Valparaíso, for example, became
known as "perhaps the most British of all the cities in South America,"
where English was widely spoken and where one could play football
and, of course, cricket.[18] British presence permeated various aspects of
Chilean society. The British had introduced horse racing, football, the
overcoat, and the Boy Scouts into Chile; the Chilean navy steamed in
British-built naval vessels, and its crews wore copies of the uniforms
of His Majesty's sailors.

Chile's intellectuals, particularly the nation's university professors,
identified themselves with France. "French," noted one Chilean, "is
our legislation, French our everyday reading and French are the fash-
ions which our women follow. France is our intellectual mother." Not
surprisingly, therefore, *El Mercurio* sadly noted that the world war
"profoundly convulsed the national soul."[19]

Located far from the fighting and recognizing its cultural and economic schizophrenia, the Moneda saw no reason to join in the mayhem. Even if it had yearned to participate, the government faced a Hobson's choice: choosing sides would clearly antagonize a significant ethnic bloc, jeopardizing the delicate political balance of Chilean society. Regrettably, the belligerents did not allow Chile to remain aloof from the war. Both the German and the British fleets flagrantly violated Chilean waters, although London, unlike Berlin, generally apologized for its diplomatic gaffes.

Because the European belligerents desperately needed Chile's *salitre* to produce explosives—each time a nine-inch artillery piece was fired, it consumed one hundred pounds of nitrate—the conflict should have brought prosperity to Santiago. Instead, the First World War made a shambles of Chile's neutrality and its economy. German submarines, the high cost of coal and maritime insurance, and the lack of transport ships prevented Chilean nitrates from reaching the Entente powers.[20] Santiago's *salitre* sales to the Central powers virtually ended with the British naval blockade of Germany and Belgium, which traditionally had imported a quarter of Chile's nitrate exports.

Chile found itself in a paradoxical situation: while the war had increased the demand for *salitre,* it prevented Chileans from profiting from the conflict. The number of functioning *salitreras* declined from 143 to 43. Closure of the nitrate mines exacerbated Santiago's already hostile relations with Lima, because the Peruvian government accused the Moneda of using the economic crisis to expel Peruvian nationals from Chile. When, by mid-1915, nitrate exports increased by 40 percent over prewar levels, some degree of economic normality returned. The slaughter on the Western Front increased demand for nitrate, and by 1917 *salitre* production reached three million tons.

While temporarily reviving the nitrate industry, the war distorted Chile's traditional economic relationships. Germany, quarantined by the British blockade, ceased trading with Chile, while England, although still purchasing Santiago's products, could no longer satisfy Chile's consumer needs. The United States seized the commercial opportunity, and, a year after the struggle began, it had replaced England and Germany as Chile's principal trading partner. By 1918, the United States purchased 64.3 percent of what Chile exported, while selling Santiago 46.5 percent of its imports.

The United States might have benefited from the war, but Chile did not fare as well. By 1916, Allied need for nitrates increased prewar prices by 20 percent. Washington's entry into the conflict increased consumption and drove up nitrate prices to twice the prewar price. In an attempt to dampen the cost spiral and to guarantee a steady supply of *salitre,* the British created a centralized purchasing agency, the Nitrate of Soda Executive. Eventually including American and other Allied representatives, the board managed to stabilize prices and to guarantee the Entente powers and the United States abundant supplies of nitrate. While benefiting the Allies, the Nitrate of Soda Executive prevented Chile from extracting the maximum profit from the war-generated *salitre* scarcity.

The Neutrality Issue

Because Chile and the United States initially decided to remain neutral, World War I at first did not noticeably affect Chilean-American relations. But, in April 1917, the United States declared war on the Central Powers. Typically, when Wilson entered the conflict, he tried to recruit the Latin Americans to his cause. The Caribbean and Central American nations, virtual U.S. protectorates, followed Washington's lead by joining the "war to end all wars." Perhaps hoping that they would gain American support in their ongoing boundary disputes with Chile, Bolivia and Peru broke diplomatic relations with Germany. But in South America, only Brazil joined Wilson's crusade, principally because it too opposed the German blockade and Berlin's promiscuous use of submarine warfare.

Wilson naturally tried to enlist Chile in its legion. But the stolidly pro-German president, Luis Sanfuentes, would not budge. Chile, his diplomatic representatives argued, hardly mattered in the world struggle. Its involvement, noted one politician, would be like adding theater extras "who swell the personnel of the chorus without singing a single note."[21] Santiago, they reasoned, contributed more by providing nitrates to the Allies than by declaring war on the Central Powers. In truth, Chile hesitated because it remained divided on the issue. The clergy—which identified France with the Antichrist—and the army abominated the Allies. President Sanfuentes and other politicians favored the Germans out of either personal preference or fear of the politically powerful Deutsch-Chilenischen Bund. Some Chileans voiced more pragmatic reasons for abstaining from the struggle. The 1917 German and Austrian breakthrough on the Italian front convinced them that the Central Powers were not moribund. Hence, while the United States might impetuously join the Allies, the more cautious Chileans opposed taking sides until they were sure who would win.

Clearly anti-Americanism motivated many Chileans. The leader of FECH, the Chilean university student federation, claimed that it was "money, [the] dollar and nothing else" that had propelled the United States into war. "Humanity—what does that matter to a businessman! The Law—what does that matter to a criminal! Liberty—what does that matter to the oppressor of Central America!"[22] Chile, which had suffered so much at the hands of Washington, had no reason to rally to its side. One politician proclaimed that since German intervention had prevented James G. Blaine from taking Tarapacá from Chile, Santiago must reciprocate: the German people "should receive the fruit of their sacrifices, efforts, and victories."[23] Others begged the Moneda to abstain from the war as a way of punishing the United States for its past misdeeds. Galvarino Gallardo Nieto, for example, urged Chile to remember American insults directed against not merely Santiago but also the entire continent and then to "decide if it wishes to side with the United States."[24]

Washington's blacklisting of German firms operating in Chile reinforced existing anti-American feelings. The American use of the blacklist, lamented one Chilean congressman, again demonstrated that "Chile has ceased being an independent and sovereign nation."[25] The United States, of course, had not invented this strategy, but critics complained that once it became a belligerent, it too "was applying these measures despite the economic and social damage it inflicts. So much for Panamericanism and for the rights of Latin American states to act independently." Some Chileans believed that a defeat of the Central Powers removed the last barrier preventing the intrusion of "American Imperialism in the affairs of our continent."[26] Certainly the Allies, bled white by the war and in debt to Wall Street, appeared powerless to restrain the United States. Indeed, some feared that Washington would cancel the Entente's war debts in exchange for them granting the United States complete freedom of action in South America.

Thus, Chileans could offer numerous explanations—divided loyalties, ethnic ties, discretion, or simply anti-Americanism—for remaining neutral during the First World War. Perhaps the best reason was that provided by President Sanfuentes. Once, when lectured by the American minister Joseph Shea "on the German menace," the Chilean replied that since the Central powers had not injured Chile, Santiago lacked a rationale for declaring war.[27] Even those politicians who disliked the Central Powers agreed that it would be craven for Chile to declare war because the United States wished it.[28] Conversely, they characterized as outrageous Washington's diplomatic offensive to force the hemispheric nations to join the war effort.

What is significant is not that Santiago wished to remain neutral but that it succeeded. The Moneda managed to implement this policy in part because Argentina, under the rule of newly elected Hipólito Irigoyen, also favored neutrality. Santiago, therefore, would not be the lone holdout. Ironically, the Moneda would discover that peace would limit its maneuverability.

The First World War merely accelerated Santiago's decline, a decline which began after 1891. Chile's most valuable resource, nitrates, had virtually lost its value, and former allies had become impotent. Germany, Chile's protector after the War of the Pacific, was a defeated nation, laden with reparations. Chile's other friend, Great Britain, was bankrupt. The British Foreign Office tacitly accepted Washington's hemispheric dominance. In 1918, London offered to cancel the visit of a British mission to Latin America if its presence offended Washington. Three years later, the British withdrew their fleet from the South Pacific. Britannia might rule the waves, but not those off Chile.[29]

Surrounded by enemies and without European allies, the Moneda lacked hemispheric friends. Peru and Bolivia had cravenly, but wisely, thrown in their lot with Washington, demanding that Wilson apply the Fourteen Points—his prescription for settling the problems of Europe —to their boundary problems. The White House had ample cause to dislike Chile, resenting its refusal both to become involved in the First World War and to resolve the Tacna-Arica dispute. Given Chile's weakness and American strength, the postwar years would further strain relations between the two countries.

5 The Social Crisis, 1920–1938

The years following World War I severely tried Chile. Its nitrate-based economy had collapsed, forcing thousands from the *salitreras* into the soup kitchens. Three decades of corruption and political instability had taken its toll: during the five years of Luis Sanfuentes's presidency, a petulant legislature had unseated seventeen cabinets. Chile lacked both the political will and the financial resources to respond to the catastrophic recession. Progressive elements often attempted to force change, but they invariably failed. Sadly, the postwar political crisis also complicated Chile's ability to resolve its foreign problems.

The Aftermath of World War I

The First World War marked a watershed in Chile's economic development. The 1918 armistice, by ending the fighting, reduced the need for Santiago's raw materials. Copper exports and prices, which had risen dramatically during the war, declined by 20 percent. Nitrate producers suffered even more. Before 1914, Santiago monopolized the world's supply of nitrates, which it exported primarily to Europe. At the war's end, the Allies possessed a six months' supply of *salitre*. The Anglo-American Nitrate of Soda Executive, after selling this inventory, disbanded in May 1919. The glut of nitrates on the world market savaged Chile's economy: in 1919, for example, sales of *salitre* declined by almost 75 percent, while prices dropped 30 percent. *Salitreros* attempted to protect themselves by forming an association to regulate production and maintain price levels. In 1920, either as a response to the cartel's action or to world conditions, the nitrate market improved, bringing joy to the northern *salitreros*. Lamentably, their happiness proved short-lived.

Peace did more than reduce demand for Chile's nitrates; it crippled the entire industry. The Haber process, which synthetically fabricated ammonia, had permitted Berlin to survive without imported nitrates. After 1918, the Allies began using this German technology to produce ammonia. The combination of synthetic chemicals, the decline in European currencies, and transportation problems devastated Chile's economy. By the end of 1921, prices, monthly production, and exports had fallen, in some cases, by 70 percent.[1] The one hundred thousand individuals who relied indirectly upon the *salitreras* for work joined fifty thousand nitrate miners in the unemployment lines. With Chile's principal source of income in what seemed a permanent depression, both the value of its peso and its credit rating collapsed.

Predictably, the United States, with its enormous capital reserves and its productive capacity, replaced the British as the principal force in Chile's economy. Not only had American companies and financial institutions expanded their postwar economic contacts, but U.S. business interests had also invested large sums in Chile.[2] Both the Chilean Exploration Company, a subsidiary of the larger Anaconda Copper Company, and William Braden's corporation, which subsequently became the Kennecott Copper Company, increased their holdings and modernized existing properties. Bethlehem Steel expanded its mining operations of iron. When the Guggenheims, who controlled much of Chile's copper, developed a new technique that inexpensively increased nitrate production, they began to buy up various *salitreras*. Initially beneficial, the new infusions of technology and capital perpetuated Chile's dependence upon the mining sector, amplifying American economic influence. The Guggenheim process, moreover, provided only a temporary respite: the nitrate industry had entered into a permanent state of depression.

Had the economic pressures generated by the collapse of the nitrate market not become so strong, the political status quo might have remained intact. By 1920, however, the political and economic situation had become so desperate that even middle-class Chileans demanded change. Presumably, the election of reformist candidate Arturo Alessandri would accomplish that purpose. Unfortunately, the new president had to rule a nation using the same political institutions that had brought the country to such grief. For more than three years he unsuccessfully tried to cajole a legislature dominated by conservatives into enacting his reform programs. When the legislature refused, Alessandri decided to subvert the electoral process in order to pack the congress with his supporters who, he believed, would approve his reform proposals. While he did win control of both chambers, he found that his supposed friends proved as uncooperative as his enemies. Partisan bickering had paralyzed Chile.

Foreign Tribulations

Although politically beleaguered, Alessandri moved decisively to resolve the Tacna-Arica dispute. His concern proved wise, because the diplomatic confrontation with Peru had deepened. Wilson's Fourteen Points advocated self-determination and opposed the acquisition of territory through force. Not surprisingly, Peruvians petitioned Wilson for assistance in regaining their lost provinces; their less genteel countrymen assaulted Santiago's consulates throughout Peru. Chileans responded by attacking the Peruvian legation in Iquique. Both capitals ordered home their consuls, in effect severing all forms of direct diplomatic communication. Scolding both Peru and Chile for closing their consulates, the U.S. president urged them to restore relations in order to address the issue of Tacna and Arica. Wilson's haughty tone infuriated the Moneda, but since Chile's European allies had tacitly accepted American hemispheric supremacy, Santiago could ill afford to allow the Tacna-Arica dispute to antagonize Washington. Anxious to woo American public opinion, Chile opened a New York information office, which flooded the U.S. press with articles defending Chile's position. Santiago also dispatched to the United States a high-ranking delegation, which, in addition to seeking loans, defended Chile's role on the boundary issue.[3] The crisis with Peru worsened, becoming so tense that in 1920 both nations rushed troops to their common border. Although the war scare subsided, Peru appealed to the League of Nations. The prospect of other nations meddling in a hemispheric question so deeply offended Washington that Peru's president, Augusto Leguía, withdrew the motion.

While it was clear that Peru wished to placate the White House, the Chileans did not. A proposal of Under Secretary of State Henry Fletcher suggested that the Moneda allow a third party to set the conditions under which Santiago would conduct a plebiscite in Tacna and Arica. Santiago, however, strongly rejected Fletcher's proposal. Chile's reluctance to act led to more hostile comments and persistent rumors that Washington might intervene in the Tacna-Arica dispute.[4]

Alessandri recognized that the frontier problem not only antagonized Latin America but subjected Chile to U.S. pressure as well. By resolving the dispute, Chile would cease being a pariah state. In 1920, during a diplomatic banquet, Alessandri expressed an interest in settling the boundary issue. He also ordered Beltrán Mathieu, his ambassador in Washington, to request U.S. assistance. Various American officials feared becoming embroiled again in this extremely acrimonious question. Others, of course, disagreed: better that Washington mediate the dispute than permit the League of Nations, to which the United States did not belong, to assert its jurisdiction. President Warren G. Harding, to whom Alessandri appealed as a fellow Mason, finally agreed to act as mediator.[5]

Informed of Alessandri's intention, President Leguía appeared willing to accept U.S. intervention. Washington, he insisted, should discuss not merely the holding of a plebiscite but "all the questions which the 1883 Peace Treaty had produced."[6] By refusing to hold the election in 1894, as originally stipulated, Lima believed that Chile had vitiated the Treaty of Ancón. Peru was questioning not simply Santiago's occupation of Tacna and Arica but its ownership of Tarapacá. The Moneda, of course, dismissed Lima's contention. Postponing the plebiscite, it retorted, did not negate the Treaty of Ancón. Indeed, an election remained the only method for resolving conclusively the status of the provinces.[7] Perhaps fearing a repetition of the 1880s,

Washington also refused to question Chile's title to Tarapacá. Indeed, after Washington threatened to withdraw from the peace process unless Lima dropped its demands, Leguía capitulated.[8] Consequently, when Santiago unofficially suggested that Washington should host a conference of the two nations, the ever-amiable Warren G. Harding happily complied. But when the Chilean and Peruvian diplomats met in Washington in 1922, it became clear that they could agree on little, including procedures for holding the plebiscite.

Three years of negotiations did not improve the situation. Unwilling to give up, both nations appealed to Harding's successor, Calvin Coolidge, to arbitrate the Tacna-Arica dispute. In March 1925, Coolidge announced his decision: contrary to Peru's allegations, Chile's actions, including its Chileanization program, had not nullified the Treaty of Ancón. And since the 1883 agreement did not set any time limit for conducting the plebiscite, the two countries could still use this agreement as a basis for determining ownership of the disputed territory. Coolidge made an important additional finding: pending the election results, Chile would administer the area and hence supervise the plebiscite. The American president insisted, however, that a committee, composed of representatives of Chile, Peru, and the United States, under the control of General John Pershing, determine voter eligibility and verify the election results.

After Pershing arrived in Arica in August 1925, he became almost immediately embroiled in a conflict with the Chilean authorities when he insisted that the plebiscite should be honest. Santiago did not share the general's goal. The Chileans needed to win the election in order to obtain legal title to the two provinces. Thus, while the Moneda was ostensibly helping Pershing oversee the electoral contest, its officials were intimidating, and even murdering, anyone who opposed continued Chilean rule. When the general protested, the Chilean authorities either denied his allegations of misconduct or accused him, the American ambassador, William M. Collier, and the secretary of state, Frank Kellogg, of being pro-Peruvian.[9] Pershing should not have been surprised. Agustín Edwards, the Chilean envoy, had earlier warned him that "if they [the Peruvians] say a thing is white, we shall say that it is black, and vice-versa." [10] Still, Chilean duplicity depressed the battle-hardened American general.

Less than a month after his arrival, Pershing concluded that if the United States persisted in its efforts to hold a plebiscite, then it "would make us the laughing stock of the world." Rather than conduct a farcical election, he suggested that Chile and Peru should negotiate a settlement. Santiago, however, still insisted that the plebiscite occur as scheduled. In early 1926, the frustrated Pershing, suffering with infected teeth, departed for medical treatment in the United States. His successor was another professional army officer, General William Lassiter. Observing that Chilean officials tolerated the persecution of Peruvian voters and perpetuated flagrant registration frauds, Lassiter also called for an end to the plebiscite process. [11] But Kellogg, fearing that everyone would blame the United States if he canceled the election, rejected Lassiter's suggestion. Instead he proposed that both sides use U.S. good offices to reach a settlement.

Fearing that they would be admitting that Santiago had perverted the plebiscite process, Chilean authorities officially rejected a negotiated settlement. Privately, however, they hoped to find a solution that would allow them to abandon the election decorously while beginning negotiations. Consequently, Kellogg's suggestion—that Chile and Peru send delegates to Washington to settle their differences—allowed Santiago to hold onto the fiction of the plebiscite while attempting to arrange an agreement.

Peruvian-Chilean talks began in April 1926. After two months of fruitless discussions, Kellogg ordered Lassiter to cancel the plebiscite. For obvious reasons, the Peruvian delegate happily sided with the American chairman. Thus, on 14 June 1926, after Lassiter blistered the Chileans for obstructing the election, the commission voted to end "the make-believe plebiscite, repugnant to the requirements of the award." Santiago, of course, was furious. Denying any responsibility, the Chilean delegate denounced Lassiter for illegally canceling the plebiscite. The Moneda became so angry that it intimated that Santiago might break diplomatic relations with the United States. [12]

Few if any of the American officials involved in the abortive plebiscite experience emerged unscathed. Secretary Kellogg, described by one Chilean critic as the Savior of Peru, was flayed for suspending the election and for trying to impose a settlement. Lassiter, occasionally compared to James G. Blaine, was accused of trying to despoil Chile of its sacred territories. The collapse of the negotiations did resemble Blaine's 1881 diplomatic effort. Chilean public opinion again accused the United States of trying to dismember the nation or using the election to establish control over the Moneda. Alessandri, who had initiated the plebiscite process, turned on Washington, likening the United States to a giant nation ruled by pygmies. Privately boasting that he had stymied the White House's plans, Alessandri announced that he would repudiate Pan-Americanism and instead work for "Latin America for the Latin Americans."[13] Santiago had again managed to brand Washington the aggressor.

Some Chileans, however, saw the Tacna and Arica issue as a "pretext to smother in blood the social revolution by playing the patriotic horn."[14] While perhaps an exaggeration, this sentiment revealed an intense frustration with Chile's political system. In 1924, the Chilean senate began to debate a project that would have granted a stipend to legislators. Since Chile's congressmen did not receive a salary, many believed that the proposed legislation would allow the less affluent to hold public office. But while a democratic reform, the measure came at a singularly inappropriate moment: the bureaucracy and the military had not received their salaries for months. They became livid, therefore, to learn that the legislature contemplated compensating its members. Angry clerks may inspire only derision, but angry soldiers, like angry policemen, cause concern.

A group of junior officers, many of whom had not been promoted for years, attended a legislative session, where they made their presence known by rattling their sabers. Alessandri attempted to pressure the legislature by capitalizing on the military's anger. He organized a new cabinet, which included various high-ranking officers. He then submitted to the legislature an omnibus bill enacting all the reform measures, including concessions to the military, that had languished for months. Initially, the congress did not respond. A member of the junta warned them, however, that the legislature either pass the proposal or face dissolution. In two hours they approved Alessandri's entire program. Once in power, the military refused to return to their barracks: they wanted Alessandri to dissolve the legislature. Instead of acceding to their demand, the president resigned. A junta of senior officers disbanded the congress and ruled the nation.[15]

By early 1925, when the reform-minded junior officers learned that the military junta hoped to impose a conservative as president, they rebelled. After forcing out the senior officers, the Young Turks invited Alessandri to resume the presidency. By the time he returned to Santiago, Alessandri discovered that the political situation had changed. During his absence, a constituent assembly had written a new constitution that restored the presidential form of government, made the judiciary independent of the executive branch, and limited the legislature's power. More significantly, the 1925 constitution empowered the government to act more vigorously in order to assure that the state would protect the health and welfare of the nation's citizens.

Although he was presumably stronger than the junior military officers, President Alessandri quickly discovered that he seemed incapable of reining in the military, particularly Colonel Carlos Ibáñez del Campo. Ibáñez, who had helped topple the junta, served as minister of war in the provisional government that ruled the nation following the 1925 coup. He continued to hold ministerial rank because Alessandri, rather than form a new cabinet, retained the provisional government's ministers. This decision proved disastrous. Colonel Ibáñez hoped to campaign for the presidency while retaining the critically important post of minister of war. When Alessandri requested his resignation, Ibáñez refused, precipitating a constitutional crisis. Rather than dismiss him, Alessandri decided to abandon the Moneda, believing that his resignation would galvanize the nation into supporting a civilian candidate for president.

Alessandri was only partially correct. Faced with the olive-drab candidacy of Ibáñez, Chileans, in December 1925, elected a civilian, Emilio Figueroa, president. Regrettably, the mild-mannered lawyer proved almost as ineffectual as Alessandri in restraining Ibáñez. Figueroa might have bested Ibáñez had the economy improved. It did not. Nitrate prices continued to fall. While the copper industry prospered, it could not compensate for the economic downturn in the *salitreras*. The president, apparently hoping to bolster his image and to tame the still-obstreperous Ibáñez, eventually appointed the officer to the post of minister of interior, the second most important position in Chile. In addition to economic changes, the new government began to oppress its critics. As part of his program to purge the nation of dissidents, Ibáñez fired various high-ranking government officials. He even attempted to dismiss Figueroa's brother, Javier, who was serving as the Supreme Court's chief justice. Rather than comply with Ibáñez's request, in April 1927 the president resigned. Although Ibáñez clearly wished to take Figueroa's place, he insisted on being elected to the presidency rather than merely seizing it. Since he ran virtually without opposition, the colonel won approximately 98 percent of the vote.

During Ibáñez's rule, from 1927 to 1931, Chile appeared to enjoy prosperity and stability. In a sense both were illusory: loans from Wall Street fueled the nation's economic good times, and Ibáñez's secret police, not contentment, assured order. In order to minimize U.S. influence, Ibáñez attempted to cultivate old friends as well as to win new allies. In the late 1920s, the Moneda sent Conrado Rios Gallardo to England in order to obtain naval weapons and diplomatic support for Chile's stance on the Tacna-Arica dispute. Britain, which had earlier considered trading naval vessels for Easter Island, broke off negotiations when it discovered that this suggestion violated the 1922 Washington Naval Armament Limitation Treaty. Ibáñez then offered Easter Island to Japan in exchange for its support in deterring the United States from intervening actively in the Tacna-Arica dispute. When his overture to Tokyo failed, the general may have recognized that he had to settle peacefully Chile's border problem with Lima.[16]

By chance, Chilean and Peruvian diplomats sailed on the same ship in order to attend the 1928 Pan-American conference in Havana, Cuba. En route, the two sides became civil, if not friendly. The shipboard relationship deepened during the conference. Officially the two nations had not exchanged diplomats, so their representatives could not speak directly. Hence, they called upon U.S. Secretary of State Frank Kellogg to act as matchmaker. After the delighted Kellogg suggested that the two nations reopen their embassies, he wisely stepped back, allowing the delegates to negotiate. In 1929, after decades of confrontation, the two countries reached a settlement. Chile would retain the port of Arica and the area to the south; Peru won Tacna, plus certain financial concessions. Peru's president, however, insisted that President Herbert Hoover should pretend that he drafted the agreement. This ploy would allow Lima to claim in the future that the United States had forced the treaty upon Peru.[17]

The American Presence

When the Great Depression engulfed most of the world in 1929, it seemed to bypass Santiago. Thanks to the cupidity of Colonel Ibáñez and the gullibility of Wall Street, Chile had enough money in reserve to sustain it into 1931. The loss of foreign funding and foreign markets, however, devastated Chile's economy: from 1929 to 1932, imports fell 80 percent and exports dropped by 87 percent. The Great Depression administered a coup de grace to the nitrate industry, which saw *salitre* prices fall 98 percent and production decline by 91 percent. Fortunately, copper, which also suffered substantial losses—including a 70 percent drop in the world price and a 68 percent decline in exports—managed to pick up some of the economic slack. With 70 percent of the vital mining sector unemployed, the rest of the Chilean economy suffered as well: by 1932, 128,000 workers, out of a labor force of 1,300,000, lacked jobs.

Such massive economic dislocation unleashed the latent political discontent that had been simmering since the First World War. The middle class and the professionals joined the workers in protesting the Moneda's policies. In July 1931, Ibáñez, facing massive civil unrest, fled to Argentina. An interim government scheduled elections to select a successor to the deposed leader. Alessandri, who was involved in the various abortive coups against Ibáñez, again sought the presidency. The Chilean public, perhaps tired of don Arturo's bombast, selected instead a more sedate professor of law, Juan Esteban Montero. Unfortunately Chile's new leader did not enjoy great success. A June 1932 coup, engineered by an air force colonel, Marmaduque Grove, and two civilians, declared Chile a Socialist republic. During their first few days in office, a series of juntas instituted some radical changes. They regulated prices for consumer goods, authorized the government to seize idle factories and nationalize banks, and promised to end the government-owned nitrate monopoly, COSACH. In September, after a hundred days of dictatorial rule, the army forced out the remaining leaders, scheduling Chile's third presidential election in two years. This time Arturo Alessandri was elected.

Although Alessandri's reelection restored political stability, Chile remained deeply troubled. The nation had to rebuild its economy as well as repay the American bankers who had funded Ibáñez's public works projects. The country discovered that U.S. citizens not only owned an uncomfortably large share of its international debt but also dominated both the copper industry and, thanks to the Guggenheim process, nitrate mining. When Ibáñez formed the government *salitre* monopoly COSACH, American investors controlled a majority of the seats on the board of directors.

Chileans resented the increasingly visible American presence. Critics complained about the copper towns, claiming that workers lived in substandard housing, in "misery, promiscuity, alcohol, and degeneration. Chuquicamata [the U.S. owned copper town]," observed one critic, "is annihilating the race." It is questionable if American employers treated their workers worse than domestic capitalists. Certainly the copper companies paid higher salaries than Chilean companies.[18] Copper miners, moreover, paid less for food and received free housing, education, and medical care. As one contemporary noted: "In all cases it appears that you can infer that the economic condition of these families is very superior to the great majority of the working families of the other industries in the nation."[19] But the workers' living conditions were not the main issue. By 1927, a Radical party deputy complained that "today, the government of Chile is subordinated to North American bankers and it cannot undertake any guarantee or sign any loans without the approval of these bankers. We are, in this respect, in the same situation as some Central American Republics which have lost their sovereignty." A Chilean historian subsequently described Chile in 1930 as "no more than a factory of the United States."[20] This economic penetration had occurred, however, because Chilean entrepreneurs chose to put their money elsewhere. Indeed, one Chilean complained that his fellow countrymen had invested some twenty million dollars in Bolivia as well as large sums in Argentina rather than risk their capital to develop local industries or resources.[21]

Chileans, moreover, did not hesitate to defend their economic interests. Immediately after World War I, Chilean nitrate producers attempted to resurrect their industry by creating a cartel, the Nitrate Producers Association. American-owned *salitreras*, fearing prosecution under U.S. antitrust laws, refused to join the association. In retaliation, the cartel forced the Moneda to pass a law discriminating against U.S.-owned mines. Although this legislation damaged U.S. interests, the State Department did not rush to defend its nationals. When the United States decided to build a synthetic nitrate plant at Muscle Shores, however, Santiago's minister in Washington vigorously protested.[22]

Clearly U.S. diplomats worked to advance American economic interests. "Our selfish national interests," wrote Ambassador William S. Culbertson, "indicates this as the time when we should adopt an active policy to safeguard our interests in markets and . . . raw materials in foreign countries." The State Department interceded on behalf of copper companies that opposed the Moneda's attempts to tax imported coal and oil, it complained when Chile tried to discriminate against U.S. insurance companies and shipping lines, and it tried to help Pan-American–Grace Airways gain access to Chilean airspace. Not every attempt succeeded. When Culbertson tried to obtain a most favored nation treaty with Ibáñez, the Chilean president refused to grant the same exemptions he had accorded other nations or to allow U.S. access to coastal shipping.[23] The American economic reach did not extend, as it did in the Caribbean and Central America, to direct intervention in Chile's political affairs. In 1931, when the Chilean navy mutinied, demanding agrarian reform and the nationalization of the nation's mineral resources, a terrified Moneda requested that the United States provide weapons as well as send some naval vessels south. Washington, however, refused.

The 1932 Socialist Republic blamed the depression on the United States, clearly threatening American economic interests. Yet, although various American businessmen expressed fear of what might befall them, the White House did not actively intervene. The United States did join France and Great Britain in warning that they would freeze Chile's assets and sever its credit lines if the new government expropriated their nationals' property. Hoover also refused to recognize the government of Carlos Dávila until it promised not to take American-owned interests without paying compensation. Washington's reaction seemed tame in comparison to that of the English, who dispatched a cruiser to Chilean waters as a warning.

Although espousing a form of state socialism, Dávila privately assured Culbertson that "my American friends . . . have nothing to fear." Within a few months the army crushed the Socialist Republic, holding new elections that restored Alessandri to power. The United States, while doubtless pleased, did not help unseat Dávila. As one scholar noted, "Although foreign overreactions compounded the junta's woes, the Socialist Republic was made and unmade by the Chilean military and a handful of civilians, not by the masses or foreigners."[24]

The Alessandri Years, 1932–1938

Chile quickly discovered that it could not shed its financial obligations as easily as it deposed Ibáñez and the Socialists. In 1931 the

Moneda had suspended servicing its international debt. When Alessandri took office, he promised to dedicate various taxes, including those on nitrates, to satisfying Chile's foreign creditors, but it was clear that he deeply resented paying these debts. Alessandri's minister of finance, Gustavo Ross Santa María, argued that the international bankers, by encouraging Ibáñez to accept loans, had victimized Chile. The Great Depression, which made debt repayment extremely difficult, aggravated these feelings. The peso's value had fallen because high tariffs and low world demand had reduced the consumption of Chilean exports. Either the Moneda's creditors renegotiated the terms of their debts, Ross warned, or they would lose everything. With Washington's tacit support, the disgruntled creditors formed the Committee of Chilean Bondholders in order to press their claims for compensation. In 1933, Ross convinced many of Santiago's creditors to accept a smaller return on both the interest and amortization. Two months after signing an agreement that reduced the value of Chilean bonds by 86 percent, he began purchasing these heavily discounted notes and in the process almost halved the national debt. While undoubtedly clever, this maneuver did not endear either the minister or his government to the American bondholders.

Bilateral trade constituted another contentious issue. Confronted with the Great Depression, both the United States and Chile hastily erected high tariff barriers to protect domestic industries and to generate revenues. Of the two nations, Chile was more economically vulnerable to such tactics. Washington's four-cents-per-pound import tax on copper reduced by almost 95 percent America's consumption of Chile's principal export. The results were immediate and catastrophic: the Moneda's exports and, therefore, its income fell. In order to husband its foreign reserves, the Moneda imposed currency controls. Chile also reclaimed some of its old European markets, primarily France and later Germany, by entering into quasi-bartering arrangements called Compensation Trade Agreements. Santiago, in essence, exchanged its nitrates in return for manufactured goods. The Compensation Trade Agreements proved so useful that Chile made similar arrangements with more than a dozen other nations. Indeed, by 1936 Germany had supplanted the United States as Chile's most important trading partner.

The State Department opposed the compensation agreements and the imposition of exchange controls because they made it more difficult for Americans to sell goods to Chile, remit profits, or receive interest payments on bonds. As a compromise, the Moneda offered a compensation agreement to the United States, but it refused to give up exchange controls. Henceforth the American copper companies, or any U.S. corporation remitting their profits to the United States, would have to buy dollars from Chile's Central Bank at an artificially high rate. The American government protested but could do little, because the tariff on Chile's copper had diminished U.S. economic leverage on Santiago. Committed to economic nationalism, the Franklin D. Roosevelt administration could ill afford the political consequences of rescinding the copper tax.

The State Department tried to sidestep Santiago's trade restrictions by seeking most favored nation status. After months of bickering, Washington won only a few concessions: Chile offered the United States equal treatment on issues of currency controls, quotas, and taxes, but the Moneda adamantly refused to accord Washington the same concessions that it extended to those countries with whom it had signed compensation agreements. Thus, not only did Alessandri deny the United States most favored nation status, but as Chile relied more heavily on compensation agreements, he also increased restrictions on trading with the U.S.[25]

Santiago continued to act, if not in defiance, then with disdain toward the United States. After 1932, the Moneda froze American credits worth about twenty-one million dollars. The supposedly conservative Ross advanced the cause of Chilean economic nationalism by increasing the taxes on American-owned copper corporations. For Alessandri and his successors, the levy on copper became the Moneda's fiscal mainstay. By 1934, for example, the owners of the Gran Minería complex paid approximately 18 percent of their profits on their mining operations in tax.

The copper miners were not the only Americans to suffer. The Chilean government forced an American-owned electrical utility company to accept a Chilean majority on its board of directors and to divide its profits equally between the government, the shareholders, and the consumers. Ross, moreover, replaced COSACH with a new nitrate corporation: the Chilean Nitrate and Iodine Sales Corporation. Like COSACH, COVENSA was created to regulate production in hope of supporting the world price of nitrate. Unlike COSACH, however, Chileans constituted a majority of COVENSA's board of directors, and hence they virtually controlled policy decisions. In addition, the Moneda received 25 percent of the corporation's profits. Regrettably, COVENSA failed; the Great Depression merely completed the process of deterioration begun by the Haber process.

The collapse of the newly formed nitrate company affected Chile's relations with the United States. The Moneda had earlier agreed to dedicate the government's share of COVENSA's income to servicing Chile's foreign obligations. Thus, the failure of the nitrate company adversely affected the Moneda's creditors. An irate United States threatened to withhold economic assistance in order to force Chile to promise that it would continue to pay its debts. Ambassador Culbertson even suggested that Washington freeze the funds Chile earned from selling its products in the United States. Fearing that Alessandri might take reprisals against American copper and nitrate holdings, Secretary of State Cordell Hull rejected Culbertson's advice.

This episode demonstrated that although Chilean nationalists complained about America's economic presence, Washington, not Santiago, appeared more vulnerable. As long as Chile held hostage U.S. investments, particularly in the copper industry, the Moneda possessed more leverage than the White House. This situation would not change after Alessandri completed his term of office in 1938 and the Popular Front came to power.[26]

6   The Radical Presidents, 1938–1952

When laissez-faire capitalism collapsed in the 1930s, numerous Latin American nations abandoned liberal democracy in favor of highly nationalistic and authoritarian governments. Sometimes, as in Caribbean and Central American countries, the United States could protect its nationals' interests. Conversely, it could not prevent a hostile Mexico from turning on American-owned corporations. The creation, in Brazil and Argentina, of regimes modeled on Fascist Italy or Nazi Germany troubled Washington more than Mexico's expropriation of U.S. assets. These Latin American nations, as well as Chile, contained large German and Italian populations, which possessed a strong sense of ethnic identity. Many Americans feared that Hitler's resurgent Germany might use these communities' political influence in order to replace the United States as the Western Hemisphere's political and economic leader. Roosevelt attempted to blunt Berlin's political influence, but Latin America's leaders did not share his sense of urgency. Not until the 1938 Pan-American Conference meeting in Lima did they express a weak commitment to hemispheric collective defense. In that same year, the Radical party came to power in Chile.

Founded in the 1860s, the Radical party rarely lived up to its ferocious name. Historically, the party confined its efforts to secularizing Chilean society, but the Great Depression drastically changed the Radical party's rhetoric, if not ideology. During its 1931 convention, the party formally denounced both capitalism and its handmaiden, imperialism, in favor of a collectivist economic system that stressed nationalism. Predictably, hostility toward the United States increased because it supposedly "had sustained dictatorships throughout the continent." A few Radicals advocated creating a Latin American confederation "capable of stopping the systematic advance of the blond colossus."[1] Left-wing members of the party's urban sector began identifying with American Indians.

Traditionally Chile's Radical, Socialist, and Communist parties—which comprised the Popular Front—had little in common except a loathing of the Right and of each other. The rise of Hitler's Germany so preoccupied Joseph Stalin that in 1935 he ordered Communists everywhere to forge political alliances with "progressive" elements in order to limit the spread of fascism. Chilean Communists obediently began cultivating the once-denigrated, largely middle-class Radicals and the slightly less bourgeois Socialists to create the Popular Front, a coalition that pledged to nurture democracy, foster social justice, and oppose imperialism. Initially, massive government vote fraud defeated many of the Front's candidates in the 1937 congressional elections, but the alliance survived. In 1938 the Front selected Pedro Aguirre Cerda as its presidential candidate. Campaigning on the slogan of providing all needy Chileans "Bread, Housing, and an Overcoat," don Pedro vowed to change Chile by stressing social justice and economic development.

Despite Aguirre Cerda's popular appeal, Gustavo Ross Santa María, Alessandri's handpicked protégé, was expected to triumph. Ross could count on the support of the Moneda, and he possessed a war chest deep enough to bribe most Chileans into voting for him. Ross enjoyed yet another advantage. Carlos Ibáñez del Campo had returned from his Argentine exile in order to join the crowded presidential race. The former caudillo, who had won the nomination of Chile's small Nazi party, was expected to siphon enough votes from the Left to allow Ross to defeat Aguirre Cerda. An unexpected event, however, altered the political equation. In September 1938, a group of Nazi students attempted to depose Alessandri. Rather than jail the young students, as most Chileans anticipated, the authorities murdered them. This gratuitously savage act shocked a nation accustomed to police who generally reserved their brutality for the workers, not the sons of the middle class. Ibáñez, who had been jailed following the abortive coup, ordered his supporters, including the Nazis, to vote for Aguirre Cerda. Thanks to the public's revulsion about the massacre and Ibáñez's last-minute support, Aguirre Cerda defeated Ross by four thousand votes.

The new president faced a daunting task: industrialize the nation, improve living standards, and expand social services. An unexpected event complicated Aguirre Cerda's first days in office. A 1939 earthquake devastated parts of Chile's south, killing perhaps thirty thousand people. Rebuilding the devastated area would require massive state intervention and funding. Aguirre Cerda solved the first problem by creating CORFO, the Development Corporation, to oversee reconstruction. Obtaining new economic resources proved more difficult. Aguirre Cerda and the legislature could have increased taxes, particularly on the landed aristocracy, or levied imposts on the foreign-owned copper companies. If the Moneda taxed the landholding elite, the *hacendados* would surely sabotage Aguirre Cerda's plans to industrialize the economy. The president clearly could not tax the emerging industrialist class, which depended on government protection. The urban proletariat and the agrarian workers also constituted a caste of economic untouchables: the former possessed too much political power to be taxed, and the latter possessed nothing worth taxing. Not surprisingly, the president turned to the copper companies: they had ample resources and, more significantly, they were foreign-owned.

The government instituted a special 15 percent tax to fund CORFO, a 9 percent impost on mining companies, and a 6 percent tax on foreign corporations. The Moneda eventually imposed a 3 percent surcharge on the latter two imposts. By December 1941, the copper companies were paying approximately 33 percent of their revenues in taxes.[2] In addition, the Moneda retained the law requiring foreign copper companies to buy their dollars, at artificially high prices, from the Central Bank. While Chile's tax policies clearly discriminated against American-owned corporations, the United States could not easily retaliate. The threat of foreign competition, particularly from Germany, limited Washington's options. The Moneda, moreover, could always confiscate U.S. copper holdings. The combination of the new imposts and exchange controls, which endangered the copper companies and distressed Washington, did not satiate the Moneda's economic appetite. Consequently, Aguirre Cerda turned to the United States for economic assistance. Washington's ambassador, Norman Armour, supported Aguirre Cerda's request for loans, arguing that American support, by improving living conditions, benefited Chile and, by limiting the growing hemispheric influence of Hitler's Germany, would help the United States.

Borrowing from Washington posed ideological problems for Aguirre Cerda. The Popular Front's program specifically denounced American imperialism, often describing its old rival, Ross, as a creature of Wall Street.[3] Additionally the Moneda believed that servicing Chile's foreign debts absorbed so much domestic capital that it stunted the nation's economy. Consequently, requesting funds from the United States perpetuated Chile's dependency on Washington while compromising Santiago's development. Thus, when Santiago finally decided to ask Washington for assistance, a conflict over priorities developed. Willing to help Santiago repair the earthquake damage, the United States refused to fund Aguirre Cerda's other projects. The Moneda retorted that it could always obtain the resources by ceasing to service its foreign debt, raising the taxes on American corporations operating in Chile, or borrowing from Germany.

Eventually the Export-Import Bank authorized a loan of between ten and fifteen million dollars, far less than the one hundred million that Santiago sought but at a more favorable interest rate. Washington, however, insisted that the Moneda use the money to purchase American-made goods. This stipulation displeased the Chileans, who unsuccessfully sought to spend the money without restrictions. Chile subsequently appealed to the United States to provide additional funds for its Corporación de Fomento as well. But the United States would advance only seventeen million dollars, a small percentage of Chile's request. Thus Washington's niggardliness, as well as its refusals to lower trade barriers or to abrogate the tariff on Chilean copper, antagonized the Moneda. On two occasions Chilean authorities threatened to stop servicing their nation's debts unless the United States granted additional loans.[4]

Traditionally, Chilean nationalists stridently denounced American domination of the country's copper industry. Yet the Chilean government, even under Aguirre Cerda, clearly expected the United States to support its extractive industries. After the Second World War began, the Chilean economy suffered as copper sales to Europe fell. Revenues declined as unemployment increased. In order to compensate for the loss of Chile's European markets, Aguirre Cerda dispatched a delegate to Washington, requesting that the United States lend money to the Moneda for the purchase of essential imports, buy Chile's nitrate, and increase American imports of Chilean copper. When the United States began to rearm, Washington stepped up its purchases of Chilean copper without encouragement. Aware that a seller had the advantage, the Moneda raised the price for the metal from ten to twelve cents per pound and increased the taxes on the copper industry.

Initially the White House tried to resist the Moneda's financial demands, but the attack on Pearl Harbor ended Washington's haggling. The Chilean government not only forced the United States to pay an additional two cents per pound for copper but also retained 60 percent of the price increase. In addition to these direct imposts, the companies still had to pay a 50 percent surcharge on each dollar they remitted to the United States. Thus, the Moneda took about 65 percent of the copper companies' profits. Washington, moreover, had to suspend its 1932 import tax on Chilean copper.[5]

Chile's economic victory proved both illusory and short-lived. Wartime demand pushed world copper prices from eleven to twenty-five cents per pound, leading Chile to complain that its 1942 arrangement with Washington had cheated it of approximately five hundred million dollars. The United States dismissed these charges. Chile, it countered, had entered freely into the 1942 agreement. Santiago, critics observed, could hardly claim that it should earn the prevailing market price for copper, because the Second World War had so warped the world economy that the market forces of supply and demand no longer applied. The United States, by purchasing Santiago's nitrates —when Americans produced these chemicals domestically and less expensively than the Chileans—had subsidized the Chilean economy.

The Issue of Chile's Neutrality

At the 1940 Havana conference, which convened shortly after the fall of France, the Moneda vaguely agreed to assist Washington in hemispheric defense. In order to fulfill that mission, Chile's armed forces needed substantial help. Regrettably, just as the Moneda and the White House quibbled over economic aid, so they haggled over military assistance. Chile requested forty million dollars worth of equipment, more than either it could afford or the United States could provide. When Washington noted that Santiago did not have the funds to pay for the war matériel, the Moneda responded that it expected the United States to lend it the money. But Washington had established its own priorities for military assistance, and Chile, located at the end of the world, did not appear high on the list. The Moneda possessed a trump card: Germany offered to sell Chile weapons that it had captured during the first battles of World War II. Santiago, moreover, intimated that it could obtain the necessary funds by raising the taxes on the American-owned copper mines. Fearful of forfeiting both its influence and its investments in Chile, Washington opened its arsenal door slightly wider.

Although the Moneda promised to cooperate in hemispheric defense, neutrality remained the linchpin of Chilean foreign policy. This decision reflected the nation's ethnic composition. Many Chileans, particularly those of German extraction, favored the Axis powers, a sentiment which the German embassy actively nurtured. Domestic politics also encouraged the Moneda's nonbelligerence. Following the 1939 Russo-German Non-Aggression Pact, Chile's Communist party obediently switched from insulting Hitler to flaying the Allies. The Socialists, however, continued to advocate support for the British and French. This policy difference, as well as conflict over control of the union movement, so bitterly divided the Socialists and Communists that it contributed to the collapse of the Popular Front in 1941. Hitler's invasion of Russia drove the Communists back into the Allied camp, but many Chileans still opposed active involvement in the European conflict.

The Japanese attack on Pearl Harbor did not produce a noticeable shift in Santiago's policies. In January 1942, the Latin American nations met in Rio de Janeiro to hear U.S. Assistant Secretary of State Sumner Welles urge them to sever their ties with the Axis nations. While most nations obliged, Argentina and Chile lobbied against Welles's proposal. Thanks to their efforts, the hemispheric countries recommended, but did not require, that the Latin American states sever diplomatic relations with the Axis powers.

If Chile's neutrality distressed Wilson in 1917, then Chile's reluctance to enter the Second World War outraged Washington. The Moneda refused to act, claiming that it feared the Japanese might retaliate by attacking Chile's largely undefended cities. While the American military attaché agreed that the Moneda's anxieties were not without some merit, he also believed that the Imperial fleet had more tempting targets than Chile's coast. The Japanese embassy, of course, played on Santiago's anxiety, promising not to attack Chile if it remained neutral. When Washington vowed that the U.S. fleet would protect Chile, the Moneda's foreign minister, Gabriel Rossetti, undiplomatically replied, "What fleet? The one sunk in Pearl Harbor?"[6] Rossetti intimated that Chile might act more belligerently if the United States supplied the weapons and aircraft to protect its vulnerable shoreline. Washington, however, had to arm dozens of nations as well as fight its own war. Chile's requests for assistance seemed excessive, and Roosevelt insisted that Santiago declare war without waiting for U.S. military matériel.

Domestic political pressure influenced the Moneda's foreign policy vis-à-vis the Axis. In late 1941 Aguirre Cerda unexpectedly died, requiring the nation to elect a new chief executive. The 1942 election deeply concerned Washington. The staunchest advocate of the Allied cause, the Socialist Oscar Schnake, fearing that his candidacy would divide the electorate and thus permit a rightist triumph, withdrew from the presidential contest. From Washington's perspective, the two remaining contenders did not seem particularly attractive: Colonel Ibáñez, who proclaimed his affection for the United States, led a coalition that included the Chilean Nazi party; and Juan Antonio

Rios, who was courting the German-Chilean community, represented the Radical party. Rossetti, himself a Radical, feared that if Chile severed its ties with Germany, then Rios would lose the crucial German-Chilean vote and hence the election. "If I return to Chile," Rossetti subsequently declared, "after having broken relations with the Axis, they may hang me in the Plaza de Armas."[7] Rossetti, therefore, resisted American pressure, and Rios triumphed.

Rios's foreign minister was Ernesto Barros Jarpa who, while pro-American, adamantly opposed breaking diplomatic relations with the Axis powers. Paradoxically, while espousing neutrality, Barros also pestered the United States to increase its military aid to Santiago. When challenged about this apparent inconsistency, Barros responded that the Moneda was merely following a policy enunciated by George Washington—that a nation should not engage in a foreign war if such action did not serve its interests. Chile, additionally, lacked a reason for breaking relations. "If the United States," he explained, "had to wait for an attack on Pearl Harbor [before declaring war], then Chile could wait, if not for an attack on its territory, then at least for an act of war which might occur inside what it considers its 'zone of influence' " before becoming a belligerent.[8] Chile alone could decide its fate. Indeed, by vigorously asserting this principle, Santiago claimed that it was defending its sovereignty as well as that of all Latin American nations.

Involved in what he perceived as a life and death struggle with fascism, Roosevelt considered the Moneda's inaction as a threat to American security and an insult to the inter-American movement. Nothing seemed capable of pushing the Moneda into war. In March 1942, off New York, a German submarine torpedoed a Chilean transport, the *Tolten*; some Americans believed this action would prompt the Moneda to declare war. The Chilean foreign minister refused to denounce the German attack and blamed the United States for the incident. Because Washington had forced the *Tolten* to travel without lights—which would have identified it as a neutral ship—the United States, Santiago argued, had caused the transport's destruction.

Refusing to declare war, the Rios government nonetheless renewed its request that the United States supply Chile with substantial amounts of weapons. Washington's envoy supported the Moneda's petition, arguing that supplying weapons would expedite U.S. efforts to make Chile a belligerent. An impasse developed because Santiago insisted that it receive military assistance before complying with the Rio treaty. The State Department shrewdly demanded that the Moneda sever relations with Axis nations as a precondition to receiving arms. In December 1942, Rios privately informed Washington that Santiago might break relations with the Axis. Fearing a Japanese attack on his nation's vulnerable coastline, however, he requested that Washington first provide Chile with military equipment. Rios's demands seemed so exaggerated that the State Department decided that Chile was using the war to extract a high price in return for its diplomatic cooperation.[9] A British diplomat reached the same conclusion, remarking that "while Argentina is not 'for sale' Chile *is*."[10]

Some Chileans, of course, favored delaying a decision until it became clear that Santiago would join the winning side. Seeing the string of Axis victories in 1942, many, including Barros, were not certain that the Allies would win the war.[11] A few Chileans actually opposed helping the Allies, believing that an Axis victory would end Santiago's economic dependence upon the United States and Great Britain. As Rios's ambassador to Germany noted, by remaining "neutral we will continue serving, together with our interests, the true interests of Iberoamerica in Europe [where] . . . integral revolutions are creating new political and economic systems, which we cannot stop by sacrificing our neutrality . . . [while] by breaking ties with the Axis we cut the secular ties of vital importance with this continent and we will deliver ourselves to only one of the belligerents."[12]

Another Chilean faction hoped to use their nation's entry into the war to extort economic concessions from the United States.[13] In 1942 Chile's ministers of finance and commerce, as well as officials of the Corporación de Fomento, informed Washington that Rios would use the sinking of the *Tolten* as an excuse to declare war, in return for American economic concessions: an increase in the price the United States paid for Chile's copper, nitrate, and iodine, and a pledge to continue purchasing these items at specified levels after the war ended. The United States also had to guarantee that its synthetic ammonia plants would not engage in ruinous competition with Chile's nitrate industries. And finally, Washington would have to lend up to one hundred million dollars to the Moneda so it could make various capital improvements.

Barros and Rios subsequently repudiated these tactics, but to no avail. The State Department felt that Chile demanded too much for what other nations had already done gratuitously. Perhaps recalling a British diplomat's remark that "the generous gesture and faith in an eventual reward does not appeal to the Chilean mind," Secretary of State Cordell Hull informed the Moneda that the United States refused to bargain on the issue of declaring war, hinting ominously that Santiago might rue its hesitation after the war.[14] The situation became so acrimonious that President Rios canceled a visit to the United States after Secretary Hull publicly chided Chile and Argentina for not breaking with the Axis powers.

The Moneda's failure to prevent Axis agents from operating in Chile also antagonized the United States. The German Air attaché in Santiago and the local North German Lloyd Line had organized a spy network, code-named Condor, to provide intelligence to Berlin. The U.S. State Department claimed that Nazi submarines utilized this information to sink Allied ships carrying needed raw materials to the United States. To substantiate this assertion, the United States submitted a list of activities undertaken by Axis agents operating in Chile. Believing that he could force the Moneda to take some action, Welles leaked a report demonstrating that the Chilean authorities tolerated Axis spying. Barros adamantly rejected these assertions. Even if Axis agents had operated from Chile, he argued, their information would not affect the safety of the shipping lanes.[15]

Welles's report antagonized various Chileans, among them three former presidents, who described it as U.S. intervention in Santiago's affairs. Conversely, Barros's inability or reluctance to root out the Axis agents so incensed the Socialist party that it demanded the foreign minister's resignation. Eventually Barros lost his post, but for ideological reasons. The foreign minister had alienated so many members of Rios's cabinet that the president decided to recast his government. But when Rios replaced Barros with Joaquín Fernández Fernández, the president noted that he was merely changing foreign ministers, not Chile's foreign policy.

In early 1943, Rios indicated that Chile would finally break relations with the Axis powers. While possessing the will to declare war, Rios lacked a credible pretext. Clearly the president could not use the torpedoing of the *Tolten* as an excuse, since this event had occurred a year earlier. Washington chivalrously provided the Moneda with a list of vessels that it claimed the Germans had destroyed as a consequence of information provided by spies operating from Chile. Armed with Washington's promise of protection and postwar economic assistance, Rios requested the congress to discontinue diplomatic relations with the Axis powers. Even this act, which occurred thirteen months after the bombing of Pearl Harbor, was a hollow victory for the United States: Rios suspended, but did not sever, relations with the Axis nations.[16]

For almost two years, Chile lived in a state of diplomatic limbo. In February 1945, however, Santiago declared war on the remaining Axis powers. The catalyst for this sudden step was not U.S. pressure but a Russian insistence that only countries that had declared war on Germany and Japan could join the embryonic United Nations. Joseph Stalin had placed Rios in an unpalatable situation: while he desperately wanted a place at the victors' table, the Chilean leader still lacked a reason to turn on Berlin and Tokyo. Eventually the lure of joining the peace conference proved so strong that Rios made the decision without consulting the Chilean congress. Two months later, the legislature retroactively ratified the president's action. Although the process had been awkwardly, if not clumsily, handled, Chile had cast its lot with the Allies in time to join the United Nations.

World War II, even more than World War I, strained Washington's ties with Chile. American leaders, who saw the conflict as a struggle between democracy and fascism, grumbled that the Chileans used the Second World War to extract military and economic concessions from the United States. These beliefs were not without foundation. Santiago charged top dollar for its products, such as gold and manganese, which the United States had to purchase regardless of cost or Washington's needs. Chile permitted U.S. naval units to refuel in Antofagasta and Valparaíso only on the following conditions: that Washington first build a tank farm, which would revert to Chile at the end of the war; that it request permission before using the refueling facilities; and that it pay an import duty on the fuel the American fleet consumed. At the end of the war a U.S. government report noted that Washington purchased more per capita from Chile than from any other Latin American nation. Chile, in addition, received twenty-eight million dollars in loans plus thirty-eight million to finance various projects.[17] Santiago, moreover, became Latin America's third largest recipient of wartime military aid. Chile insisted that the United States not reveal that the Moneda paid only 30 percent of the twenty-three million dollar cost of the matériel it received in lend-lease. Thus the White House viewed the Moneda's reluctance to join the war with contempt, suspicion, and disdain. Indeed, Santiago's last-minute break with the Axis powers—in order to win an undeserved place at the victors' table—merely confirmed Washington's belief that Chile was not an ally.

The United States had emerged from the war with its economy revitalized and with a monopoly on the atomic bomb. This sense of security quickly dissipated when the Soviets occupied Eastern Europe. The White House then took steps to ensure that its Latin American ties, which had developed over the course of the war, would not unravel. The United States needed Latin American raw materials; it also wanted to earn back the dollars that various hemispheric nations had accumulated during the course of the war. Finally, it sought Latin American support, which composed 40 percent of the General Assembly of the United Nations.

Although important, Latin American economic needs did not preoccupy Washington as much as events in Europe, where Russian pressure seemed the most urgent. Within the State Department, a generation of cold war policy makers debated U.S. priorities in Latin

America—economic development or military security. Although Latin American governments preferred butter to guns, they accepted military agreements, such as the 1947 Inter-American Treaty of Reciprocal Assistance, in the belief that economic aid would be forthcoming. The assistance, at least in the amount desired by the Latin Americans, did not materialize. Preoccupied by the threat of communism in the Western Hemisphere, the United States began favoring conservative over liberal Latin American regimes, especially if the latter tolerated Communist activities.

Chile Turns Right: Gabriel González Videla, 1946–1952

Gabriel González Videla came to power just as the United States was fashioning its anti-Communist strategy. Chile, by contrast, began 1945 beyond the pale. Not only had Chile unenthusiastically and tardily declared war, but it possessed one of the continent's largest Communist parties. After Hitler attacked the Soviet Union, Chilean Communists dutifully endorsed the anti-German struggle, urging the Rios administration to cooperate in the crusade against fascism. Just as quickly, the once pro-American Communists urged the Moneda not to join Washington's anti-Soviet crusade, which they dismissed as capitalist fantasy.

Strife between the Communist and Socialist parties, both of which courted the workers' vote, precipitated substantial unrest in Chile. Both sides organized strikes that often degenerated into bloodshed. Socialists used their positions within the postwar government of Vice President Alfredo Duhalde, who assumed power following Rios's death in 1946, to suppress the Communist party, which accused the government of acting as a lackey of the United States. While this action doubtless pleased Washington, the White House had not urged Duhalde to move against the Communists. Nor had the Moneda indulged in Red-baiting simply to obtain economic credits from the United States.[18] The Chilean, Radical, and Socialist parties had moved against the Communist party for purely domestic political reasons.

Communism subsequently reemerged as an issue in Chile. Rios's death necessitated conducting another presidential election. The ruling Radicals nominated Gabriel González Videla, who also attracted the support of the Liberals and Communists. While perhaps admiring his political agility in forging such a bizarre coalition, the State Department nevertheless regarded González as hostile to U.S. interests. Despite Chilean requests for U.S. intervention, the State Department remained aloof from the election, even ordering private American companies not to provide funds to anti-González elements.

When González won a plurality in a four-way presidential race, he fulfilled his political obligations by giving the Communists three portfolios: the ministries of communications and public works, land and colonization, and agriculture. Although these were minor departments, they represented the first cabinet posts held by Communists. Within months the three parties were feuding among themselves. Such a struggle was expected, since the Liberals loathed the Communists; the Communists hated the Liberals; and the Radicals despised both of them. In April 1947, the frustrated González dissolved his cabinet. The Communists, who expected to return to the government, became incensed when González staffed his new cabinet with exclusively rightist politicians.

González refused to appoint Communists to his second government because he did not want them to use his administration to widen their political base within Chile. Unlike the Conservatives and Radicals, the Communists had done well in the 1947 municipal elections. By excluding them from his government, González simultaneously solved two pressing problems: the president hoped that he could limit the Communists' domestic political popularity; and purging the Communists increased his chances for obtaining U.S. economic support.

Chile's foreign policy often mirrored that of Washington. In 1947, González signed the Inter-American Treaty of Reciprocal Assistance and the following year joined the Organization of American States. In 1952, Chile signed a bilateral military assistance agreement with the United States. Similarly, Chile's U.N. representatives followed American leadership. But while the Radical party's leaders hoped to avoid confrontation with Washington, Chile's foreign policy was not completely passive. González extended Chilean territorial waters to two hundred miles. To protect Chile's nitrate industry, he successfully pressured Argentina and Brazil to abandon plans to build synthetic nitrogen plants.[19] In 1950, the Moneda compelled both the United States and the copper companies to accept Chilean terms when negotiating a new agreement.

Predictably Chile's support for Washington's economic and military programs caused domestic problems for González. The Communists manifested their anger by launching more strikes. One of these, in August 1947, paralyzed the nation's coal mines. Since this work stoppage occurred in the midst of winter, it threatened the nation's economic and public health. In order to keep the mines working, González sent in the military and mobilized those miners who belonged to the army's reserves. Furious at the Communists, the president arrested various members and shut down the party's press. The discovery of plans for a Communist coup prompted González to break diplomatic relations with the Eastern bloc. In 1948, the legislature, at the president's request, passed a measure—the Law for the Defense of Democracy—banning the Communist party and striking its members from the voting rolls.

González's actions pleased the U.S. government. Indeed, some argue that the Chilean leader moved against the Communist party either to curry Washington's favor or in response to U.S. political pressure. Certainly the State Department had become chary of González since his election. In September 1946, a Communist-led strike paralyzed the Kennecott mine at Sewell. The United States interceded on behalf of the company, threatening to withhold economic credits from Chile unless the Moneda intervened to settle the work stoppage. González refused, insisting that Kennecott use existing Chilean legal mechanisms to resolve its labor dispute. Thus, while willing to appoint an arbitrator who would be fair, the Chilean president refused to capitulate to Washington. On the contrary, he warned the State Department that its crude attempts to influence a Chilean labor dispute would strain relations between the two nations, while providing the Left with a new excuse to attack the United States. The State Department retreated, encouraging Kennecott's management to compromise. Apparently González's refusal to crush the strike persuaded some of the State Department staff that he was a Communist dupe. Consequently, when Chile requested that the United States provide coal and approve its application for a forty million dollar loan, the State Department refused. Assistant Secretary of State Spruille Braden, whose father had once owned the Sewell mine, vehemently opposed granting Chile additional financial credits. Santiago, he warned, would receive neither funds nor coal until it reorganized its foreign debts, ceased discriminating against the copper companies, and broke with the Communist party.

It remains unclear whether U.S. or domestic pressures determined González's decision to suppress the Communists. But when he declared that Chile's "future, industrial development, [and] economic welfare depended in great part on the friendship and collaboration of the United States" and ended his alliance with the Communists, Chile quickly received urgently needed economic assistance.[20] Washington immediately shipped one hundred million tons of coal to Chile, and when the Moneda increased the tax on the copper companies by 20 percent, the State Department did not protest. On the contrary, Washington authorized almost forty million dollars in loans.

Despite their shared view on the "Red menace," Chile and the United States differed on international issues. When the United States entered the Korean War, it hoped that the nations of the Western Hemisphere would provide troops. This time Chile was not alone when it, and most of Latin America, refused to contribute to the war. American control of copper also came under increasing attack. As early as the 1940s, one politician had advocated that Chile nationalize the mines in order to "liberate ourselves from Yankee tutelage which today we must endure and adopt attitudes decidedly nationalistic in the area of economics."[21] The outbreak of the Korean War revived charges of U.S. economic imperialism. When the conflict began, prices rose. Needing raw materials, the United States again negotiated a special price with the copper companies. Still smarting over the 1942 copper agreement, Santiago became incensed when it learned that the United States had dealt directly with companies rather than with the Moneda. The Chilean government demanded that Washington rescind its agreement with the copper corporations and renegotiate the arrangement with the Moneda. The State Department acquiesced: henceforth Santiago would receive a higher price for its copper, a portion of which the government would retain, but Chile would begin to market its copper directly. As González Videla later explained, he had bested the American bureaucrats, "who have the mentality and egotism of cowboys when dealing with Latin America."[22] Unable to obtain assistance as part of a greater "Latin American Marshall Plan," Chile nonetheless received help: $6.2 million in grants and $6.7 million for military aid, plus credits and loans from the Export-Import Bank totaling about $104.2 million, representing 3 percent of U.S. economic assistance, 14 percent of military aid, and 16 percent of credits to Latin America.

American largesse and the revived copper market could not calm the political unrest. In 1949 and 1950, for example, demonstrations degenerated into riots requiring military intervention. Even the military toyed with the idea of overthrowing the government. Although the Communists continued to function, albeit under a different name, they did not bear sole responsibility for these disturbances. Obstructed by a hostile legislature, González's regime could do little to arrest the economic decay, the continuing dependence upon copper, and the escalating inflation.

The Radical presidents had failed to fulfill the promises of the Popular Front. In part this failure occurred because the nation's resource base could not support Aguirre Cerda's goals, because the gerrymandered political system frustrated reform, and because the Radical party itself sought patronage rather than change. Dissatisfied with the Radical party's inability to guarantee economic progress and social justice, Chile's increasingly cynical electorate turned again to a caudillo from another era.

7 From Caudillos to Christian Democracy, 1952–1970

In the same year that Chileans chose a paternal military officer to lead them, Americans elected Dwight D. Eisenhower president of the United States. Unlike Ibáñez, Eisenhower had no previous political experience, but he had demonstrated his managerial skills as commander of the Allied war effort. Eisenhower's successful rise from modest economic circumstances, moreover, gave some credence to his embrace of the Republican party. The return of Carlos Ibáñez del Campo represented the triumph of emotion over reason, of personality over ideology. The retired officer's platform, which he did not read prior to its publication, was deliberately vague, reflecting the candidate's own preferences. Chileans, Ibáñez once averred, did not need parties or ideologies, only a "noble and disinterested sense of patriotism and social justice."[1] Ibáñez's reasoning and appeal were simple: since he was a patriot, above partisan considerations, he deserved to occupy the Moneda. His cure for the nation's increasingly difficult problems was a combination of fortitude and grit. Eisenhower pledged to "go to Korea"; Ibáñez solemnly announced, "I will stop this inflation. I will be able to do it because it is my will."[2] The American accomplished his goal by threatening to use atomic weapons. Ibáñez, who lacked this alternative, failed.

As a candidate, Ibáñez was known as the General of Hope, but once settled in office, his apolitical mysticism could not overcome Chile's crushing reality. The war-generated copper boom collapsed in 1953, and inflation reached epidemic proportions: the cost of living increased 50 percent in 1954. When workers went on strike, Ibáñez responded, as he had in the 1920s, by jailing union leaders. The president's resorting to violence misfired: public demonstrations became more frequent and more violent.

Foreign Pressures and Domestic Realities, 1952–1958

Ibáñez's relations with the United States did not begin auspiciously. He had once opposed Chile's 1952 military assistance pact with Washington, labeling it "a criminal act on the nation's dignity."[3] American officials became more distressed when a high-ranking aide to Ibáñez announced that Chile might identify more with the developing world than with the United States.

Despite these ominous beginnings, Ibáñez drew closer to the United States. Describing the regime of Guatemala's Jacobo Arbenz as a threat to hemispheric liberty, he endorsed Washington's 1954 overthrow of the leftist leader. Ibáñez's virulent anticommunism seemed the result more of his personal feelings than of American pressure. In his 1957 presidential message, he declared: "My government's foreign policy has unalterably maintained itself within the Western orbit. In this way, we contribute to reinforcing the democratic system of the free world against the . . . threats of intentional Communism."[4] Paradoxically, Ibáñez had accepted the support of the clandestine Communist party and, in return for its help, abrogated the Law for the Defense of Democracy in 1958. Yet, Ibáñez's government also received substantial amounts of U.S. aid. American generosity alone could not cure Chile's enormous economic difficulties. When the postwar business expansion abated in the early 1950s, the Moneda had refused to restrict spending. Hence Chile suffered from enormous fiscal deficits and inflationary pressures.

Regrettably, Ibáñez lacked the sophistication or technical skills to cope with the problem. The impost, including exchange controls, on the copper industry, which produced approximately 30 percent of the nation's income, and the tax on imported goods constituted the Moneda's fiscal arsenal. A suggestion from the minister of finance —that "the powerful also pay" its share of the taxes—provoked a firestorm of protest from "the powerful."[5] Thus the few changes that Ibáñez's ministers instituted—including a regressive but highly productive sales tax—could not satiate the government's budgetary appetite.

Under enormous economic pressure, Ibáñez predictably turned to Chile's favorite resource: the copper companies. In 1953, he increased their taxes from 50 to 60 percent. This law and the government's ability to market the copper directly allowed the Moneda to take approximately 86 percent of the companies' gross profits.[6] But the combined effect of higher taxes and fierce world competition prompted the companies to reduce their investments. When mine output and revenues declined, the Moneda altered its tactics, by basing taxation on the companies' productivity. In 1955, Ibáñez announced the "New Deal"—El Nuevo Trato—for copper. Henceforth, companies would pay a minimum of 50 percent of their profits. Failure to increase output would require them to pay a surcharge of 25 percent. In addition, the Chilean government would control the production and the sale of copper.

Ibáñez's innovations failed. Although the nation enjoyed a budgetary surplus in 1953, it suffered an eight billion *escudo* deficit in 1954, a deficit which doubled the following year. The cost of living rose from 58 percent in 1954 to 88.7 percent in 1955. Regrettably the Moneda continued to use copper revenues to fund ordinary government expenses, not to diversify the country's economy. Thus, Chile merely increased its fiscal addiction to the mining sector. It became clear that the General of Hope must do something.

When Ibáñez could not resolve the problems, he called upon a foreign mission for guidance—the American firm of Klein and Saks. Klein and Saks was internationally respected, but the Chileans had chosen the American company in part because it was not identified with specific national interests. Believing that Klein and Saks enjoyed close ties with Washington, they hoped that the State Department would look favorably upon Chilean loan requests if the Moneda implemented the consulting firm's suggestions. An equally important, but unstated, consideration was that by selecting a foreign consultant, Chile's politicians would not have to bear the responsibility for the mission's more onerous suggestions. Known for favoring laissez-faire economic solutions, the Klein and Saks advisers suggested that the Moneda reduce the cost of government, restrict credit, reorganize the exchange controls, and end price subsidies and automatic salary increases.

The Chilean congress enacted only some of these recommendations. By a scant one-vote margin, it limited salary increases to 50 percent of the rise in the cost of living, but softened the impact of this measure by instituting a minimum wage and providing higher family allowances. Similarly the legislature restricted credit and revamped the exchange controls. Limiting cost of living increases broke the inflationary fever, but restrictions on credit smothered the construction industry, and the abolition of exchange controls exposed Chile's domestic industries to foreign competition. Thus, while inflation declined, unemployment increased. The main burden of the reforms fell upon the poor, who rioted, in April 1957, to protest the government's policies. Fearful of political unrest and facing elections in 1958, the legislature passed pay increases, thus undoing the effect of the mission.[7]

Only right-wing parties endorsed Ibáñez's reform measures. Their support was predictable, since the Conservatives favored any motion that placed the burden of an austerity program onto the backs of the poor. Not surprisingly, the Klein and Saks mission became identified not merely with Ibáñez and Chile's domestic Right but with the United States as well. The Radical party, for example, made the foreign mission into a major campaign issue, while the Left described the consulting firm as a tool of U.S. imperialism. Chile, one politician demanded, should resolve the problem of inflation not by sacrificing the workers but by ending the privileges of "those elites who have remained tragically backward in their understanding of the social dilemma."[8] Ironically, bashing the Klein and Saks mission became the one tactic that all the presidential candidates in the 1964 campaign employed.[9]

Predictably, the Klein and Saks mission tainted Chilean-American relations. As a Chilean noted, Klein and Saks were "pristine exponents of the American liberal individualistic mentality," which was patronizing and which assured Chile's continued status as a "semi-colonial" state.[10] Yet precisely because it advocated such unpalatable solutions, the firm shifted the onus for the economic crisis from Chile's Right to the United States. Serving as a scapegoat, Washington also acted as Ibáñez's benefactor, providing approximately sixty-nine million dollars in economic aid, thirty-four million in military help, and fifty million in loans. Despite this assistance, Ibáñez became less compliant. In 1954, he attacked Washington for demanding political support without granting Latin America economic assistance, joining other hemispheric nations to press Washington to fund the Inter-American Development Bank. Ibáñez defended Chile's claim for a two-hundred-mile limit and, when the United States imposed a tax on Chile's copper, he canceled a proposed trip to Washington.[11]

Increasingly Chileans blamed their nation's economic problems not on the country's refusal to restructure the old economic order but on more insidious external forces. Advocates of this school of thought attributed Chile's economic underdevelopment and social inequality to an exploitive world. The developed nations, the argument went, purchased Chile's natural resources at very low prices. Eventually the same countries sold back to Chile, at much higher prices, the same natural resources after they had been processed into manufactured goods. This updated version of mercantilism, it was claimed, condemned Chile and other Third World nations to perpetual underdevelopment and therefore to eternal exploitation. This argument served an important function: it attributed Chile's underdevelopment to foreign interests while virtually exculpating the nation's elite. Yet Chile's political system, more than external economic forces, appeared responsible for the nation's underdevelopment.

The government in post-1925 Chile shared many of the same flaws as the Parliamentary regime that preceded it. Insulated from the electorate by political corruption and restrictive institutions, the political parties did not have to address the nation's social and economic ills. And because these problems proliferated and deepened as the population grew, the situation became increasingly volatile. Despite the appearance to the contrary, Chile remained a politically backward nation. Since illiterates and, until 1949, women could not vote, only

14 percent of Chileans were registered electors. Enfranchising women did not dramatically alter that situation. It was not until the 1958 presidential election that 20 percent of the nation could vote.

Other factors limited suffrage. The 1925 constitution instituted the D'Hont system of proportional representation, which favored the established political parties, making it extremely difficult for the left-wing or reformist elements to win seats. In the 1949 legislative elections, one scholar concluded, the D'Hont system deprived the Socialists and the Falange Nacional—which eventually became the Christian Democratic party—of 73 and 56 percent of their votes respectively.[12] Since Chile never reapportioned its legislature to reflect demographic changes, rural voters wielded disproportionately more power than did the urban electorate.

Widespread corruption, moreover, distorted the political system. Not until 1958, when the Chilean government provided the ballots for elections, did the rural landlords lose control of the *inquilino* vote. Four years later, the state simplified the registration process, revamped the voter rolls, and made voting mandatory. These reforms dramatically altered Chile's electoral process. Political participation increased enormously and voters could, perhaps for the first time, honestly manifest their opinions. But until the electorate could express its desires, the nation could not address outstanding social and economic issues.

The 1958 presidential election reflected the changed political environment. Chile's electorate increased by a third, and, for the first time, the Left emerged as a powerful force in national politics. The presidential race was crowded. The Socialists and Communists created the Frente de Acción Popular (FRAP), which championed Dr. Salvador Allende. The centrist Radicals and the Christian Democrats each selected candidates, while the Right coalesced around Arturo Alessandri's son Jorge. Allende's campaign, in addition to proposing numerous domestic reforms, advocated that Chile abandon its alliance with the United States in favor of nonalignment and closer economic ties with Latin America as well as with the Eastern bloc nations. He also promised to nationalize the American-owned Chilean Electric Company and to abrogate Ibáñez's "New Deal" agreement with the copper companies. A FRAP triumph appeared likely until a defrocked radical priest, Antonio Zamorano, supposedly encouraged by the United States, entered the presidential campaign. The former cleric siphoned enough votes from Allende to allow the conservative Alessandri to win a narrow victory.[13]

The Alessandri Years, 1958–1964

Jorge Alessandri's election constituted the last hurrah of the Chilean old order, a desperate attempt to solve the nation's economic and political ills without confronting its basic problems. Alessandri honestly tried to address Chile's lack of a substantial industrial base, the inequitable landholding system, underemployment, and chronic inflation. Regrettably, Chile had changed too much for Alessandri's solutions. Even if he had wished to be innovative, the Great Engineer first had to craft a political power base. Electoral reforms of the late 1950s, which simplified the process of voter registration and made voting easier, had by 1964 almost doubled the electorate. Mobilized by the Left, these new voters became acutely aware that the established political parties had traditionally ignored their needs. They demanded, therefore, that the state provide them with needed social services and opportunities to achieve a better life.

Inflation constituted perhaps Alessandri's most pressing problem, which he blamed not on the government's deficit spending but on the lack of production. The state, he reasoned, could stop the spiraling cost of living by permitting the free entry of foreign goods, which would be less expensive than domestically produced items, and by stimulating industrial and agricultural output. When productivity rose, prices and inflation would abate. Hence, Alessandri sought to smother inflation by stimulating domestic output while holding salary adjustments to a minimum.

To revive the stagnating economy, Alessandri announced projects to provide homes for the middle class, build public works, and reconstruct those areas of the nation savaged by a 1962 earthquake.

He encouraged Chileans to repatriate the money they had illegally sent abroad. Once deposited in special savings banks—Asociación de Ahorros y Prestamos, which would index the interest rate to match inflation—these funds could help finance the nation's economic recovery. Initially Alessandri's plans seemed to work. Housing starts rose close to 500 percent in one year.

The price of Alessandri's policies was increasingly high deficits. Imports rose by 30 percent. Serving the nation's increasingly large foreign debt consumed 70 percent of Chile's export earnings. The combination of the trade imbalance and debt service devoured the nation's foreign reserves. The country's economic health suffered when an earthquake ravaged the nation and the price of copper fell. By 1962, the government suspended foreign exchange operations, forcing Alessandri to devalue the Chilean *escudo,* which the president had vowed to keep on par with the U.S. dollar.

While imperative, the devaluation devastated the Chilean economy and national psyche. Earlier, Chileans had accepted reduced salary increases, believing that this sacrifice would restrain the inflation. Initially the combination of the smaller *reajustes* and the increase in imports dampened the rate of inflation. By raising the price of imported goods, devaluation increased the cost of living. Interpreting devaluation as a sign that the government had abandoned its antiinflationary crusade, Chileans demanded higher wages in order to compensate for past increases in the cost of living and to protect them against a future loss of purchasing power. The inflationary spiral accelerated. Within three weeks, consumer prices increased by 50 percent. Food costs rose so quickly that by 1963 at least half the Chileans were considered malnourished. Just as predictably, strikes turned into riots as people finally demonstrated to obtain some measure of relief.[14]

The Cuban Question

These troubles occurred just as the United States attempted to enlist Latin America in its crusade against the Cuban leader Fidel Castro.

Some expected that Chile would have willingly joined the American cause, because since 1945 Santiago, with rare exceptions, had generally accepted Washington's leadership of the inter-American system.[15] Given his nation's internal difficulties, Alessandri felt no desire to deviate from these policies. Chile, he admitted, was too weak to launch any foreign policy initiative that would "depart from reality in its direction and in its proportions. The scarcity of our resources and of our means of action are incompatible with the undertaking of large initiatives, as well as with resounding attitudes on great world problems."[16] Although distant and with few economic ties to Chile, Castro's Cuba nonetheless caused a dispute between Santiago and Washington, forcing the Moneda to rethink its policy of following the international lead of the United States.

The Chilean Left had endorsed Castro's revolution. The Communist and Socialist parties considered Castro's regime as part of a revolutionary process occurring throughout all the Latin American nations. As such, it provided an example for others to follow. Hence when the U.S. government called for economic sanctions against the island, Allende argued that Santiago should protect Havana from American aggression. "Any aggression against Cuba," he argued, "is an aggression against the small nations of the world, against Latin America, and against Chile."[17]

Although the rightist Liberal and Conservative parties indisputably hated Castro, the newly emerging Christian Democrats reacted ambivalently. While criticizing the Castro state's totalitarian nature, the party did not repudiate the revolution's goals nor would it countenance any foreign attempt to overthrow the regime. Given the political influence the various parties could bring upon Alessandri, the president had to walk a narrow line when dealing with the Cuban issue: if he followed Washington's lead, Chile's Left would turn on him; if he did not, the United States might withdraw its support.[18] Predictably, Alessandri's Cuban policy emerged as an issue in Chile's domestic politics and its 1964 presidential campaign.

Alessandri had no great love for Havana. The 1959 arrival of Raul Castro, replete with an armed guard, did not endear him to the

Moneda. The activities of various Cuban diplomats, including the foreign minister, which often bordered on the insulting, also antagonized Santiago. Although the Moneda had declared a Cuban diplomat persona non grata, Alessandri refused to turn on Havana. Chile, he claimed, had historically favored national self-determination; it would not deviate from this policy even on behalf of human rights.[19]

The president was only partially correct. While previous administrations may indeed have opposed intervention, Alessandri did not. In the late 1950s, Venezuela accused the Dominican dictator Rafael Trujillo of ordering the assassination of President Rómulo Betancourt. Anxious to topple the venal Trujillo regime, an understandably distressed Caracas demanded that the OAS impose sanctions on the Caribbean nation. Alessandri's government joined with most of Latin America to vote for sanctions on the Dominican Republic. The decision on the Dominican issue marked a substantial shift in Chile's foreign policy, providing a precedent that the United States would cite when it attempted to convince Chile to impose sanctions on Castro's Cuba.[20]

Cuba became the principal topic of the January 1962 meeting of the OAS. In a series of votes, the majority of the organization declared Marxism-Leninism incompatible with the inter-American system, praised the Alliance for Progress, established a committee to help nations fighting against communism, and called for strengthening the Committee on Human Rights. While the Chilean delegate, Radomiro Tomic, agreed with many of these proposals, he abstained on the vote to exclude Cuba from the OAS, to suspend weapons sales to that nation, and to consider the possibility of imposing sanctions. Sanctions, he claimed, rarely worked and should be invoked only in the case of external aggression. Santiago's envoy, moreover, legitimately inquired if the same nations that avidly sought to punish Cuba for its authoritarian policies were themselves paragons of democracy. Many Chileans shared Alessandri's hostility to the U.S. position. On the basis of the State Department's logic, Tomic argued, Argentina, Peru, and Bolivia would have the right to invade Chile if it had elected a

Marxist in 1958. Santiago, therefore, refused to suspend its commercial ties with Cuba.[21]

Yet, later that year, Alessandri, acknowledging that the installation of missiles in Cuba dramatically altered the hemispheric political balance, supported John F. Kennedy's quarantine of the island during the October missile crisis. As the Moneda's UN representative averred, Chile's vote did not violate its traditional policies because an extracontinental power was using Cuba as a base to deploy nuclear weapons. Alessandri's decision, while pleasing to the Right and to the centrist Radicals, infuriated the Left, which charged that Alessandri was playing with the lives of Chilean citizens. The United States, they argued, had used its vast power to undermine Chile's independent foreign policy. The Left need not have worried: Alessandri, while still supporting the U.S. antimissile policy, nonetheless joined Mexico in defending the principle of nonintervention.

In 1964, after discovering a weapons cache on Venezuelan soil, authorities of that country demanded that the OAS investigate to determine possible Cuban involvement. When an ad hoc committee concluded that Havana had indeed attempted to foment a rebellion in Venezuela, Caracas requested the OAS to impose sanctions against Cuba.[22] This vote occurred as Latin America's political climate was turning toward the Right: a 1964 military coup in Brazil replaced the government with a more conservative regime, which the United States soon began favoring with economic aid. If Chile—one of the four nations that still maintained a legation in Havana—opposed sanctions, it ran the risk of becoming a hemispheric pariah, thereby losing the support of the Alliance for Progress.

When the inter-American states convened a meeting in Washington in July 1964, Alessandri's position had become distinctly more uncomfortable. He hoped to avoid heating up Chile's already turbulent political environment by taking a strong stand against Cuba. Yet, he did not wish to antagonize the Moneda's international friends. Seeking a middle ground, he condemned Cuba's intervention in Venezuela while declaring Chile's opposition to sanctions. Speaking to the meeting of the inter-American states, Chile's foreign minister, Julio Philippi, argued that the 1947 Rio pact's definition of aggression did not apply to the Cuban situation. Hence Santiago would not abandon its longstanding diplomatic policy merely to conform to hemispheric opinion.

An unrelated and unexpected problem forced Alessandri to reconsider his opposition to sanctions. The Moneda's perennial border dispute with Buenos Aires suddenly became acute when Chilean carabineros clashed with Argentine troops in Palena, located in Chile's south. Clearly this was not the most propitious moment for the Moneda to disagree with the United States and the other Latin American nations, especially if such a disagreement jeopardized Chile's standing in its dispute with Argentina.[23] Alessandri adroitly tried to sidestep the issue. While the Moneda's delegate voted against sanctions, he nonetheless pledged that Chile, as a member of the OAS, would enforce them. This tactic was disingenuously self-serving: Chile agreed to break economic and diplomatic ties with Havana, while simultaneously reiterating its legal objections to the OAS's policies. Chile's retreat from diplomatic confrontation with the United States and the OAS illustrated an important fact. Even if the Moneda had wished to placate its domestic critics by forging an independent foreign policy, the Palena incident demonstrated that Chile either had to abide by the OAS decision or had to withdraw from an organization that guaranteed its integrity from an aggressive neighbor.

Alessandri's attempt to pacify his internal critics and the United States failed. Eduardo Frei, Alessandri's successor, announced that he still opposed sanctions. Every country, he argued, even Cuba's totalitarian regime, must have the right to self-determination. Other Christian Democrats attacked Alessandri's action, claiming that it demonstrated that the United States completely dominated both Chile and the continent. The Left, of course, agreed, arguing that the decision humiliated the Moneda.[24]

The Alternative Economic Model

Ironically Washington's insistence that Santiago initiate domestic reform produced even more hostility in Chile than the status of Cuba. The Alliance for Progress, which called for Latin American economic modernization, democracy, and social justice, provided Alessandri with the economic incentive to reform society. In early 1962, he introduced a measure to purchase the large landed estates and divide these among the work force. Unlike earlier attempts at agrarian reform, Alessandri's proposal offered compensation to the landowners in a combination of cash and long-term bonds, which obviously permitted the government to acquire more land. Serious flaws blunted the thrust of the Moneda's agrarian reform. The proposal, for example, permitted the state to acquire property only when the individual or corporate owners of the land had inefficiently cultivated or abandoned it. The measure, furthermore, did not provide for agrarian credits. Thus, by 1964, only 1,066 peasants had received sixty thousand hectares of land, 70 percent of which had formerly belonged to state organizations.[25]

Although the landed oligarchy's holdings remained virtually intact, Alessandri's measure nonetheless infuriated the Right. Politically powerful landed interests resented what they perceived as an American intrusion into Chile's internal affairs. In retaliation for the U.S. support of social reform, the landed oligarchy turned on the American-owned copper companies. Chile, one conservative senator cynically argued, did not require hare-brained schemes like agrarian reform to improve the nation's social well-being. Increased copper production and higher taxes on the copper companies would provide the nation with ample financial resources to help the poor. And, he warned, if the U.S. corporations refused to increase their output, the Moneda should nationalize them. Liberal and Conservative politicians even advocated that the Moneda borrow funds from the Alliance for Progress to buy control of the copper companies. The Left, which for years had denounced the Gran Minería as a foreign enclave, echoed the Right's condemnation of the copper companies. Precisely because the mines produced approximately 75 percent of the Moneda's foreign exchange, employed thousands, and purchased large amounts of domestically produced items, many Chileans believed that they were too important a resource to remain in private, particularly foreign, hands.[26]

Because levying taxes on the nation's oligarchy appeared unthinkable and unpatriotic, the copper companies became the Moneda's primary political bête noire and economic resource. Whenever the state required additional funds, it invariably turned to the foreign-owned corporations. Twice during Alessandri's presidency the legislature imposed surcharges on the copper companies to pay for earthquake reconstruction and higher salaries for government employees. Although American investment had increased the mines' productivity and hence their tax payments, Chile's share of the world market had fallen by a third. If the nation hoped to regain its prominence as a copper producer, the American companies would have to modernize their mines. The corporations refused to invest additional funds unless the government promised first to freeze taxes for the next twenty years. This suggestion outraged all political parties, whose members then called for nationalizing the mines.

Alessandri dared not go that far, but his minister of mines demanded that the copper companies increase production and domestically refine most of the copper extracted from their Chilean holdings. The president eventually silenced his outspoken minister, but the opposition Conservative politicians carped that the United States should protect Latin America from communism rather than impose alien changes like equitable taxation and agrarian reform.[27]

A terrible dilemma confronted the United States: any policy that it advocated antagonized the Chilean political or economic elite. Its proposed reforms infuriated the Conservatives who, having the most to lose, tried to hold hostage the American copper companies. At the same time, the Left, which wanted more drastic social reforms, complained about U.S. meddling in Chile's internal affairs.

The 1964 Election

By the time Alessandri's term of office ended in 1964, Chile's economy and political systems were in chaos. The previous year's municipal elections had demonstrated that, despite the electoral reforms,
a large portion of the electorate disdained the political process and
that those who voted had turned to the Left. When the new election
procedures allowed the *inquilinos* to vote freely, they repudiated the
Liberal and Conservative parties. Both the Right and the centrist Radical party suffered losses. While conservative parties feuded with each
other for the public's favor, the Left emerged from the elections with
a greater sense of unity.

In 1964, as in 1958, FRAP nominated Dr. Salvador Allende. As he
had before, Allende promised to enfranchise illiterates and those between the ages of eighteen and twenty-one and to nationalize the
mines as well as the nation's banks, utility companies, and insurance
firms. He vowed, furthermore, to stimulate the creation of national
industries and, by instituting a program of agrarian reform, to increase agricultural productivity while providing land to the tenant
farmers. Two candidates opposed Allende: Julio Durán, a Radical, and
Eduardo Frei, a Christian Democrat. Because they advocated change
—agrarian reform, renegotiating the Moneda's agreement with the
copper companies, stimulating national industries, and implementing a more independent foreign policy—the Christian Democrats appeared on the verge of supplanting Durán's once powerful party.

Although Frei advocated a reformist platform, enormous differences
distinguished him from Allende. The Christian Democrat sought
agrarian reform, but, unlike his Socialist rival, he advocated paying
compensation for any land taken and favored retaining the family
farm. Similarly Frei promised not to expropriate the mines but to
negotiate a new agreement with the copper companies. Finally, the
Christian Democrat, while determined to chart an independent foreign policy, refused to be pro-Cuban like Allende.

Confronting a divided opposition, Allende appeared assured of
winning the presidency. A congressional by-election for a vacant seat

in the grain belt of Curicó, however, altered the electoral equation. Declaring that it regarded the election as a plebiscite on the performance of the Alessandri government, the conservative-centrist coalition, the Frente Democrático, nominated a Radical as its candidate. Seeing that the contest had attracted national attention, the Christian Democratic party also entered the fray. The FRAP candidate won in this normally conservative district; the Christian Democratic nominee, who had belatedly joined the electoral campaign, placed a strong third. The loss demonstrated that a Radical candidate, even one running with conservative support, could not defeat a leftist candidate. It became clear to the anti-Allende forces that they must either rally around Frei or lose.

Recognizing that only the Christian Democratic candidate could stop Allende, Washington became an avid supporter of Frei, providing economic and technical assistance. Durán's continued candidacy, however, threatened to fragment the anti-FRAP bloc, and rumors began circulating that the United States would pay him to resign from the presidential race. Allende tried to win Durán's endorsement by offering ministerial portfolios to the Radicals. Ultimately Durán decided to withdraw from the election, and this decision, regardless of its motivations, permitted the anti-Allende forces to coalesce around Frei.

The United States might have viewed Frei as the "last best hope," but Chilean conservatives recognized that they could either accept Frei's moderate reforms or suffer Allende's draconian changes. The Christian Democrat's campaign adroitly created and then capitalized on a climate of fear. His supporters predicted that Allende would do to Chile what Castro had done to Cuba: introduce godless communism, institute a wave of summary executions, and ship Chilean children to Russia for education. The Frei camp played recordings of Castro's sister Juanita attacking Allende. The FRAP candidate responded by feverishly trying to shed his Marxist image, depicting himself instead as a benign, avuncular reformer.

Washington invested approximately three million dollars in Frei's electoral jaunt. Of course, the United States was not alone in this activity. Various European Christian Democratic parties contributed to their Chilean colleague's effort. Nor was Allende an orphan: both Cuba and Russia provided the FRAP candidate substantial funds.[28] In the American case, the money was well spent. In September 1964, almost 90 percent of the Chilean electorate voted. Allende attracted only 38.9 percent of the electorate. Frei received 56.1 percent of the ballots cast. Durán, who at the last moment had reentered the campaign in hope of being a power broker, collected a puny 5 percent of the vote. While clearly Frei's victory indicated support for reform, his triumph should not be misinterpreted. Many of those who voted for Frei did so not because they favored Christian Democracy's goals but because they feared radical Socialist change. This attitude not only diluted Frei's power base, but it also limited his ability to maneuver.

The Christian Democratic Years

Washington considered a Christian Democratic–ruled Chile as an experiment, demonstrating that the United States could help a nation implement social and economic change within the framework of liberal democracy and capitalism. While Frei fervently championed economic justice and development, which Washington lauded, he also hoped to wean Chile from the United States. Forging an independent foreign policy, he believed, would simultaneously liberate Chile from U.S. domination and prove his administration's commitment to change. Regrettably, Frei's agenda clashed with Lyndon Johnson's programs, which called for military intervention in Southeast Asia and militant anticommunism in Latin America.

From its inception in the 1930s, the Christian Democratic party (PDC), then called the Falange Nacional, attempted to break with the past by finding a middle way between communism and capitalism. Its solution, "communitarianism," called for the state and the workers to share in the profits and in the decision-making process. In the international arena, the Falange defended Chile's right to self-determination, denouncing the Moneda's declaration of war in 1945 as an example of Chile's craven subservience to the United States. Rejecting the

United States' Manichaean worldview, the PDC's leadership repudiated Washington's harsh post–World War II anticommunism and cold
war posturing. Predictably the PDC opposed González Videla's 1947
break with the Eastern bloc.

While critical of Washington, Frei was not anti-American. The
Anglo-American nation, he argued, shared little other than the same
continent with its Latin neighbors. The United States was Protestant
and northern European in origin; Latin America was Catholic and Hispanic. Given the disparity in size and power, the hemispheric scales
could never be balanced. The United States was an economic giant
that exploited the less-developed nations. At best, Latin America was
merely a game piece to be deployed and, if needed, sacrificed to serve
Washington's cold war strategy.[29] Disdaining to choose between the
unappetizing alternatives of *entreguismo*, a supine reliance upon Washington, and *odio estrátegico*, a mindless loathing of the United States,
Frei called for the *asociación digna*, identifying with Western values
without accepting American tutelage. As a counterpoise to the overwhelming U.S. presence, Frei suggested that Chile either use existing
international organizations to foster a sense of hemispheric solidarity
or strengthen its bilateral relations with other Hispanic nations.[30] He
recognized, however, that Chile's outstanding border problems with
Argentina, which contested Santiago's claim to the Beagle Canal, and
Bolivia, which still yearned for a seacoast, precluded such an organization.

Frei thus pursued two apparently paradoxical goals: to maintain a
cordial relationship with Washington and to separate from the United
States. He naively hoped that Washington would understand and cooperate in achieving these objectives. If the inter-American system
was to become an organization of equals, the Christian Democrat believed, then the United States must provide economic assistance to
Latin America and help integrate the hemispheric economies. The
Marshal Plan had done this for Europe, and, if the White House
wished to solve the hemisphere's problems, the United States should
do the same for Latin America. Should the United States prove reluctant, alternatives did exist. Other friendly governments could provide

bilateral assistance. Alternatively, Latin America could create units, like a common market, to foment economic growth. Although Frei did not prohibit foreign investment in the Chilean economy, he insisted that his nation's economic needs, not the pocketbooks of overseas investors, constituted his government's primary interest.[31]

As an expression of Chile's new independent foreign policy, Frei planned to establish diplomatic relations with all governments regardless of their political orientations. By cultivating new allies, as well as by maintaining old friendships, Chile compensated for its relative weakness when dealing with the more powerful nations, particularly Argentina and the United States. Consequently, Frei began wooing the nonaligned nations and the Third World by supporting more actively the UN's attempts to eradicate the remaining vestige' of imperialism. Closer to home, Santiago worked to foster the economic and political integration of Latin America, which, it believed, would strengthen Santiago's geopolitical position vis-à-vis Washington.[32]

Superficially Frei's goals resembled those of the American government. He tried to stimulate the economy, particularly the nation's industries, while reducing and then eventually ending the debilitating inflation. More significantly, Frei aspired to divide the large landed estates among the *inquilinos,* thus converting the traditionally underprivileged agrarian laborers into independent landowners and simultaneously encouraging agricultural productivity. He sought a more equitable tax system, planning to use the increased revenues to expand existing social services, particularly education. But Washington's support for agrarian reform, which the U.S. ambassador, Ralph Dungan, called "an act of humanity," infuriated the Chilean Left and the Right. The oligarchy described the land reform as Communist-inspired, while the Left resented the United States for sponsoring bourgeois changes that delayed the economic Armageddon.[33]

Both the Left and the Right retaliated by attacking the most glaring example of the U.S. presence in Chile—the copper companies. Because Chile's existing domestic tax base lacked the resources to finance an agrarian reform program and expand social services, the government decided that the copper companies would have to bear a large burden in paying for Frei's programs. The Moneda suggested that if the state became part owner of the mines, then Chile would share in the profits from both the refining and the eventual sale of copper on the world market. Chilean technicians, moreover, would learn how to operate the mines. Ultimately the Chilean government proposed to purchase a 25 percent interest in existing mines and a 51 percent share in any new companies. The Moneda refused to expropriate the copper companies, because it did not wish to antagonize the United States and because it lacked the means to pay compensation as well as the expertise to run the mines.

The American copper interests, although irritated, did not adamantly oppose the government's plan. Kennecott agreed to help develop Minería El Teniente, which would be 51 percent Chilean-owned, by promising to invest the money it received from the sale of its assets to increase the mine's output and to improve the work force's living conditions. In return for Kennecott's reinvesting its funds, the Moneda reduced the tax on the copper company. Instead of the old 50 percent minimum levy, the American corporation would pay a 20 percent tax on its capital investment plus a 30 percent tax on its profits. The Moneda also gave Kennecott a ten-year contract to manage the mine. Anaconda Copper Company, with two-thirds of its corporate assets invested in Chile, reacted less enthusiastically. While willing to increase production levels and to sell a quarter interest in its Exotica holdings, it wished to retain its corporate integrity. Rather than make the Chilean government a partner, it decided to finance the expansion program by borrowing $30 million from the Export-Import Bank and $72.5 million from private banks. But since Anaconda did not sell a portion of its holdings to the state, it continued to pay the same taxes as stipulated in the 1955 agreement.

The entire process, which became known as "Chileanization," provoked widespread criticism. Predictably, nationalists and leftists, who denounced the agreement, argued that the sum Kennecott received for selling its share, based on the mine's replacement value, exceeded the corporation's book value of its holdings. Critics also complained that the Moneda had not only invested its own funds but had also guaranteed Kennecott's $110 million improvement loan from the Export-Import Bank. If the government subsequently expropriated Kennecott's holdings, then it, not the American company, would be responsible for repayment. They charged that Kennecott had invested no money in the new joint venture, although in fact the U.S. company used the approximately $80 million that it had received from the sale of its share to modernize its holdings. Nonetheless, Frei's conciliatory policy permitted Chile to acquire an interest in the copper mines and obtain funds to modernize these holdings (thereby increasing output) without offending Washington.[34]

Problems over copper still developed. In early 1966, the American companies raised the price of copper in the United States from thirty-six to thirty-eight cents per pound. Chile, of course, was delighted, since each cent of increase meant higher revenues. Fearing that higher costs would be inflationary, the Johnson administration forced the American companies to reduce their prices to thirty-six cents per pound. Washington also sent Averill Harriman to Santiago in order to convince the Moneda that it too should lower the cost to thirty-six cents. Predictably, the Moneda preferred the higher price. Noting that copper sold for between sixty-five and ninety cents a pound on the London Metal Exchange, Chilean nationalists even opposed the thirty-eight-cents-per-pound price. After much discussion Chile agreed to sell its copper for the less inflationary thirty-six cents. Although nationalists angrily denounced Frei for capitulating to the White House, the Moneda had extracted substantial concessions. The Johnson administration suspended the duty on Santiago's copper, promising to purchase approximately one hundred thousand tons of Chilean copper for the U.S. strategic stockpile. Anaconda, moreover, had to pay an additional tax. The United States also waived certain restrictions on Americans wishing to invest in Chile. In addition, Washington lent Chile ten million dollars under such generous terms that it was tantamount to a gift. Santiago, moreover, received an eighty million dollar loan from AID, and an additional twenty-three million to purchase two Boeing 727 jet aircraft. Despite these concessions, the Left accused the Moneda of surrendering to the Americans.[35]

Chileanization appeared to work: production at Gran Minería increased. As commodity prices rose, the Moneda prospered, although far less than it either wished or expected. When the Left, as well as the more radical Christian Democrats, discovered that the American copper companies' profits had risen dramatically, they demanded that Frei renegotiate his agreement with the U.S. mining corporations. The decision to reopen the proposal violated the provisions of the Chileanization agreement, which had frozen the rate of taxation for twenty years. This fact did not deter the Chileans. Higher world prices for copper, they argued, had altered economic conditions so dramatically that the Chilean government had the right to renegotiate the contract. The copper companies, which had already invested their funds in Chile, could do little but acquiesce. Had they balked, they would have risked nationalization. In May 1969, Frei demanded that Anaconda sell its holdings in its El Salvador and Chuquicamata mines. The purchase of the company's 51 percent was based upon an evaluation that the government had calculated unilaterally. Anaconda disliked the Moneda's actions but, given the political environment, believed that resisting would be imprudent.

The copper issue did not strain U.S.–Chilean relations. Indeed, the State Department, which had abandoned the copper companies in the late 1940s, seemed ready to do so again. More fundamental problems did exist: while Washington and Santiago may have concurred on the need for social and economic reforms in Chile, they did not share the same motivations. Frei advocated reforms because he sincerely believed in social justice. Washington supported change because it did not want Chile to turn too far to the Left. Frei, moreover, resented what he perceived as American imperialism, criticizing Washington's overthrow of the leftist Jacobo Arbenz regime in Guatemala in 1954. Although the Christian Democratic leader eventually accepted U.S. funds, he initially opposed Chile's applying for Alliance for Progress aid.[36] Thus, from the onset of his regime, Frei attempted to distance himself from Washington but not from its pocketbook.

The Estrangement Begins

The divisiveness began before Frei's inauguration. During the latter part of 1963, the United States Army commissioned an ambitious research project, picturesquely named Project Camelot, to discover why insurgencies erupted in underdeveloped nations and how the United States could either abort the rebellions or crush them after they began. The list of nations to be studied did not include Chile, but in April 1965 a naturalized American citizen, Professor Hugo Nutini, was planning to visit Chile, his place of birth. The project's leaders asked him to determine if any Chilean scholars would participate in Project Camelot. One of those who had been invited to join was Johan Galtung, a Norwegian academic. Considering the research an intrusion into the internal affairs of Latin American nations, the angry Galtung informed his Norwegian and Chilean colleagues about Camelot, even showing them a government memorandum on the proposal. Thus, by the time Nutini arrived in Santiago, many Chileans already knew about Project Camelot.

The outcry was predictably loud. The Left accused the United States of spying on Chile. Even the American ambassador demanded an explanation. An embarrassed U.S. government canceled Project Camelot, although it was too late to prevent the damage. Many Chileans resented that their nation would be subject to a political autopsy for the benefit of American counterinsurgency programs. Thus, while the program never encompassed Chile, it compromised, if not tainted, the White House's ties to the Moneda.[37]

The Dominican Intervention

Regrettably Project Camelot was not the last cause for confrontation between Chile and the United States. In April 1965 President Lyndon Johnson, fearing another Cuba, ordered U.S. troops to invade the Dominican Republic. Having intervened, he requested that the OAS retroactively sanction America's actions and, more tangibly, contribute troops to an inter-American defense force that would control the turbulent island. Chile proved to be less than malleable on the Dominican issue. Students protested by attacking the American consulate in Santiago, and the Moneda urged the OAS to repudiate Washington's unilateral intrusion in the Caribbean republic. Curiously, Frei did not oppose OAS action, but he wanted the organization to represent more accurately the intention of hemispheric nations rather than to serve as Washington's docile instrument. Thus, unlike the most intractable opponents of the United States, Santiago did not call for the immediate withdrawal of American troops. Instead it sought their evacuation as soon as the removal was consistent with maintaining order.

But Frei's conciliatory policy did not appease Washington. The United States insisted not only that it had the right to intervene but also that it should control any proposed inter-American occupation expeditionary force. Chile's ambassador to Washington, Alejandro Magnet, demurred. Like Frei, Magnet did not oppose collective action; he did, however, dislike the notion of Washington's unilaterally deciding when and how to intervene. Consequently, when the OAS acceded to Washington's request to create an inter-American force, Chile, as well as Cuba, Mexico, Uruguay, and Peru, refused to contribute troops. In retrospect, Frei's decision proved politically wise. By opposing the White House's call for troops, he demonstrated that Santiago was not Washington's lackey. Even the normally vitriolic Socialist politician Carlos Altamirano endorsed Frei's decision. Fortunately for Frei, Washington did not harbor any grudges. Thus, what potentially could have been a disaster instead became a minor incident. Chile still needed the United States, and the United States still needed Chile.[38] This community of interest soon ended.

Chile's Quest for Diplomatic Independence

Frei's plan for diplomatic independence initially focused on two issues: establishing ties with the Eastern bloc nations and supporting the admission of the People's Republic of China into the UN.

Soon after his election, Frei exchanged envoys with the Soviet Union, Poland, Czechoslovakia, Hungary, Bulgaria, the People's Republic of China, and Romania. Believing that closer ties with European nations would allow Chile to lessen its dependence on the United States, Frei traveled to Western Europe, where he consulted with various heads of state and entered into numerous international accords as well.[39] But if the Chilean hoped to find new diplomatic allies and sources of funding in Europe, then he was disappointed. Europe, still requiring U.S. help to keep the Soviets at bay, regarded Latin America as Washington's sphere of influence. Hence, Europe spurned Frei's overtures. Radomiro Tomic, then serving as Chile's ambassador to Washington, warned the Moneda that its attempt to fashion an independent foreign policy merely strengthened the antireform element in the U.S. State Department. Given Chile's need for American economic assistance, it would be better, Tomic urged, not to alienate Washington.[40]

If the Moneda's decision to recognize the Soviet Union and its Eastern allies did not provoke a confrontation with the United States, then Santiago's criticism of Washington's China policy and, more significantly, its involvement in the Vietnam War did. Initially Chile's foreign minister, Gabriel Valdés, had not condemned American participation in the war in Indochina. By 1967, however, his tone became increasingly hostile, and the next year he chided Washington for refusing to end the conflict.[41]

The issue of recognizing the People's Republic of China precipitated even more acrimony. Frei did not wish to alter Chile's traditional policy, which had been to support the United States in denying Peking a place in the United Nations. The PDC Left, led by Renan Feuntealba, Chile's delegate to the world body, however, argued that Santiago would gain prestige by adopting a more independent stance on this issue. Thus, rather than merely rubber-stamping Washington's refusal to support Peking, Fuentealba suggested that both Taiwan and Peking should be allowed to sit in the United Nations. The first example of this new policy was Fuentealba's 1965 decision to abstain from voting rather than reject an Albanian proposal to admit the People's Republic. This vote, however, did not reflect official Chilean policy. When the Moneda neglected to inform Fuentealba to oppose the Albanian proposal, he abstained, believing that this action best represented the PDC and Frei's desire for diplomatic independence. Fuentealba's decision distressed Frei. In 1966, when the Albanians reintroduced their motion, Frei ordered Fuentealba to join the United States in opposing Tirana's proposal.

Frei's decision to second Washington's China policy did not endear him to his Christian Democratic colleagues. Thus, Valdés and Fuentealba were delighted when other UN members introduced measures to allow Peking to enter the international organization while permitting Taiwan to remain as well. These compromises, they believed, provided an opportunity for Chile to separate from the United States. But Chile still needed U.S. economic support, so Frei ordered his delegates to reject Peking's admission. Fuentealba still yearned to distance Santiago from Washington. The Christian Democrats, he argued, had to act more independently in order to demonstrate to Chileans, particularly the Marxists, that their party was not an American lickspittle.[42] Fuentealba's proposals, while perhaps encouraging domestic support for the PDC, angered the United States, which requested that the Chilean delegate oppose the proposal to admit Peking to the United Nations. American insistence that Santiago repudiate the Albanian resolution so upset Fuentealba that he resigned in protest.

Eventually the various nations supported a compromise proposed by the Italian delegation and several Latin American nations, including Chile, calling for a committee to study the possibility of allowing the People's Republic of China to join the UN. The United States, in a substantial policy shift, accepted the Italian–Latin American compromise because it allowed the White House to oppose the Albanian proposal while the international committee studied the matter. The compromise measure also gave the Chileans a little leeway. They joined the United States in rejecting the Albanian resolution while voting for the Italian plan. If Chile's attempts to forge a China policy demonstrated a certain élan, then it clearly measured the limits of Santiago's leash.

Regrettably, the Moneda's experiment also antagonized both domestic and foreign elements: Frei's tentative steps toward diplomatic independence failed to appease the nation's Left, which had argued for support of the Albanian plan, while angering the United States, which had opposed the proposal. Eventually Frei and Tomic recognized their nation's diplomatic vulnerability vis-à-vis the United States. Chile, they agreed, had become involved in an issue that was not vital to its interests, was too ambitious for a small country to espouse, and threatened to complicate its relations with Washington.[43]

Economic Aid or Regional Security

Additional conflicts developed in November 1965, when the OAS convened a general meeting of its members. The United States, still sensitive following the Dominican episode, sought to legitimize its doctrine of sanctioning hemispheric intervention if it ensured regional security. Consequently, in conjunction with Brazil's president, Humberto Castelo Branco, the United States advocated amending the OAS charter in order to create a permanent inter-American defense force. These troops would ensure that no domestic incident could mushroom into a movement that jeopardized regional stability. Chile's delegate to the meeting, Gabriel Valdés, opposed the American suggestion, arguing that the OAS should not alter its charter simply to accommodate Washington. Fundamentally, the Chilean noted, Latin America and the United States pursued different objectives: Washington wanted military security; Latin America, economic development. Thus, if Washington wanted to conform to the wishes of Latin America, it should restructure the OAS to foster growth, not facilitate military adventures. Working with Mexico, Chile forced the United States to abandon its proposal to create an inter-American force, convincing Washington to accept a general set of principles—the Economic and Social Act of Rio de Janeiro—that encouraged regional economic development.

The debate over aid versus security resurfaced in the 1966 meeting of the OAS in Panama. Much to Chile's pleasure, the delegates moved to require the member states to assist each other in order to resolve their outstanding economic or social problems. During the 1940s the Pan-American movement had promised to help repel foreign aggression; now the OAS made a similar commitment to vanquish economic underdevelopment. Henceforth member states should provide assistance on "flexible terms," while refraining from using economic pressure to extract concessions. Predictably, the United States continued to stress regional security by seeking to make the Inter-American Defense Board part of the OAS. It also tried to enhance the power of the OAS to resolve any dispute that threatened hemispheric security.[44]

Various Latin American nations, including Chile, feared that the U.S. proposal would give the OAS carte blanche to intervene in the internal affairs of the member states. Santiago had particular reason to dislike the U.S. proposal: the OAS might use Bolivia's ongoing dispute over its lost seacoast to intervene in Chile. Thus, instead of granting the international body such broad political powers, Chile preferred to strengthen the OAS in areas of protecting human rights and encouraging reforms. The members drafted a proposal that underscored the need for economic development, including insisting that OAS members assist the poorer member states, while deleting the U.S. request for increasing the power of the Inter-American Defense Board.

Again, although there was substantial disagreement, Chilean-American relations did not deteriorate. In part this was because Cuban truculence forced Frei into a more accommodating position vis-à-vis the United States. Santiago, moreover, needed American goodwill as both nations undertook to develop jointly Chile's copper reserves. But Frei's hemispheric vulnerability increased. When the Argentine armed forces overthrew the government of Arturo Illia, Chile's diplomatic situation became more precarious. As the Palena incident demonstrated, Santiago and Buenos Aires still had outstanding border issues to resolve. The rise of the Argentine military, which had long advocated a strong stance on the frontier dispute, might exacerbate this problem. Santiago also feared that the military governments in Brasilia and Buenos Aires would seek a confrontation with Santiago, which they considered soft on communism. Faced with problems so close to home, the Moneda could ill afford to antagonize Washington.[45]

Another issue forced Santiago to act more benignly toward the United States: Bolivia still yearned for a seacoast and access to the Pacific. Washington, while not advocating that the Moneda cede land to La Paz, nonetheless supported creating a Bolivian zone in the port of Arica. This issue, coupled with American economic and military involvement in Bolivia, worried Santiago. That La Paz seemed intent upon generating support among Chile's neighbors was predictable. Santiago worried, however, that Bolivia might try to complicate Chile's relations with Washington.[46] In this respect, the Moneda's situation in the 1960s seemed not unlike that of the late nineteenth century, when Chile feared U.S. intervention on behalf of Peru. Santiago, therefore, felt compelled to cultivate the United States. Happily for Chile, Washington, facing substantial opposition to its attempts to amend the OAS charter, seemed more receptive to Chile's attempt to improve bilateral relations. Frei had shelved, but did not abandon, his attempts to force the United States to deal with the hemispheric nations' economic and social problems.

Frei still shared the general doubts of Latin American leaders about the advisability of using the methods of the Alliance for Progress and Washington's economic strategies. At a 1963 meeting in Argentina and a UN conference on trade and development the following year, the Latin nations demanded greater access to world markets and more control over their economic future. The vehicle selected for voicing the hemisphere's demand for economic equity would be CECLA, the Special Commission of Latin American Coordination.

The recently elected Richard M. Nixon shared the hemisphere's suspicion of the Alliance for Progress and in fact sympathized with the idea of Latin American economic integration. He responded favorably to the plea of the Ecuadorean Galo Plaza Lasso for a high-level mission, to be headed by Nelson Rockefeller, to visit the continent. The American president spoke of a "new partnership," saying that Latin America wanted trade not aid. But it became clear to many nations, including Chile, that Nixon's soothing words masked a decision to alter Washington's Latin American economic policies.

Just as the United States had altered its hemispheric economic strategy, CECLA's 1969 Consensus of Viña del Mar revealed the extent of Latin America's resentment toward Washington. Rather than promote Latin American development, the consensus accused American corporations and banks of siphoning more money from the hemisphere than they invested. When Washington offered help, it generally imposed too many conditions. Latin Americans, for example, had to buy American-manufactured goods, which were often more expensive than those fabricated elsewhere. The U.S. Congress also imposed import taxes on Latin American products. Rather than perpetuate the old economic order, Washington should reduce its tariff barriers, provide financial assistance, and impose fewer restrictions on how Latin America spent development funds.

CECLA's delegates selected Santiago's Gabriel Valdés to present their demands to the United States. His address marked yet another watershed: no longer would the Latin American states preface their petitions with a litany praising the inter-American system. On the contrary, he, as well as the other representatives, pronounced this system outmoded. Henceforth, Latin America would have the right, as a unit, to confront the United States rather than deal with it on a bilateral basis.[47] At a subsequent meeting, held in Port of Spain, Trinidad, the U.S. minister, Charles Meyer, while making a few minor concessions, rejected the CECLA consensus. This action reflected a dramatic change in Washington's policy. Under Kennedy and Johnson, the United States attempted to push Latin America to accept reform; after 1968, the hemispheric nations would seize the initiative.

The Estrangement Deepens

The Rockefeller Report, which noted the limitations of foreign aid in curtailing the spread of communism, anticipated Nixon's approach

to the hemisphere. Rightist governments, like that of Brazil, got per-
functory and generally meaningless criticism; the populist military
administration of Peru—which, after seizing power in 1968, had initiated an agrarian reform program and nationalized the American-
owned International Petroleum Company—received much rougher
treatment. Perhaps preoccupied with Brazil and Peru, the United
States increasingly ignored Chile. Frei ceased being Washington's
"last, best hope."

In part, Frei's inability to fulfill his own campaign promises precipitated his fall from grace. He had vowed to reduce inflation, stimulate nontraditional exports and national industries, provide 360,000
housing units, introduce agrarian reform, increase farm productivity,
implement an equitable tax program, and build more schools. Frei
simply could not realize such ambitious goals. His agrarian reform
program, which did not receive congressional approval until 1967,
called for the expropriation of all improperly cultivated estates and
their conversion into collectives, *asentamientos*. After five years, the
land could be divided among the former *inquilinos*. Clearly the age
of the haciendas had ended. But the new measure simultaneously
antagonized the Left, which carped that it cheated the landless, and
the Right, which screamed that it despoiled the landowners. Between
1967 and 1970 the Moneda expropriated approximately six million
acres of land, slightly more than 25 percent of what Frei had originally
sought, on which it settled twenty-six thousand families.

Converting *inquilinos* into yeomen farmers cost ten thousand dollars
per family, including technical assistance and support, but did not increase farm productivity. The amount of land under cultivation and
farm productivity fell. Not all the decline was attributable to bureau-
cratic incompetence. A 1968 drought devastated the farm sector, fear
of expropriation discouraged *fundo* owners from cultivating their land,
and, finally, the state lacked the resources to provide the *asentamientos*
with technical assistance needed to increase the yield. Similar problems hampered industrial development. In the beginning, the nation's
factories, encouraged by government policy and the public's increased

purchasing power, had increased their output, but when the government began restricting credit and tightening the money supply, industrial production slowed.

In addition to encouraging economic development, the Moneda had expanded its social expenditures. When the higher copper revenues and taxes could not finance such ambitious goals, Frei turned to the United States for economic assistance. Anxious to ensure the Chilean leader's success, the Johnson administration initially proved quite generous. By 1965–1966 Chile received approximately $250 million in loans, becoming the second highest per capita recipient of American aid in the world. For a short time, the combination of domestic reform and U.S. funds seemed to work. The nation's G.N.P. increased by 6.1 percent in 1965 and by 9.2 percent the following year; consumer prices, however, rose by 23 percent and 18 percent in 1966 and 1967 respectively. While quite impressive, the increases in G.N.P. failed to meet Frei's avowed goals. By 1967, moreover, Frei's economic miracle collapsed. The combination of declining copper prices, labor unrest, and inclement weather had stunted the economy. When inflation surged, Frei tried to limit wage adjustments and force Chileans to save, but he could not convince the opposition to support his program: the Left insisted that the workers' purchasing power should not suffer; the Right opposed forced savings. Capitulating to both, Frei turned on the printing presses. When inflation rose and productivity declined, international loan agencies that had once showered Frei with money insisted that he curtail his ambitious social projects, reduce government deficits by ending price subsidies, and encourage foreign investment in the economy. These demands deeply antagonized the Frei administration, which believed that the United States had retreated on its commitment to Santiago.

The Cuban Rapprochement

In the late 1960s Chile moved to improve its relations with Havana. This rapprochement with Havana constituted a major policy shift for

Frei, who had earlier denounced Cuba's authoritarian government and its blatant intervention in the affairs of other Latin American nations.[48] Apparently he adopted this stance because it demonstrated Chile's diplomatic independence as well as provided a way to manifest Chilean hostility toward Washington. Ironically, this ploy failed on both counts.

In 1967, Chile's foreign minister, Gabriel Valdés, tried to negotiate an agreement to smooth Cuba's return to the community of Latin American nations. In exchange, Castro had to promise not to intrude into the affairs of his neighbors. When Cuba indicated that it preferred to export revolution and soon began fomenting unrest in Venezuela, Valdés's plan collapsed. Three years later the Chilean government agreed to sell agricultural products to Cuba. While acknowledging that some might construe this act as a violation of OAS sanctions, the Moneda argued that changing political conditions permitted Santiago to reevaluate its Cuban policy. Since Havana had ceased intervening in the internal affairs of its neighbors, the Moneda believed that the OAS sanctions, while perhaps once valid, no longer applied. Ironically Havana did not want to restore diplomatic ties. While Cuba avidly sought technical assistance as well as trade, establishing formal relations would require Havana to renounce exporting revolution. Castro refused to abandon his role as the paladin of movements of national liberation simply to win the Moneda's approval. If Castro accepted Frei's offer, then the Christian Democrats might gain a political victory over Cuba's allies in Chile. Hence, Fidel refused the Chilean proposal.

Most Latin American governments, fearful of alienating Washington, did not join the Moneda's crusade. Hence Frei's Cuban initiative accomplished little, other than antagonizing the United States: Nixon dispatched Assistant Secretary of State Charles Meyer to chastise Frei for violating the OAS sanctions and defying America's wishes. Nixon's reaction understandably incensed Frei. Though Frei deferred to Washington on issues like the admission of Communist China to the UN, the Chilean resented American attempts to dictate Chile's political and commercial relations with hemispheric nations. Realistically Frei could do little but fume: Washington possessed the economic and political power to prevent Santiago from opening relations with the Caribbean island.[49]

From the onset of his regime, Frei sought essentially two incompatible goals for Chile: to maintain a cordial relationship with the United States and simultaneously to attempt to separate from Washington. Since he had opened relations with the Eastern bloc, opposed U.S. occupation of Santo Domingo as well as the U.S. attempt to create an inter-American defense force, championed Peru, and favored Latin American integration, Frei could argue that he had successfully broken his nation's dependence on the United States.[50] In fact, Frei had only reshaped U.S.–Chilean relations. He could not fundamentally loosen Washington's hold on Chile.

The Chilean president enjoyed few political or diplomatic options. Frei had achieved power because both the Chilean people and the United States feared the alternative—Salvador Allende—more than they loved Christian Democracy. Initially the United States provided economic assistance because it believed that it had no choice: Frei seemed the only alternative to the Cuban revolution. The rise of the militantly anticommunist governments of Brazil's Castelo Branco and Argentina's Juan Carlos Onganía, however, offered Washington another option. Apparently capable of achieving economic change within a more traditional political environment and without causing inflation or alienating foreign private investment, these regimes became U.S. models for hemispheric development. When these alternatives appeared, Frei lost his leverage. He had pushed too far and too fast; he no longer was the "last best hope."

8   Socialism Triumphant: Allende Versus Nixon

By 1970, it became clear that six years of Christian Democracy and millions of American dollars had not solved Chile's problems. Frei's failure not only depressed Chileans, but it also distressed President Richard M. Nixon. Involved in Vietnam and intensely preoccupied with Europe, the American leader wanted peace in his hemispheric backyard. Success in Chile might have convinced other Latin American nations to embrace, if not Frei's ideology, then at least his methods. Conversely, the Christian Democrat's failure seemed to encourage Latin Americans to abandon liberal democracy in favor of more extreme alternatives. In 1968, Peruvian army officers overthrew the government of Fernando Belaunde Terry, installing an extremely nationalist and anti-American populist regime. In Uruguay and Argentina, revolutionary groups threatened to install extreme leftist governments. The Western Hemisphere, rather than being an oasis of geopolitical tranquility, had become a source of concern to Nixon. Worse, the unrest that had befallen so many countries threatened to spread to Chile. In 1970, Chileans would select another president, and it became clear that radical Salvador Allende might win the election.

The son of a comfortable and politically prominent family, Allende saw firsthand his nation's endemic poverty while he was a medical student. Perhaps out of guilt or idealism, he considered socialism as the principal, if not the only, means of changing Chile. An extremely affable bon vivant and notorious womanizer, he enjoyed political success from the start of his career, serving as a deputy and a minister before he was thirty. Elected to the upper house as a leader of the Socialist party, which he helped found, Allende eventually became

159

president of the senate and twice sought the presidency. For Nixon, who had made anticommunism his personal political ideology, the prospect of Allende's election seemed almost a personal insult.

Allende's competition provided little reassurance to Nixon. The increasingly unpopular Christian Democrats had nominated Radomiro Tomic, Frei's former ambassador to Washington and a member of the Christian Democratic Left, as its presidential candidate. Conservative Chileans, who had never liked Frei, fervently embraced Jorge Alessandri, who, they believed, would save the republic from Socialist terror and Christian Democratic bungling.

The Election

Although Chile's 1970 presidential campaign appeared to be a reprise of the 1964 campaign, the political situation had changed. The Unidad Popular (UP) replaced FRAP, broadening its base to include the Radical party. Unlike his past experiences, Allende's most immediate problem was winning the support of his Socialist *compañeros*. Mistrusted because he seemed so bourgeois, Allende won his nomination by a margin of only one vote—his own. The fact that Allende could not count on the enthusiastic support of his colleagues would complicate the formulation of his domestic policies and the conduct of his foreign relations, particularly with the United States.

Allende's promises to nationalize the copper mines, the banks, and the large national industries distressed the White House and those American corporations with substantial holdings in Chile. In order to defeat the Socialist menace, the CIA's Forty Committee authorized the expenditure of $425,000 to help Alessandri's campaign. It would have disbursed more if the State Department had not intervened. Ultimately the U.S. government spent over $1,000,000 to sway the Chilean electorate. Private U.S. companies, including International Telephone and Telegraph Company (ITT) and Anaconda Copper Company, contributed over $600,000 to Alessandri. Allende also had his benefactors: the CIA estimated that Cuba donated more than $300,000 to the

UP candidate, a sum which the Russians apparently either matched or exceeded.[1]

The 1970 electoral campaign lacked civility, let alone elegance. The Right predicted that a triumphant Unidad Popular intended to convert Chile into another Cuba, plunging the nation into a bloodbath of godless terror. The Left genteelly described Alessandri as a senescent homosexual, the passive instrument of U.S. economic interests. Tomic, whose campaigning style consisted of screaming and violent hand gestures, directed most of his anger at Alessandri rather than at the UP candidate. When the ballots were counted, Allende had collected 36.2 percent, Alessandri, 34.9 percent, and the bombastic Tomic, 27.8 percent of the vote. Allende clearly won the election not because he was the most beloved but because, unlike 1964, this time his political opposition was divided.

Chile's constitution stipulated that congress choose the president if none of the candidates won a majority of the vote. Since Allende's supporters numbered only eighty of the legislature's two hundred members, he would have to woo the PDC, which controlled seventy-five votes. While theoretically it could elect anyone, the congress traditionally selected the man who had won a plurality of the votes. Consequently, if the legislature adhered to precedent, Allende would occupy the Moneda even though almost two out of three Chileans had voted against him.

As proved typical of the next three years, precedent counted for little. Unlike past defeated presidential candidates, Alessandri campaigned among the PDC legislators, promising that if the congress chose him president, then he would immediately quit. Alessandri's resignation would have necessitated another presidential election, and Frei could participate in the new contest, since he would not be succeeding himself in office. Given the Christian Democrat's widespread appeal, particularly when compared with the alternative of Allende, he would have easily won. But Allende, who had waited for two decades for this triumph, threatened to unleash a civil war if the legislature broke with political precedent.[2] His warning certainly gave the congress pause.

The specter of a "Red" in the Moneda distressed various American corporations. International Telephone and Telegraph, for example, twice approached National Security Advisor Henry Kissinger with a plan to prevent Allende from taking power. Although the future secretary of state rejected the proposition, he did not oppose covert action against the UP candidate. Kissinger apparently believed that Allende would convert Chile into a Marxist dictatorship. This prospect frightened the United States because Chile was not an island that, like Cuba, could be easily quarantined. Allende, Kissinger feared, could make his nation into a center for exporting communism into nearby Argentina, Peru, and Bolivia, countries with which Washington did not enjoy the most cordial relationships. Thus, Santiago might emerge as the leader of a fractious Southern Cone, thereby shattering the already fragile inter-American system. If Chile nationalized American holdings without paying compensation, it could set a dangerous precedent. There were also unsettling implications for U.S. policy in Europe, where NATO officers were becoming concerned about Eurocommunism and the prospect that democratically elected leftist governments would have access to the alliance's military secrets. If Allende could win an election in Chile, then it might encourage European nations to elect a radical.

While Nixon agreed with Kissinger, the president had to act gingerly; he could ill afford to give Allende an excuse to unleash a wave of anti-American propaganda. Hence, any U.S. response would have to be covert. The Central Intelligence Agency mirrored Nixon's concerns, warning that an Allende triumph would fragment "hemispheric cohesion [and] create considerable political and psychological" problems for the United States.[3] A coup could stop Allende, but the American ambassador Edward Korry, as well as the CIA, indicated that the only group capable of undertaking this action, the armed forces, seemed reluctant to act. The CIA's Forty Committee, therefore, decided to exploit Alessandri's ploy, authorizing Korry to persuade Frei to accept the former president's offer. It also orchestrated a public opinion campaign to convince Frei to cooperate. To reinforce the importance of taking action, the CIA encouraged a series of newspaper articles and radio broadcasts, warning that if elected the Allende government would plunge the nation into an economic abyss.

Initially Frei appeared willing to cooperate, but one man stood in his way. General René Schneider, the army's most senior officer, considered Alessandri's attempt to subvert the electoral process unconstitutional. He also took seriously Allende's threat to precipitate a civil war if he were not permitted to take office. Given Schneider's opposition, Korry recommended that the White House accept Allende's victory as gracefully as it could.

When Frei rejected Alessandri's plan, the Forty Committee implemented a program designed to create economic panic. An ITT official claimed that he had received a memo from the CIA advising the company, as well as other American-owned corporations, how to exert economic pressure on Chile. While there is some question about this plan and the involvement of companies other than ITT, the CIA did fund opposition political groups so that they could continue to resist Allende.

Soon after the September election, an economic panic engulfed Chile, as depositors withdrew approximately a billion *escudos* from the nation's banks. One cannot be sure, however, if the United States either precipitated or exploited this hysteria. Historically, in uncertain times—and many might have considered Allende's election as unsettling—Chileans invested their money in gold, hard currency, or basic commodities. Hence, American responsibility for the flight of capital remains unclear.

Without Korry's knowledge, Nixon had authorized CIA head Richard Helms to use whatever means he required to stop Allende from taking office. Code-named Track II, this covert operation sought to enlist the Chilean military in an anti-Allende putsch. The CIA office operating in Santiago informed Washington that such a conspiracy might succeed if it could generate support among the junior officers. Two possible leaders emerged: General Roberto Viaux, leader of the abortive 1969 mutiny of the Tacna Armored Regiment, had apparently been plotting against Allende as early as May 1970. Viaux's forced retirement from the army limited his effectiveness, forcing the CIA to look for a serving officer, with access to troops, to lead the coup. While the local military attaché discovered numerous possible candidates, the most promising was General Camilo Valenzuela, commander of the Santiago garrison. Valenzuela's plan called for the conspirators to seize General René Schneider and form a governing junta, composed of the general, Admiral Hugo Tirado, General Vicente Huerta of the carabineros and General Joaquín García of the air force. To facilitate the coup, the American military attaché provided Valenzuela's men with three machine guns as well as some chemical grenades.

Valenzuela's planning came to naught when General Schneider twice evaded his kidnappers. Perhaps dejected, the Valenzuela group returned their weapons to the U.S. military attaché and apparently abandoned the idea of kidnapping Schneider. News that the Valenzuela cabal had canceled its plans emboldened Viaux to try to seize the general. On 22 October, Viaux's followers waylaid Schneider as he was traveling to work. When he resisted, the panicked kidnappers opened fire, mortally wounding the officer.

The degree of U.S. complicity in the Schneider assassination remains unclear, since U.S. agents had broken off contact with Viaux before his attempt to kidnap Schneider. Nor had the United States provided the general's gang with weapons. At best, however, Washington could deny involvement in, but not foreknowledge of, the Viaux conspiracy. Regardless, the assassination of General Schneider galvanized support for the constitutional process. The military closed ranks around the government, and even Alessandri urged his congressional followers to vote for Allende so that the nation could avoid a civil war. Thus, Salvador Allende took his oath of office and was formally inaugurated in November 1970.

Allende's Foreign Policy Goals

Allende's worldview profoundly influenced his foreign policy. The new president divided the globe into two uncongenial, if not antagonistic, blocs: the developed capitalist world—Western Europe, the

United States, Canada, Japan, and Israel—and another, the Socialists —the Soviet Union, the People's Republic of China, Eastern Europe, as well as the nations of the Third World. The latter countries, he argued, including Chile, remained mired in stagnation and poverty largely due to the greed of the developed nations' multinational corporations and their domestic lickspittles. These two groups had conspired to keep Chile "a capitalist nation, dependent on the imperialist countries, dominated by bourgeois sectors who are structurally tied to foreign capital, and who cannot resolve the fundamental problems of the nation, from which derive precisely their class privileges."[4]

Allende's analysis externalized the cause of his nation's wretched economy by blaming foreign capitalists and their Chilean allies. Instead of recognizing Chile's imperial experience, Allende concluded that his country did not develop because outsiders had looted the nation's resources. His solution to the nation's problems was quite simple: "To affirm the complete political and economic independence of Chile . . . a firm sense of identity of Latin American interests and resistance to imperialism will be fostered by means of a foreign policy which relates to people rather than to Foreign Ministers."[5]

As part of this new policy, Allende increased his nation's diplomatic missions from forty-eight to fifty-seven. He also established diplomatic relations with Cuba, the German Democratic Republic, North Korea, North Vietnam, Albania, the People's Republic of China, and, much to the distress of the United States, the Viet Cong. To reinforce its identification with the Third World, Chile joined the nonaligned movement, providing Allende a forum to attack the role of foreign capital investment in developing nations. In 1972, Santiago hosted the UNCTAD III conference, where Allende called for a restructuring of the existing and inequitable world order. Predictably, Chile reaffirmed its support for the Andean Pact, particularly the measure seeking equal treatment for foreign and domestic investors.[6]

Allende did more than merely attend international meetings. In retaliation for ITT's illegal meddling in Chile's affairs, Allende called for measures empowering nations to limit the activities of multinational corporations. Under his prodding, the United Nations and the

Conference of Non-Aligned Nations endorsed stronger restrictions on multinational corporations. Allende also called for a moratorium on collecting the onerous economic burden of the Third World's foreign debt, declaring that these nations contracted the loans "in order to offset the damage done by an unfair trade system to defray the cost of the establishment of foreign enterprises in our territory, to cope with the speculative exploitation of our reserves."[7]

Even before Allende came to power, the Moneda already deeply distrusted the White House. While Allende recognized that the United States would not directly intervene militarily, he worried that Washington might use surrogates to attack Chile just as it had used client states to overthrow the Arbenz regime in Guatemala. If so, Chileans had ample cause to fear their neighbors. To the east lay Argentina, a militantly anti-Marxist nation with which Santiago shared a still unresolved boundary. Brazil, also in the hands of a conservative military government, might serve as Washington's surrogate. Nor could Peru, Santiago's other perennial foe, be considered friendly. Although ruled by a group of "progressive" military officers, the Lima government exhibited a strong anti-Marxism and still resented Chile's War of the Pacific victories. Bolivia, happily, appeared a congenial neighbor since the leftist General Juan José Torres had taken power, but given the unstable nature of Bolivian politics, there was no guarantee that Torres would remain in the presidency. His successor might be wooed into the anti-Chilean camp with U.S. promises to assist Bolivia in gaining a seaport. Thus, President Allende labored to avoid continental isolation by strengthening Chile's ties with all the Latin American nations.

To neutralize potential hostility and to guarantee its own legitimacy, the Moneda espoused "ideological pluralism": the acceptance of all sovereign states regardless of their political systems. It reaffirmed, moreover, the principle of self-determination and nonintervention. Such policies, Foreign Minister Clodomiro Almeyda Medina claimed, would make it difficult for other nations to act against Chile.[8] Demonstrating his commitment to hemispheric solidarity, Allende visited his spiritual mentor, Cuba, the continent's maverick, Mexico, as well as all the members of the Andean Pact: Peru, Colombia, and Ecuador. In

each of the three countries, he urged the Latin Americans to open relations with Cuba, reject "economic pressure as a tool of foreign policy,"
and seek joint Latin American action for economic development.[9]

While cementing distant relationships, Allende moved to mend
nearby fences by seeking a rapprochement with Buenos Aires. Ostensibly Chile had little in common with Argentina's military leaders,
who had seized power illegally and had launched a dirty war to ex-
terminate the nation's Left. Fearing the United States and a hostile
Brazil, however, Allende began cultivating Argentina. As part of his
policy to create an "independent, free, and sovereign" Latin America,
Allende visited Salta, Argentina, in July 1971, where Compañero Presidente embraced the "Gorilla," General Alejandro Lanusse. A few
months later, Lanusse reciprocated by touring Antofagasta. Allende
went to enormous efforts to placate the general, even requesting that
left-wing students desist from demonstrating against the dictator and
his brutal government. Allende's fence-mending neutralized one of
Chile's potential adversaries, and Buenos Aires even granted Santiago $350 million in credits. By 1973, Argentina had replaced the
United States as an export partner. Curiously the Moneda enjoyed
more success in establishing closer ties to Brazil, which Allende originally feared might fill the continental vacuum created by Nixon's "low
profile" policy.[10] While ideological differences prevented a political
accommodation, Santiago nonetheless obtained $30 million in short-
term economic credits. Ironically, the 1973 contributions from conservative Brasilia and Buenos Aires saved Santiago from having to seek
emergency economic aid as it had in 1972.[11]

In addition to improving Chile's bilateral relations with various
Latin American nations, Santiago sought to reduce Washington's clout
by limiting its role in the OAS, the "servant of the Cold War, against
the interests of Latin America."[12] Allende considered the OAS less a
union of equals than a mechanism for the United States to impose its
will on the hemispheric nations. Latin America and the United States,
he declared, shared nothing in common. Nor were they juridically
equal, because Washington often used its superior position within
the OAS to subordinate Latin America economically. Although Chile

would remain in the OAS, Allende warned that it would strive to limit U.S. influence in that body as well as try to replace the OAS with an exclusively Latin American organization. In 1971, for example, he called for Latin America to adopt a common political and economic agenda that, as a united front, it would try to negotiate with the United States.[13] At a 1973 OAS meeting, Foreign Minister Clodomiro Almeyda moved to cancel the sanctions against Cuba. He also hoped to abolish those organizations, such as the Inter-American Defense College, which he described as fossils of the cold war. Equally important, Almeyda wanted to restructure institutions like the Inter-American Development Bank so that the Latin American nations, not the United States, controlled them. He also encouraged the OAS to adopt the Consensus of Viña del Mar as a goal.

Allende's efforts produced some results. He substantially increased Chile's trade with Latin American nations: Argentina, for example, eventually satisfied more of Chile's import needs than did the United States.[14] In a 1973 meeting, the Economic Commission of Latin America denounced the economic policies of the United States and the European Economic Community. To remedy the existing defective system, it called for increased participation by the underdeveloped nations in setting trade and monetary policy and in staffing the international banking institutions and for suspending temporarily the collection of debts. These measures received the backing of such ideologically diverse nations as Brazil and Cuba. By 1973, it appeared that the OAS had split into two antagonistic blocs: the Washington-Brasilia clique, which consisted of the United States, Brazil, Central America, Paraguay, and Bolivia; and the Havana-Lima group, in which Chile wielded considerable power. Allende's advocacy of such policies as the two-hundred-mile limit, support for Panama in the controversy over the canal, and opposition to U.S. protectionist measures and its sale of stockpiled strategic metals, all won hemispheric support.

Cultivating hemispheric alliances and currying favor with global friends protected Chile's flanks so that it could deal with its principal enemy, the United States. Anti-Americanism constituted the cornerstone of Allende's foreign policy. For Chile to become free, he believed that it had to destroy capitalism domestically and end Santiago's condition of international "dependent capitalism." The Moneda could only achieve these goals by exorcising the United States. Given the extent of American financial investment in Chile and Washington's self-appointed role as protector of the Western Hemisphere, conflict between the two nations appeared inevitable. The United States, according to Almeyda, had become the "armed policeman" of the capitalist status quo, defending "the common and the general interests of the entire capitalist world against the threat of revolution and socialism." By publicly embracing socialism and by encouraging resistance, Chile challenged Washington's power. Indeed, taken in the context of Latin America in the 1970s—the emergence of Torres in Bolivia, the rise of Velasco Alvarado in Peru, and the possibility of the election of the Frente Amplio in Uruguay—Chile appeared to be on the verge of creating a Socialist "bridgehead in the southern part of the continent . . . [that] would deprive the United States of its control over the situation."[15] Chile, in short, would lead a Latin American crusade against the American economic golem.

Copper Expropriation

One of the best ways to accomplish this goal was to attack the American copper companies. Copper became Chile's most important export, providing the state with 80 percent of its revenues and approximately 80 percent of its hard currency. To allow foreigners to control such a strategic area of the nation's economy eventually became an issue that Frei's program of Chileanization could not ameliorate. Allende had vowed to nationalize the mines in 1958 and 1964, and he repeated his promise in 1970. Less than two months after his inauguration, Allende introduced legislation to nationalize the mines. His proposal empowered the state to purchase the outstanding shares in the Gran Minería mines. In return, the companies would receive thirty-year interest-bearing bonds as compensation. In July 1971, the legislature approved Allende's measure. That the Left and Center ratified this policy was predictable, but the adherence of right-wing parties, which traditionally sanctified private property, proved surprising. The conservatives had no choice: their refusal to support the motion would have called into question their patriotism. The largely agrarian-based conservatives, moreover, used the nationalization measure to punish Washington for supporting Frei's agrarian reform program that had broken up the large estates.[16]

While many Latin American nations had nationalized their subsoil resources, Allende's proposal contained two controversial provisions. One empowered the president to reduce the amount of the final compensation award by deducting any excess profits the companies might have earned after 1955, the year of the passage of the Nuevo Trato legislation. This provision, which applied exclusively to foreign corporations, came into play only if the president decided to invoke it. The mining companies could appeal the president's action to a special Copper Tribunal. This court, however, could neither rescind nor modify the president's findings about excess profits. Before making his calculations, Allende warned that he would consider any profit excessive if it exceeded 12 percent of the corporation's book value or if a company earned more money on its Chilean holdings than it did from its other mines. Utilizing these standards, Allende announced that Kennecott and Anaconda had amassed over $770 million in excess profits. Because this sum exceeded the amount owed by the Chilean government, calculated by the comptroller of the republic at $333 million, it became clear that the copper companies would receive no compensation for their Chilean holdings.

Allende's decision unleashed a wave of protest. The copper companies denied that they, on an average, had earned more on their Chilean operations than on their American holdings, and they also denied that their profit margins exceeded 12 percent. Finally, they disputed the government's right to act so arbitrarily. Various scholars sided with the copper companies. Even one of the Unidad Popular's attorneys acknowledged that the Moneda's attempt to deduct the excessive profits did not conform "to the prevailing legal rules."[17] Allende subsequently argued that a 1962 United Nations resolution provided a legal rationale for his action. Essentially, however, the Moneda asserted that it could act as it did because the Nuevo Trato measures, although perhaps once acceptable, had "with the perspective of time, appeared as unconscionable to the national interest."[18]

Fundamentally the issue was not excess profits but politics.[19] The Chilean government wanted to sever the economic sinews that bound it to the United States. To accomplish this goal Allende had to domesticate the American copper corporations just as in Cuba Castro had to break the U.S. sugar companies. Thus, Allende retroactively and unilaterally declared illegal actions that Chile's legislature had earlier sanctioned. Furious at what they perceived as the confiscation of their holdings, the American corporations appealed Allende's actions to the Copper Tribunal. Since Allende appointed all of the court's members, the U.S. companies did not expect to obtain any judicial relief. Consequently, they also requested that American courts impound the assets of the Chilean Copper Corporation, CODELCO, as well those of the Chilean government. Kennecott went further, suing Chile in the courts of France, Germany, Italy, and Sweden in an attempt to seize the copper produced by its El Teniente holdings. Unsuccessful in U.S. courts, Kennecott enjoyed better fortune in Europe, where a few tribunals ruled in its favor, forcing the Moneda to appeal the decisions. Kennecott's lawsuits cast enough doubt on the right of CODELCO to sell the metal that buyers refrained from purchasing Chile's copper.

Predictably, the U.S. State Department also opposed Chile's nationalization decree, which, it maintained, deviated from "accepted standards of international law." Fearing that the Allende Doctrine would encourage other Third World nations to confiscate American-owned private property, Secretary of State William Rogers noted: "Should Chile fail to meet its international obligations, it could jeopardize the flow of private funds and erode the base of support for foreign assistance."[20]

Economic as well as ideological differences fueled Washington's hostility toward Chile. Since the American government–backed Overseas Private Investment Corporation, OPIC, had insured the copper companies' Chilean investments, Allende's policies threatened to cost the United States dearly. Edward Korry, who had earlier negotiated the amicable nationalization of other American holdings in Chile, proposed that the copper companies accept less compensation for their holdings. In return, the Moneda would pay Kennecott and Anaconda for their property in bonds, backed by OPIC. This tactic allowed the companies to convert the bonds immediately into cash. In a sense, all sides would compromise: OPIC, while having to guarantee Santiago's bonds, at least would not have to pay the copper companies' full claims; the corporations, while receiving less than Frei's Chileanization agreement stipulated, nonetheless would obtain some compensation; and the Moneda, although having to pay something, would have reduced the size of the compensation award while preserving its international credit standing.

Given the clear hostility of the Nixon regime, the settlement agreement seemed rather conciliatory. All Washington sought was a token payment from Chile in order to avoid a dangerous precedent. Kissinger reputedly said to Orlando Letelier, Chile's ambassador to the United States, "Pay just a dollar, but pay something." [21] But under pressure from his Socialist colleagues, who wanted to avoid any hint of compromise with either the Americans or the copper companies, Allende ultimately rejected the compromise. Politics dictated his decision. At the outset Allende appeared willing to accept Korry's proposal. But as would happen often during Allende's regime, the left wing of his coalition, the Socialists, vetoed the arrangement. They could not tolerate compromise, or even the appearance of compromise, with the copper companies. For the Socialists, nationalization was an act of manhood; retreat, therefore, constituted betrayal. Thus, if Allende wished to maintain his coalition, he had to accede to the demands of the extreme Left. This action, while placating the hardliners in Chile, encouraged the hard-liners in the United States, who urged Washington to retaliate.

Allende wanted state ownership not only of the copper mines but also of the most significant portions of the nation's industrial output, the banks, and the insurance companies. Ultimately he envisioned an economy consisting of three parts: the Social Property Sector (ASP), state-owned and operated factories; the Mixed Sector, in which the state and private interests would participate equally in the ownership of a concern; and the Private Sector, those companies in which the state had no interest. Once in power, the Moneda moved quickly to create the ASP. In some cases it accomplished this goal by purchasing outstanding shares in publicly held corporations. Certain companies, however, were privately held; others, like the local General Motors Corporation, belonged to Americans. If the owners did not evince a willingness to sell their shares, the state could not purchase these corporations.

But the Moneda discovered a subterfuge in a 1932 fiat—Decree Law 520—issued by the Socialist Republic of One Hundred Days, that permitted the state to take over a factory if the owners either failed to operate it or if they operated it inefficiently. Occupation of the plants, however, did not confer legal title. Unless the state paid compensation, it could operate these concerns, employing a manager called an *interventor*, on a temporary basis. Another law, a leftover from the Aguirre Cerda period, allowed the state to requisition and operate a factory temporarily if a labor dispute disrupted production.

The Moneda utilized both measures to seize "monopolistic" domestic industries and foreign, especially American, concerns. (While opposed to foreign capitalism, Allende carefully avoided taking the property of companies from whose governments he solicited credits.) In such circumstances several American firms unwillingly joined the Social Property Sector. Although Nixon denounced this process, he feared that Chile might use any American overreaction as an excuse to repudiate its nearly one billion dollars of debt.[22] For that reason, Nixon did not invoke the provisions of the Hickenlooper Amendment, which called for sanctions when a foreign government refused "prompt and adequate compensation" after seizing U.S.-owned property.

Nixon instead retaliated by urging private American banks to restrict their loans to Chile and by vetoing Santiago's applications for loans from international lending institutions—the Inter-American Development Bank, the World Bank, and the International Monetary Fund. Curiously, private U.S. banks had not curtailed their loans to

Chile when Allende came to power. Indeed, in a few instances, some had even increased Santiago's credit line.[23] But the copper expropriation and the deteriorating domestic Chilean economy so frightened the banks that they reduced their loan commitments.

The White House also had other means to punish Chile. In March 1972, when the Congress approved a measure to fund various international development banks, it added the González Amendment. This rider empowered the president to order American representatives serving on international banks to oppose any loan to a nation that had nationalized U.S. property without paying compensation. This economic embargo remained in place until the offending country paid compensation, entered into negotiations with Washington, or agreed to submit any outstanding claim to arbitration. While not initially damaging, these restrictions significantly damaged the Chilean economy in Allende's last months.

Allende's Domestic Crisis

Allende tried to redress decades, if not centuries, of social and economic inequality. He accelerated Frei's agrarian program of confiscating and dividing the large estates. Unfortunately, the Moneda also tolerated *tomas,* the unauthorized seizures of farms legally exempted from confiscation. The combination of *tomas* and the generalized fear of the agrarian reform made landowners neglect their lands. Predictably agricultural output declined, a process exacerbated by the inefficiency of the communal farms.

Nationalized industries and copper mines fared little better. Hoping to reduce unemployment, the Chilean government ordered the state-run factories and mines to hire more people. These bloated factories and mines often functioned poorly because the government had replaced the former owners with managers whom it had selected more on the basis of political affiliation than technical skills. For political reasons, Allende could dismiss neither the incompetent staff nor the inefficient workers. Eventually, the state-owned factories consumed 30 percent of the government's budget.

Certain other problems surfaced. In order to redistribute the nation's income and to improve the living standards of the lower classes, Allende increased salaries while freezing prices. Initially this policy seemed to work: the laborers' share of the national income rose. The nation's poor, who for decades had occupied the margins of the economy, finally earned decent salaries. With prices frozen, the workers' standard of living improved, and the Moneda managed to limit the 1971 increase in the cost of living to 22 percent. But in redistributing national income, the Moneda inadvertently precipitated a revolution of rising expectations. Chilean workers enjoyed their newly acquired buying power by embarking on a spending spree. Initially, state factories satisfied consumer demand by utilizing the nation's unused industrial capacity and by drawing upon existing inventories of raw materials. By 1972, however, both had been consumed. Production began to fall while inflation increased.

Eventually, the Moneda's political fortunes mirrored the downturn in the economy. In April 1971, during the heyday of the good times, the UP slate of candidates won close to 51 percent of the vote in municipal elections. These contests, however, marked the Allende government's high-water mark of popularity. Although he did not know it then, the president and his coalition began to falter. In June 1971, a group of extremists, the Vanguardia del Pueblo Organizado (VOP) assassinated Edmundo Pérez Zukovic, a former minister in the Frei government. The murder infuriated the already exasperated PDC when it learned that Allende had earlier granted amnesty to some of the assassins. Although Allende was not involved in the murder, the PDC still blamed his government for releasing political sociopaths from jail. The Christian Democrats soon had additional cause for anger. In 1970, when it agreed to support Allende for the presidency, the PDC had demanded that he promise, in writing, to respect democratic practices. The Moneda's toleration, if not active encouragement, of *tomas*, the illegal seizures of factories, and the arming of left-wing extremists frightened many Christian Democrats. This anxiety increased when it became known that Cuba, in collusion with the UP officials, had illegally smuggled weapons into Chile.

The PDC capitalized on the growing uncertainty when, in July, the government held a by-election to fill a vacant seat in a Valparaíso congressional district. Accepting the support of the conservative National party, the PDC's nominee edged out the UP candidate for the coveted place. In January 1972 two additional congressional by-elections occurred. Most Chileans regarded the contests as unofficial plebiscites on the UP government, so the PDC-National alliance's impressive triumph in both reduced Allende's prestige while emboldening the opposition. As antigovernment forces grew stronger, they increased their pressure on the Moneda. The PDC introduced measures limiting the government's ability to transfer property to the Social Property Sector and its right to invoke Decree Law 520. The legislature also impeached Allende's minister of the interior, José Tohá. When Allende rejected the legislation to limit his economic power, the congress voted, by a simple majority, to override his veto. This move plunged the nation into a constitutional crisis. Allende claimed that the legislature needed a two-thirds majority in order to override his veto; his congressional opponents responded that under a 1970 constitutional amendment a simple majority was sufficient. This dispute virtually paralyzed the government.

Allende also had to confront a balky economy. Anxious to gratify its supporters' growing appetites and to perpetuate the illusion of well-being, the government imported food to compensate for the rising agrarian deficit—up one hundred million dollars just in 1971.[24] The state, moreover, had to divert funds urgently needed by the industrial sector to purchase consumer goods. Unfortunately, the price of copper fell more than 25 percent just when the government most desperately needed higher export earnings. Allende dared not impose austerity measures. Rather than retrench, he increased salaries in order to convince workers that their standard of living had not declined. Eventually the burden proved too great: in July 1972 the Moneda increased the price of many foodstuffs and devalued the *escudo* by half, which doubled the rate of inflation in just one month. By September, the cost of living had increased by 100 percent since January.

Political and labor unrest followed in the wake of economic catastrophe. Refusing to farm collectively, angry peasants petitioned the Moneda to apportion the estates among the former *inquilinos*. The Frei agrarian reform legislation had granted land primarily to the former resident workers, not to the casual labor force, the *afuerinos*. Allende tried to modify this policy by attempting to extend agrarian benefits to both. Resident peasants strongly resisted this move, insisting that the government fulfill its earlier promise and grant the *fundo* land to individual *inquilinos*. Allende refused, instead founding collective and state-owned farms. When the peasants complained, Allende, the son of the middle class, accused them of being conservative, if not counterrevolutionary.

Ironically, Allende began to clash with those elements he professed to represent. Santiago's homeless often occupied vacant urban property. After his election Allende ordered the police not to evict the squatters. The MIR—Movement of the Revolutionary Left, an extreme Marxist organization—took advantage of this policy by encouraging other land seizures. In July 1972, the authorities raided one of these settlements. A fight erupted during which one shantytown resident was shot. The extreme Left labeled Allende a murderer of the people, demanding that he apologize for the squatter's death. When the president expressed his regrets, many Chileans interpreted this incident as proof that the UP government would not enforce the law. Problems also developed in the copper pits. The miners, historically the most privileged of Chile's labor force, sought higher wages to compensate for the increase in the cost of living. Arguing that they now worked for the nation, not the hated copper companies, Allende appealed to them to scale down their demands. Instead they declared a strike, thereby depriving the state of needed revenues. Allende's position became almost ludicrous: Compañero Presidente found himself denounced by the same workers he had promised to protect.

The most serious labor stoppage occurred in October 1972, when a group of independent truckers, fearing a government takeover, went on strike. The administration responded by jailing the strike's leaders, but the action provided a focal point for the opposition. Small businessmen, shopkeepers, professionals, and factory workers joined labor groups in launching sympathy strikes, which eventually involved more than six hundred thousand workers and paralyzed the nation's economy. Extremists in MIR and the Socialist party retaliated by ordering their supporters to seize and operate any factory closed in solidarity with the striking workers. These takeovers became the nucleus of the *cordones industriales*, urban enclaves where the workers', not the government's, appointees ruled and sought to keep the factories operating. Increasingly these centers became hotbeds of political extremism.

Allende needed to restore order and revive the economy if he wished to survive the congressional elections scheduled for early 1973. To this end he invited the armed forces to join his cabinet. The results were almost miraculous. The new minister of the interior, General Carlos Prats, settled the truckers' strike by canceling the government's plan to control their industry. In November 1972, when the truck owners finally returned to the roads, their walkout had cost the nation some $150 to $200 million, severely reducing agricultural and industrial production. By year's end, the Moneda had spent $383 million to import food, a sum equivalent to 50 percent of Chile's foreign earnings. Because copper still did not command high prices, Chile's economic crisis deepened. In eighteen months Allende had spent most of the $343 million that the Frei administration had accumulated.[25]

To sustain a faltering economy, Allende increasingly turned to international lending agencies and sympathetic foreign governments. Domestically the Moneda established a food distribution system called JAPS, Juntas de Abastecimientos Populares. Critics charged that the UP-controlled JAPS, designed to stop speculation in food, favored only the regime's supporters. Those who did not belong to the UP parties, or who did not live in what heretofore had been considered the wrong part of town, either waited in line or turned to the black market. This policy did not seem unusual: since Allende had often stated that he was the president of only the workers and the peasants, it would not be surprising that the government used the JAPS to win political support and to punish the middle and upper class.

As the economic situation deteriorated, the Moneda held the 1973 congressional elections. These were crucial contests: if the opposition won more than two-thirds of the legislative seats, it could override Allende's vetoes and, if necessary, impeach him. Conversely, if Allende attained a majority, he planned to convoke a constitutional convention in order to restructure the government so that he could more easily implement his policies. After a spirited election, Allende's foes won 55.7 percent of the vote; the UP earned 44 percent. Both sides claimed victory, but the opposition charged that the Moneda had committed widespread vote fraud. Given the Allende government's history of bending the law, many Chileans believed this allegation, which convinced the anti-Allende forces that they must either endure three more years of a sectarian, if not venal, regime or rebel. Conversely, Allende's supporters insisted that he accelerate the pace of change.

Reassured by his tenuous victory, Allende complied, replacing his military cabinet with individuals who shared his ideological goals. One of these, the minister of education, introduced a measure—the Escuela Normal Unido (ENU)—to require all Chile's schools, public and private, to adopt a curriculum repudiating the "bourgeois pedagogy . . . the traditional teaching which serves the class interests of the oligarchy."[26] Many Chileans feared that the government sought to politicize the students. Even the Roman Catholic Church's hierarchy, which had rarely criticized Allende, requested that the government postpone implementation so that the nation could debate the measure more fully. More ominously, a group of eight hundred military officers openly attacked the reform measure.

Faced with widespread protest, Allende agreed to postpone implementing the ENU legislation. But taking advantage of the fact that the minister of education was abroad, extremists within the UP government nonetheless published the decree authorizing the implementation of the controversial changes. Although unsanctioned, Allende's enemies saw this act, following so quickly upon the heels of the disputed congressional election, as yet another example of the Moneda's duplicity.

Violence became increasingly commonplace. An administration attempt to suppress a strike by El Teniente's copper miners, for example, led to fighting in the provinces as well as in Santiago. In late June 1973, an armored regiment rebelled. Although quashed, the mutiny symbolized the gathering unrest, providing left-wing workers an excuse to seize more factories in order to increase the number of existing *cordones industriales* as well as to create new ones. Allende encouraged such activities, urging workers to push on as part of *el poder popular*, "popular power." The opposition interpreted the president's encouragement as an attempt to subvert established political institutions. Fearing the government's next step, the legislature refused to grant Allende power to declare a state of siege that, if implemented, would have suspended civil liberties.

Events seemed to gather a momentum of their own. Angry at the government's inability or refusal to provide spare parts, which they interpreted as part of a program to destroy them economically, the truckers went on strike again in July 1973. Perhaps the most flagrant example of political instability occurred in August, when MIR smuggled some of its members aboard two naval vessels in hope of sparking a rebellion and eventually a popular uprising. Hoping to restore some semblance of order, Allende reshuffled his cabinet, giving three portfolios to military officers, including appointing General Prats to the post of minister of defense. Selecting officers for ministerial posts, the president reasoned, might satisfy the PDC, which increasingly believed that it could only count on the armed forces to act in a nonpartisan fashion. Since this tactic had settled the 1972 truckers' strike, it appeared that it might work in the 1973 work stoppage as well.

But the military had changed. The officer corps believed that Allende had manipulated them to his advantage in 1972 and that he would do so again. Savagely criticized by their own class for preserving a government that they believed was destroying Chile, the officers discovered that the Left was urging the enlisted men to rebel or to disobey their commanders. Angry at the administration's policies, the officer corps successfully pressured those generals and admirals serving as cabinet ministers to resign. By early September, after having forced the resignation of Prats as well as the head of the navy, anti-Allende forces controlled the three branches of the armed forces.

The military became a target of violence. Left-wing militants murdered an army officer; unknown elements assassinated Allende's naval aide-de-camp; naval units had to subdue a riot at Valparaíso's Catholic University; and the workers at a textile plant fired on troops searching for illegal weapons. The random violence reinforced the military's resolve to act while encouraging professionals, including the nation's physicians, to join the truckers' strike. As the opposition circulated a petition calling for his resignation, Allende announced that Chile possessed only enough flour to feed the nation for at most four days.

The military finally rebelled on 11 September. The fleet, presumably on maneuvers, slipped back into Valparaíso, occupying the port. Allende, aware of suspicious troop movements and the navy's unscheduled return to port, learned of the rebellion early in the morning. Accompanied by his aides and a few faithful supporters, he went to the Moneda. Offered the opportunity to leave, he refused. Following rocket barrages by air force jets, the army attacked. Deserted and betrayed, Allende fulfilled an earlier promise by killing himself.[27]

Allende's supporters have invariably blamed external, not domestic, forces for their leader's overthrow. Incapable of tolerating a Marxist Chile, they argue, Richard Nixon choreographed the crisis that ultimately deposed Allende. Not only do these elements claim that Washington fomented the rebellion, but they also argue that Americans organized and implemented the coup: the Pentagon drew up the contingency plans, and American air force pilots provided communication support and flew the planes that rocketed the Moneda. Even the Chilean military's postcoup brutality would be attributed to the training that they had received at U.S. military schools in the Panama Canal Zone.[28] This scenario conveniently places the blame for Allende's collapse and fall almost exclusively upon the United States, not on Chilean elements. Implicit in this argument is the belief that

Chileans are so incompetent that they cannot overthrow their own government without foreign assistance. As history has demonstrated, however, the Chilean armed forces can act in a brutally efficient manner. Clearly the United States had tried to prevent Allende's election. But how much, if at all, did American antipathy contribute to his downfall?

The United States and Chile

While ostensibly adopting a "low profile," the White House launched an active program, providing economic assistance to Allende's foes, in order to prevent Chile from becoming a Marxist state. This aid took a variety of forms. CIA funds, for example, allowed the Christian Democrats and the more conservative National party to purchase radio stations and publish newspapers. The intelligence agency also funneled large sums of money into *El Mercurio*, the nation's largest and perhaps most influential newspaper. Such support seemed necessary because the Allende government had moved to curtail the opposition's access to the press and the media. The Forty Committee, moreover, provided assistance to opposition political groups such as the PDC and the National party. It subsidized their participation in the 1971 municipal elections, the crucial legislative by-elections that occurred in 1971 and 1972, as well as the 1973 congressional contests. Various private organizations, generally groups representing small business interests, also received American subsidies. Washington, however, explicitly denied subsidizing the truckers' strikes, although apparently the union did receive some U.S. money through intermediaries.

In addition to funding the political opposition, Washington exerted economic pressure on the Moneda by depriving it of access to funds. Previously authorized loans continued: the Inter-American Development Bank disbursed some fifty-four million dollars and, in January 1971, funded another eleven million for university aid. Washington began reducing its economic assistance and curtailed its loans to Santiago, arguing that Chile had illegally seized U.S. property. In August 1971, exactly one month after the Chilean legislature passed the copper nationalization bill, the American-controlled Export-Import Bank informed Allende's ambassador, Orlando Letelier, that it had postponed acting on Chile's application for a twenty-one million dollar loan that Santiago hoped to use to purchase three Boeing 727 jets.

Allende's doctrine of "excess profits" provided the excuse for Washington to do publicly what it earlier had attempted to accomplish covertly. Nixon soon had additional causes for anger. Alleging that ITT operated inefficiently, the Moneda nationalized the firm in September 1971. But while the United States blocked certain international loans, it continued to fund the Peace Corps and even increased its support for the Food for Peace program. More ominously, Washington's ties with Chile's military remained close, and there was an increase in funding for the armed forces. Chile, for example, received a C-130 transport plane plus equipment for an airborne unit.

The combination of a deteriorating economy and the Moneda's continuing expropriations produced a predictable result. American banks that had initially acted in a restrained fashion pulled back. Various banks, for example, citing inflation, trade deficits, lack of new investment, the declining value of copper exports, and finally the debt moratorium, curtailed credit lines.[29] Numerous international nonprofit institutions responded in a similar fashion. The World Bank, which had lent Chile some $250 million since 1946, became increasingly wary of investing additional funds, insisting, in early 1971, that the Moneda demonstrate "economic rationality" if it wished to receive more money. The World Bank refused to finance an electrification project when Allende declared that he would not increase rates to the consumer. In late 1971, a World Bank report, citing the accelerating rate of inflation, lack of domestic investment, and depletion of the nation's foreign reserves, concluded that Chile would be unable to service its existing debts.

The bank's prediction materialized. In November, Allende announced that Chile would no longer pay its international obligations. Yet, when World Bank officials hesitated to advance additional funds, an official of Chile's Central Bank accused the international organization of unleashing an economic pogrom against Santiago. Robert McNamara, president of the World Bank, denied that politics or the nationalization issue had dictated this decision. Chile, he stated, did not receive a loan because it lacked "a soundly managed economy with a clear potential for utilizing additional funds efficiently." Santiago, he argued, had to curtail inflation and restore order to its domestic economy as the price for additional assistance.[30] Although the World Bank refused to provide additional funds, Chile nonetheless received forty-six million dollars in previously authorized loans.

Various scholars have claimed that the United States, particularly the Treasury Department, choreographed the refusal of the multilateral lending institutions to lend money to Chile. Certainly John Connelly, then secretary of the treasury, made no secret of his anti-Allende animus. But other authorities, including various officials of international organizations, deny this allegation.[31] Chile's lack of creditworthiness, they argued, the result of Allende's policies and not external factors, doomed the Socialist experiment.

Did the U.S. denial of credit—the "invisible blockade"—bring down the UP government? Allende often described U.S. economic response as "an always oblique attack, covert, sinuous, but nonetheless harmful for Chile."[32] In retrospect, the curtailing of American economic assistance, while doubtless hurting Allende, should not have destroyed his regime, because Chile had alternative sources of foreign assistance. The Eastern bloc, including the Soviet Union and the People's Republic of China, provided Chile $263 million; other Socialist countries offered an additional $360 million in long-term credits.

While large, this sum displeased Allende, who expected Moscow to subsidize him much as it had supported Castro's Cuba. Indeed, this became one of Allende's principal threats: "If the United States denies us its credits, we will seek other credit lines in other nations wherever it is possible. I do not imagine that the United States would oppose other nations lending us money."[33] While willing to take advantage of Washington's discomfiture in the Southern Cone, Moscow wished to avoid any direct confrontation with the United States. More significantly, it recognized the logistic and economic problems of supplying Chile's needs. Thus, when Allende, Almeyda, and Socialist politician Carlos Altamirano made pilgrimages to Moscow, they discovered that Moscow was not an economic Lourdes. Santiago did receive technical assistance, some small grants, a few loan commitments, credits to purchase Soviet products, and vague promises to build some factories, but no large sums of money. In 1972, for example, when the Moneda required $500 million in short-term loans in order to purchase food and raw materials, the Soviets offered only $27 million and the renegotiation of an already outstanding $80 million debt. Only when Allende apparently became so angry that he threatened to cut short his visit to the U.S.S.R. did the Soviets come up with an additional $20 million.[34] Nor did the remaining Socialist nations react more generously. Cuba, which proclaimed that "we are ready to give [Chile] not only our blood but even our bread," in fact gave neither. Instead Santiago had to make do with forty thousand tons of sugar.[35] Ironically, it was the European and American capitalists, not the Socialist comrades, who provided the most economic assistance. The vilified bankers, by granting Chile a moratorium on its debt payments, allowed the Moneda to save $165 million in 1971 and 1972 and an additional $135 million in 1973–1974.

Thus Chile had access to substantial amounts of short-term credits. Indeed, in August 1973, Allende had accumulated $574 million in assistance, substantially more than the $340 million that he acquired upon taking office. Almeyda noted that by 1973 "Chile . . . had obtained enough normal bank credits from this continent [Western Europe] to buy there enough merchandise that it could not purchase in the United States." A Communist official confirmed Almeyda's statement. The often-denounced economic blockade, he noted, though causing difficulty, was, "in the main, foiled."[36]

Rather than a lack of capital—the Moneda had expended only seventy million of the five hundred million dollars in credits that it had accumulated—the Moneda's economic policy mortally wounded the Chilean economy. The Allende regime encouraged consumerism, not capital development. Even Almeyda admitted that Chile could have

obtained needed spare parts but elected to spend its money on consumer goods. This short-sighted policy, in turn, created the conditions
that led the military to move against the Moneda.

Supporters of the UP government tend to ignore the economic factors, alleging instead that the CIA and the U.S. military encouraged
Chile's armed forces to rebel, provided logistical support, and even
joined in the fighting that deposed Allende. These charges are not
unexpected, particularly when a former CIA officer, Thomas Karamessines, admitted that the infamous Track II organization, which
tried to stop Allende in 1970, "was really never ended." Some believe
that Washington did not have to participate actively in the rebellion
in order to be held responsible for Allende's downfall. The Church
Committee, for example, concluded that merely giving the impression
that Washington would welcome a coup was enough to implicate the
United States. Officials in the CIA, the U.S. military, and the State
Department and former ambassador Nathaniel Davis, however, deny
complicity in the 1973 coup. Faced with conflicting evidence, the issue
of U.S. involvement becomes a question of faith. Both sides have their
paladins, but until Washington opens its archives, we will not know
the degree of American complicity, if any, in Allende's fall.[37]

Concentrating on Washington's presumed involvement, however,
ignores the Chilean component in the equation. Chile's armed forces
had a history of deposing civilian governments. It is patronizing to
argue that a professional military, keenly aware of the government's
nationalist traditions and jealous of its autonomy, would become the
passive instrument of a foreign government. Chile's officer corps had
already demonstrated its independence when it resisted U.S. pressure
to block Allende's inauguration in 1970. Thus, it is more likely that
three years of chaos and the fear of a rebellion, not Richard Nixon,
inspired Chile's armed forces to depose Allende in 1973.

Clodomiro Almeyda, for example, saw U.S. participation as periph-
eral. Even if Washington had successively suborned the military, he
argued, Allende could have aborted the putsch, if he had crushed
the counterrevolutionary elements in the officer corps. "If the armed
forces had not been predisposed to oppose the UP government,"

Almeyda observed, "the Pentagon's call for a military uprising would have gone unheeded." Thus, Washington's "efforts designed to destabilize the UP government—activities which U.S. authorities have cynically acknowledged—did not create the factors which caused the UP government to fall but rather increased and intensified the impact of those factors."[38]

Allende's foreign policy toward Washington failed in part because the Chilean leader did not understand either the United States or its leader. Allende saw the U.S. as a monolithic country dominated by monopolistic economic interests. Since he was sure that the large corporations controlled the White House and the Congress, he believed that the American government loathed him. In a sense, this conclusion granted Allende license to act without restraint, since he believed that a confrontation with Washington was inevitable. Allende's domestic and foreign policies suffered from the same flaw—an unpragmatic romanticism. He tried to make Chile economically self-sufficient while continuing to receive foreign technical and financial assistance and to increase popular consumption while stimulating capital investment. Castro could not achieve these goals with foreign largesse and domestic austerity. But Castro endured because the Cuban military sustained him. Allende lacked that support.

9 The Corporate Caudillos and the Return of Democracy, 1973–1990

Few Chileans and even fewer foreigners anticipated a violent coup; most expected the restoration of civilian government following a bloodless putsch. Both presumptions proved erroneous. The new regime's first priority was to purge the nation systematically of leftist influence. Having assured domestic order, the largely military junta virtually abandoned the economic and political imperatives established by the 1925 constitution and expanded by the Popular Front and its successor governments. Laissez-faire capitalism and totalitarianism replaced statism and liberal democracy.

No one knows precisely how many people perished during the 1973 coup. Government critics described Santiago's streets littered with dead and the Mapocho River running red with blood. Others estimated the number killed, including foreign extremists, between one thousand and ten thousand.[1] Such violence, some argued, was atypical of Chile. As one U.S. government official said of the new regime, "We didn't mean for the junta to run wild."[2] In truth, the severity of the military's takeover and its decision to retain control should have surprised no one. The Chilean armed forces—whether in 1905 Santiago, 1907 Iquique, 1925 Puerto Natales, or 1966 Salvador—have repeatedly demonstrated a willingness to use force to maintain order. In 1973, the officer corps concluded that they had to remain in power in order to cauterize the festering wound that Marxism had inflicted.

The violence continued. The government arrested thousands more, and perhaps as many as twenty thousand fled during the junta's first two years.[3] Like Spain's Francisco Franco, General Augusto Pinochet inflicted more damage shaping his government than in seizing power.

By the 1980s it was estimated that perhaps as many as three hundred thousand Chileans lived in political exile, and that additional thousands fled, largely for economic reasons. A few remained in jail; others chafed in internal exile. Periodically people were found murdered; others simply disappeared.

Although labeled Fascist and employing *squadristi* tactics, Pinochet and his comrades lacked an ideological North Star. Fundamentally, the junta's members yearned to return to the good old days: traditional values, an established social order, and an economy regulated by Adam Smith's "unseen hand" and Milton Friedman's free-market doctrines. Predictably, their political icon was Diego Portales, who had brought order to the early republic following the supposed postindependence Liberal excesses. For a few months, the government even discouraged women from wearing pants.

Relations with the United States

The junta and General Pinochet have outlasted four U.S. presidents. Precisely for this reason, it is difficult to speak of a single American policy vis-à-vis Chile. While Richard Nixon and then Gerald Ford, who remained in power until 1976, favored the new government, Jimmy Carter did not. Even Ronald Reagan, who began his presidency extolling the virtues of the Pinochet administration, eventually ceased supporting the general. The reasons for this policy shift were quite simple: the general had not changed, but the world and the United States had. By the mid-1980s, Latin America repudiated dictatorships in favor of democratic government. Hence Washington's endorsement of a conservative military regime appeared increasingly anomalous, particularly as the threat from the "evil empire" declined. As the United States became more tolerant of the Soviet Union, the Pinochet government became more of a liability. Thus, if Washington's relations with the junta were initially warm, they eventually ended with anger and alienation.

President Nixon, while not openly exulting, clearly was not displeased that the Chilean military had rid the hemisphere of the Marxist menace. U.S. economic credits, long denied Allende, cascaded upon Chile, which received funds as well as almost half the foodstuffs authorized by the Food for Peace program for Latin America.[4] Washington joined the Club of Paris in rescheduling the payment of Chile's international debts. Nixon's successor, Gerald Ford, acted generously as well, providing Santiago more than $160 million in economic aid, $23 million in grants, and $18.5 million in military assistance. Additionally the Export-Import Bank lent Chile $141 million, while the World Bank and the Inter-American Development Bank extended another $300 million in credits.[5]

The Nixon and Ford administrations became the junta's champions in the international community. Allende's overthrow, particularly the subsequent bloody repression, outraged certain sectors of world opinion. The United Nations as well as its organizations passed numerous resolutions criticizing Chile's abuse of human rights and its treatment of political prisoners. Washington generally abstained on these votes. The junta responded positively to American support. Although it did not return the property that the Allende government had nationalized, the Moneda did pay compensation. Both Anaconda and Kennecott, for example, received payment in cash and bonds for their mines and equipment. Chile also opened wide its doors to private investors. In 1974, it passed a measure allowing foreign corporations to remit more easily their profits abroad. Since this new policy conflicted with the policies of the Andean Pact, to which Chile was a signatory, Santiago withdrew from the agreement.

Thus, while much of the world broke diplomatic ties with or reduced their staffs in Chile, Santiago and Washington generally enjoyed cordial relations.[6] The U.S. Congress did not share the White House's enthusiasm for General Pinochet. Many in the United States admired Allende. A 1975 Gallup poll indicated that approximately 60 percent of Americans believed that Chileans lived better under the UP government than under the Pinochet administration.[7] Not surprisingly, some of these people petitioned the U.S. Congress to force the junta to alter its policies. Senator Edward Kennedy became one of the first to champion the antijunta forces, proposing a cessation of economic assistance to Chile, other than for humanitarian aid, until it improved its human rights policy. Kennedy's motion failed, but the Senate urged President Nixon to cajole Pinochet to stop brutalizing his countrymen. The following year, when it became clear that quiet persuasion could not improve Chile's domestic environment, Kennedy moved to end all military assistance unless Chile changed its human rights record. When Pinochet refused to alter his policy, Santiago received no military assistance during the fiscal years 1976–1979. In 1974, when the news from Chile turned especially grim, the Congress stipulated that Santiago could receive no more than twenty-five million dollars in economic assistance. The president, refusing to accept the legislature's financial restrictions, easily circumvented the congressional limitations by ordering his delegates to authorize additional loans from international banks to Chile. As a consequence of this tactic as well as a series of innovative legal interpretations, the White House increased the economic assistance to ninety million dollars.

But by late 1976 the Moneda's blatant abuse of civil rights and its repressive policies had finally disillusioned even the White House. William Simon, then the U.S. secretary of the treasury, warned Chile that the junta's brutal policies jeopardized the flow of American aid, and Henry Kissinger declared that Santiago's human rights abuses strained Chile's diplomatic relations with the United States. If the Moneda's policy failed to change, Kissinger warned, the damage would be considerable. By then, however, Washington had lost much of its leverage on Chile. So much foreign private capital—nearly three billion dollars from 1974 to 1978—had flowed into Santiago that Pinochet not only did not require American economic assistance, but he even publicly belittled the American offer of twenty-five million dollars in aid.[8]

Nor did the U.S. arms embargo discommode Santiago. From 1973 to 1977, for example, Washington provided only $107 million worth of military equipment, mainly light aircraft and transport planes, while from 1978 to 1982 U.S. military assistance declined to $20 million.[9] But

Santiago encountered little difficulty in replacing American weapons. The Moneda purchased warships from Germany and Great Britain, armored vehicles and fighter aircraft from France, transport planes and trainers from Spain, and assorted weapons from Brazil. The United States military assistance, in short, had become superfluous. During the period 1973 to 1982, Washington provided less than 10 percent of the $1.4 billion that Chile spent acquiring weapons. Increasingly Santiago manufactured its own weapons as well as assault and armored vehicles. Chile's Cardoen Industries produced a variety of cluster bombs and ammunition, even developing an attack helicopter. Chile thus joined Brazil and Argentina as an arms exporter.[10]

The Carter Years, 1976–1980

Because human rights constituted one of the essential planks of President Jimmy Carter's foreign policy, Chile became one of his administration's principal targets. And since the junta refused to end domestic repression, diplomatic interchange between the two nations remained correct but barely cordial. Preferring to work within the OAS, Carter nonetheless supported various UN declarations condemning Chile for curtailing human rights. Unlike his two predecessors, Carter also worked to oppose multilateral development bank loans to Chile.[11] The State Department manifested its dislike for the Pinochet administration by entertaining a stream of the general's foes, ranging from Eduardo Frei to Allende's former minister of foreign relations Clodomiro Almeyda. The United States also accepted large numbers of Chilean political refugees, including many of those who had once supported Allende.

Pinochet retaliated. In September 1976, a car carrying Orlando Letelier, Allende's former ambassador to the United States and minister of defense, blew up on the streets of Washington. Letelier and a companion, an American woman named Ronni Moffitt, perished in the explosion. Although he had been jailed following the 1973 coup, Letelier had left Chile, eventually taking refuge in the United States, where he worked at the Institute of Policy Studies.[12] The former ambassador was not the first enemy of the Pinochet regime to die violently. An assassin, presumably in the employ of the junta, had murdered retired general Carlos Prats and his wife in Buenos Aires. In Italy, thugs also maimed Bernardo Leighton, a prominent Christian Democratic politician, and killed his wife. Since Letelier had vigorously criticized the Pinochet administration, American authorities rightly suspected the Moneda of ordering his assassination.

The FBI traced the car bombers back to Chile, where they were identified as Michael Townley, an American resident of Chile, four Cubans, and three Chilean army officers: General Manuel Contreras, Colonel Pedro Espinoza, and Captain Armando Fernández Larios. Confronted with the evidence, Pinochet's subsecretary of interior, General Enrique Montero, signed an agreement promising to help the U.S. investigation of the murder. But when Washington requested the extradition of the suspects, the Chilean courts refused. Furious, Carter temporarily withdrew his ambassador, George Landau, and reduced by 25 percent the U.S. embassy's staff. Military assistance ended, and the Chilean navy was not allowed to participate in UNITAS maneuvers with the U.S. fleet. The U.S. government, moreover, canceled outstanding credits destined for Chile, refused to insure private investments in that nation, and vetoed Santiago's loan applications.[13]

American diplomatic pressure occasionally forced the junta to release some political prisoners, among them a dozen Christian Democratic leaders whom Pinochet planned to exile. Most of Santiago's concessions were cosmetic. The Moneda, for example, changed the name of its secret service from Dirección Nacional de Inteligencia (DINA) to the more anodyne Centro Nacional de Informaciónes (CNI). This ploy did not work. In late 1977, the United Nations voted to condemn the Pinochet government for its human rights abuses. By now even the general recognized that he had to improve his image. Consequently, in July 1977 he promised to restore democracy to Chile in 1991. This lengthy process would occur in stages. From 1978 to 1980 the military would rule. During the next five years, General Pinochet would still command, but presumably in conjunction with civilians and subject to constitutional prohibitions. Eventually, in 1989, the junta would nominate a candidate for president. If the public ratified the junta's selection, he would rule for an additional eight years. Should the nation reject him, another election would take place in which the opposition could nominate a candidate.

In 1980, the junta conducted a plebiscite on whether to accept a draft version of the constitution and to retain General Pinochet as president. On 11 September 1980, 93 percent of the eligible voters cast their ballots. Of these, 67 percent approved the new constitution. The general had chosen his time well. The nation's economy had improved; the political atmosphere appeared congenial. Thus, if DINA could become the more innocuous CNI, then General Pinochet could become president. Pinochet, of course, had put himself into an untenable situation. If he won the plebiscite, few outside Chile—and not many within—would believe that the election was honest. Skeptics had ample reason for their cynicism: the government denied the opposition access to the media and to the public. Pinochet promised the electorate that they would be awash in color television sets and automobiles if they approved the constitution. Given the government's refusal to permit outsiders to monitor the election, many feared that the plebiscite would be little more than a political face-lift to beguile Washington.[14]

General Pinochet demonstrated how easily Chile could sidestep Carter's well-intentioned human rights policy. Much to Carter's dismay, Brady Tyson, an aide to UN Ambassador Andrew Young, publicly apologized for America's supposed role in upending the Allende regime. Since such statements complicated Washington's foreign relations, the State Department ordered Tyson to resign. Carter also attempted to distance himself from Tyson by retracting his own preelection statement alleging U.S. complicity in Allende's overthrow. The president had similar difficulties with Congress. Congressman Henry Reuss introduced a measure that required Washington to cease funding aid programs for nations that violated human rights. Arguing that the measure deprived the White House of diplomatic flexibility, Carter opposed Reuss's suggestion.

If Carter's domestic supporters sometimes went too far, then the White House discovered that the international community, contrary to public statements, did not advocate a strong human rights policy in Chile. When the U.S. government attempted to prevent Chile from obtaining loans from international lending banks, reaction was quick and hostile. Both Mexico, which had broken diplomatic ties with Santiago in 1974, and Venezuela, which trumpeted its support of human rights, opposed Carter's attempt to mix morality and assistance. Economic considerations, not politics, they argued, should be the primary criteria for judging whether to approve loans.[15]

During its four years in office, the Carter administration granted Chile only one-third of what the Ford administration had provided in two years, while virtually ending military assistance. The pressure did not succeed: only Pinochet's title, not Chile's political climate, had changed. Essentially Carter's highly visible blockade failed because Pinochet had access to private credit. From 1976 to 1980, the U.S. government provided the Moneda $114 million in loans, grants, and donations. During the same time period, Chile borrowed approximately $15 billion, mainly from private banks.[16] With such financial sources available and with foreign governments selling weapons to Chile, Carter became a voice in the wilderness.

Washington's abortive attempt to isolate Chile succeeded only in antagonizing General Pinochet. Ironically, the Chilean leader likened Washington to Moscow, chastising both nations for trying to impose their political system upon the world by selectively invoking human rights. After flaying U.S. imperialism, the Moneda then criticized Washington for not taking the lead in a world crusade against communism.[17]

The Reagan Years

The 1980 election of Ronald Reagan doubtless delighted Pinochet, who believed that the new American president and the old Chilean general would lead a crusade against the "evil empire." Augusto

Pinochet finally had an ideological soulmate in the hemisphere other than Paraguay's Alfredo Stroessner. During President Reagan's first two years in office, his administration annulled many of Carter's actions: it permitted American-controlled development banks to lend money to Santiago and replaced Ambassador George Landau with the more conservative James Theberge. The White House also jettisoned Carter's human rights program. An American delegate to the UN's Commission on Human Rights, for example, while admitting that Chile's record on human rights was perhaps not ideal, declared that it was less bestial than that of other nations. Not surprisingly, in 1981, for the first time, the United States voted against a UN resolution condemning Chile for human rights violations.

Following a visit to the United States by Chile's secretary of foreign relations, the White House dispatched its UN ambassador, Jeane Kirkpatrick, to Santiago. While in Chile, Dr. Kirkpatrick disclosed that Washington might end its investigation of the Letelier and Moffitt murders. The reason was simple: if Chilean officials were involved in the assassinations, which she doubted, then their participation was indirect.[18] Ambassador Kirkpatrick's logic did not impress Senator Edward Kennedy, who prevented the Moneda from acquiring U.S. weapons by introducing an amendment to the Foreign Assistance Act of 1981 that required Chile to meet three preconditions before obtaining military assistance. President Reagan would have to certify that Santiago had made "significant progress" on the issue of human rights; any military aid provided to Chile must be in America's national interest; and Pinochet would have to help bring before a grand jury those individuals involved in the Letelier assassination.

The romance between Santiago and Washington became a casualty of change in the hemisphere's political climate. During the early 1980s, military governments in Argentina, Brazil, Peru, and Bolivia gave way to civilian administrations. U.S. State Department support of these budding democratic regimes exposed a fundamental contradiction in the White House's policy toward Chile: the Reagan administration could not advocate the democratization of Latin America while ignoring Chile.

The Moneda's policies, moreover, seemed deliberately provocative. The Pinochet regime expelled various moderate Chileans, including the head of the Chilean Commission on Human Rights. It turned a blind eye toward, and perhaps even assisted in, the assassination of a dissident trade union leader, Tucapel Jiménez. It refused to cooperate with investigation of the Letelier and Moffitt murders. Rather than publicly criticize Chile, Reagan advocated a policy of "quiet diplomacy" toward Santiago in hope of nudging Pinochet into adopting a more liberal domestic policy. Three senators—Howard Baker of Tennessee, Paul Laxalt of Nevada, and Ernest Hollings of South Carolina—visited Chile in early 1982 in order to express Washington's displeasure about the continuing dictatorship. Later the same year, Secretary of State George Shultz reopened the Letelier investigation. In January 1983, a visit to Chile did not convince a congressional delegation that Santiago had improved its human rights record.[19]

Without abandoning "quiet diplomacy," the State Department became more assertive. It protested the Moneda's continued human rights abuses, including the arrest of the leader of the copper workers' union, Rodolfo Seguel. In November, it dispatched to Chile two functionaries, Edward Derwinsky and Robert Morely, in hope of arranging some political discussions between the government, the trade unions, and opposition leaders. Their failure to obtain a settlement led Vice President George Bush to warn Chile that it would not receive certification until it permitted free elections and restored democratic institutions. Much of this talk was bombast: the State Department, by its own admission, had "minimal" influence on the Moneda and "thin" credibility with its opposition.[20]

Occasionally Pinochet did make some conciliatory gestures. In August 1983, the Moneda ended the state of emergency that had existed in Chile since 1977. President Pinochet promised to permit exiles to return to Chile, to ease censorship, and to allow more political activity. The president's generosity backfired. Once granted limited freedoms, the opposition groups formed a coalition in order to increase their power. Political dissent, so long restricted, escalated. Antigovernment demonstrations became more common and more stri-

dent, particularly as the nation approached the tenth anniversary of
Allende's fall. Pinochet reacted to this dissent by brutally suppressing
the protestors. Since the government's draconian acts clearly demonstrated that the Moneda would neither permit a return to democracy
nor treat its citizens more humanely, various opposition groups called
upon President Reagan to intervene.

During 1983 the United States abandoned "quiet diplomacy," and
the Chilean economic miracle collapsed. After a period of painful
post-Allende adjustment, prosperity appeared to return to Chile. The
Moneda instituted a laissez-faire policy that deprived domestic producers of formidable tariff barriers. Initially this policy seemed to
work: inflation fell from 300 to 30 percent, the G.N.P. increased as
copper prices surged, and Chile's nontraditional exports thrived. But
the prosperity was superficial: foreign loans, not domestic productive
forces, sustained Chile's economy. Regrettably, these sums were invested not in the economy's infrastructure but in fueling a massive
binge of buying consumer goods. For the first time in Chile's history,
the lower middle class, even workers, had access to credit. House-
holds that once aspired to possess a transistor radio now owned color
television sets. Few of these consumer goods were locally produced.
International banks lent money to Chilean banks, which in turn lent
to Chilean consumers to purchase foreign-made products.

This economic round-robin continued only as long as foreign banks
were willing to be generous toward their Chilean counterparts. By
1981, however, they belatedly recognized that Chile had amassed one
of the world's highest per capita debts. Recognizing their error in
showering money on Chile, these institutions tried to recover their
investments, but Santiago had little worth repossessing. Hence, the
foreign banks slashed their credit lines to Chile.

During the years that Santiago's debts mounted, Chile's national
economy stalled. Without protection, the nation's domestic industries first retrenched and then disappeared. Businesses that depended
upon these local factories also collapsed. The G.N.P. fell by 15 percent, and 25 percent of the work force lacked jobs. Eventually the crisis
spread to the financial sector. In 1981, the government took over four

banks and four credit institutions. By the end of 1982, 10 percent of the nation's loans were in default and three more banks failed. The crisis forced the state to become the unwilling owner of thirteen banks —two of these were Chile's largest—and five credit institutions. By 1983, less than half the country's banks and slightly fewer credit institutions had survived the economic purge. Ironically the most laissez-faire of Chile's regimes now controlled 50 percent of the nation's credit institutions. Unemployment reached 34 percent.

While the supposed prosperity of the late 1970s did not convert the Chilean public to *Pinochetismo*, it had made the dictatorship at least palatable. The economic crisis, however, turned once docile elements into vocal critics of the junta. Supposedly banned trade unions held work stoppages. In the *barrio alto*, the middle class expressed their hostility toward Pinochet as they had toward Allende—by beating their pots and pans. The recession begat violence. In early 1984, Pinochet used a wave of bombings as an excuse to impose another state of emergency, thus curtailing political demonstrations and restricting the opposition media.[21]

Pinochet's repression distressed Washington. In April 1984, James Michel, an under secretary of state, publicly advocated "the return of a democratically elected civilian government in Chile." Because the Chileans themselves lacked a consensus on what to do and because the United States feared Communist participation in any new government, Washington could only urge the creation of a middle-of-the-road government and advocate a "smooth transition to democracy." Washington's complaints about Chile's human rights and labor policies antagonized the Pinochet government. Since Washington had failed to contain communism in Nicaragua or Vietnam, Chile's foreign minister tartly observed, it was hardly in a position to preach to Santiago. Rather than listening to hysterical labor union leaders, civil rights advocates, and left-wing Democrats, the U.S. Congress should recognize Chile's contribution to the free world.[22]

The diplomatic situation appeared to improve when President Reagan rejected a congressional attempt to levy an import tax on Chilean copper, but this euphoria dissipated. In late October 1984, as public demonstrations increased, Pinochet again imposed a state of emergency, arresting members of the political opposition. The old scenario was reenacted: the more Pinochet attempted to limit debate, the more the opposition protested. In November, he restored a state of siege, thereby diminishing an already limited number of civil liberties as well as closing opposition newspapers and media. A new method of repression appeared—the mass arrest—in which police and military units surrounded the neighborhoods of the poor, detained all the men over age fifteen, and searched the homes. Most of those held were released within a day, others were not. Arrests, which between 1976 and 1982 had annually numbered less than one thousand, began to rise, reaching five thousand in 1984.[23]

The resurgence of violence in October 1984 forced the United States again to denounce Pinochet's human rights policy. High-ranking government officials, among them George Shultz, criticized Santiago, noting that the Moneda's repressive policies "disillusioned" President Reagan. In November, James Michel returned to Chile, where he spoke to government officials and opposition leaders in hope of forcing the Moneda to hold congressional elections. In December 1984, a group of Hispanic-American legislators requested that Pinochet suspend the state of siege, restore union rights, cease censoring the press, and hold elections in order to select a congress. Even President Reagan joined the chorus of critics, publicly condemning Santiago's civil rights policies.

These efforts failed to budge General Pinochet. Santiago, of course, did not regard this publicity with favor. Chilean officials suggested that the United States cease meddling in their government's affairs lest they antagonize Pinochet or make him more intransigent. The U.S. ambassador advised the State Department not to pressure the Moneda publicly or to veto any of its loan applications.

Despite these warnings, Washington adopted a new, more confrontational policy toward Santiago. Elliott Abrams replaced Langhorne Motley as assistant secretary of state for inter-American affairs. Since Abrams had earlier served as assistant secretary of state for human rights and humanitarian affairs, he knew intimately many of the abuses of the Pinochet regime. Abrams made it clear that "the policy of the United States government toward Chile is direct and unequivocal: we will cultivate the transition toward democracy."[24] To manifest its disappointment, the State Department called home Ambassador James Theberge, the hard-line former colleague of Jeane Kirkpatrick. His successor was Harry Barnes, who, unlike Theberge, did not favor the Pinochet government. He and other American diplomatic functionaries began cultivating contacts with members of Chile's opposition parties.

To add substance to otherwise symbolic acts, the U.S. government adopted a more overtly hostile policy. In February 1985, it abstained on a vote to grant a BID development loan to Chile. Nestor Sanchez, a high-level functionary in the Department of Defense's inter-American section, visited Chile with an offer, some believe, to exchange American weapons for Pinochet's promise to respect human rights. When the general refused, Washington's attempt to link financial assistance to a more enlightened human rights policy failed. American representatives to the World Bank and the Inter-American Development Bank abstained from approving loans to Chile. In June the State Department increased the pressure by voicing its reluctance about voting funds for a World Bank loan to Chile. As George Shultz noted, the United States wished to demonstrate its concern about Chile's domestic situation and to express how deeply it wished to see that nation reform.

Chile's precarious financial situation made it vulnerable to economic pressure. In 1985, its banks required infusions of approximately two billion dollars in loans from the World Bank and the Inter-American Development Bank. The United States made its position quite clear: if the Moneda wanted the money, then it would have to meet "certain conditions," conditions which the State Department refused to publicize. Pinochet knew full well the nature of these conditions. On 16 June, he abolished the state of siege. Two days later, the World Bank approved a loan for Chile. Washington also permitted various private banks to open discussions with Chile about obtaining additional funds.

The gap between the two nations widened during late 1985. The State Department chided the Moneda, claiming that it cynically used the issue of terrorism as a pretext to abridge legitimate political activity. In December, Reagan used a UN Human Rights Day address to complain about Chile. Four months later, he expressed "deep concern" over the "troubling human rights situation in Chile." Henceforth, Reagan observed, the United States would urge that all nations, not simply left-wing dictatorships, institute democratic reforms. A Chilean denunciation quickly followed. The State Department defended Washington's acerbic statements about the Pinochet regime: the president had privately advised General Pinochet of his displeasure, and he chose to express publicly his disappointment only after private entreaties failed. If General Pinochet was distressed, then various opposition leaders seemed quite grateful, particularly toward Ambassador Barnes.

Opposition to the Pinochet government became more outspoken in Chile. During one antigovernment incident, Chilean troops arrested two demonstrators who may have been carrying bottles filled with gasoline. For reasons that remain unclear and utterly incomprehensible, the soldiers poured the gasoline on the two young people and set them afire. One, Cármen Gloria Quintana, survived, albeit horribly disfigured; the other, Rodrigo Rojas, a U.S. resident, died of his burns. A State Department protest demanded an investigation, and Ambassador Barnes attended Rojas's funeral. This act of official sympathy outraged not only President Pinochet but also U.S. senator Jesse Helms, who denounced the American diplomat for participating in what he perceived as a Communist demonstration.

In mid-1986 the Frente Popular Manuel Rodríguez, a Communist-backed terrorist group, tried unsuccessfully to murder Pinochet. The attempted homicide, in conjunction with the discovery of a large arsenal of Soviet-bloc weapons, indicated that a Communist conspiracy did in fact threaten Chile. Pinochet cleverly used the botched assassination and the weapons cache to make a simple point: if he did not remain in the Moneda, then Chile would fall into the maw of world communism. Just as the events of late 1986 enhanced Pinochet's position, so they complicated Washington's situation. The United States desperately wanted to ease Pinochet out of office, but obviously it did not want Chile to become like Nicaragua, where leftists had taken over after the dictator Anastasio Somoza fled in 1979. Consequently, Washington had to walk a fine line, maintaining pressure on the Pinochet government without plunging Chile into anarchy. Typical of this maneuver was U.S. abstention on votes by the World Bank and the Inter-American Development Bank to grant loans to Chile. The new policy had limitations. Although Chile could no longer threaten to expropriate U.S.-owned copper mines, the Moneda possessed a more fearsome retaliatory weapon: it could repudiate its debts to American-owned banks. Consequently, the United States abstained from voting rather than veto a Chilean loan application.

Continued suppression of strikes and the arrest of dissident political figures in 1987 only increased U.S. problems and American ire. Washington still demanded that Chile extradite Manuel Contreras and Pedro Espinoza. In protest, the State Department refused visas both for Pablo Rodríguez, an extreme right-wing friend of Pinochet, and for a Chilean Pan-American Games athlete after it became known that he may have been involved in human rights violations. Washington also worked to prevent Chile from acquiring weapons from other nations. Perhaps as an indication of the state of relations between the United States and Chile, President Pinochet refused to attend the dedication of a joint American-Chilean project because Ambassador Barnes would be present.[25]

As the date of elections neared, the United States turned up the pressure. In December 1987, it abstained on a vote in the World Bank to grant a loan to Chile. Many argued that the Pinochet regime would collapse if Washington vetoed these loans. The White House, however, did not want Pinochet to fall unless a moderate democratic government took his place. Hence, it continued to abstain on loan requests in order to rebuke, but not maim, Santiago. More punitive measures were in store for Chile. In April 1987, Senator Edward Kennedy and Representative Thomas Harkin introduced proposals that, if implemented, would have cost 620,000 to 800,000 Chilean jobs. At year's end Reagan, citing the detention of union leaders, suspended the duty-free status of various Chilean imports. Ambassador Barnes warned Santiago that the White House might prevent Americans from investing in Chile.

Eventually, the United States did to Pinochet what it had been denounced for doing to Allende: in June 1988, Washington admitted that the government-funded National Endowment for Democracy gave the opposition six hundred thousand dollars to defeat Pinochet's election.[26] Curiously, Americans seemed more concerned about human rights than the Chileans. A 1985 opinion poll by a distinguished Santiago research institution, FLACSO, indicated that Chileans ranked torture and human rights eleventh in importance on a list of twelve problems.[27] As one Santiago taxi driver noted, "I live here more or less well. There is not much democracy, but I do not lack for food."[28]

The irony of the situation slowly emerged. Roles had reversed. Since 1973, Chile had intervened actively in the United States by hiring public relations experts to influence the American legislative process and public opinion, organizing pressure groups and ad hoc committees and, when necessary, murdering its enemies on the streets of Washington. At the same time, the United States became home to some of Allende's most vehement adherents. The deceased president's widow periodically delivered antiadministration speeches in the United States. Vocal groups, which earlier sang their support for Allende, sang the same songs in the United States, where they praised the deceased president. Similar transformations occurred in Chile. Leftists who had earlier excoriated American intervention in Chile during the government of the Unidad Popular implored Washington to do everything, short of invasion, to topple Pinochet. Conversely, the right wing, which had earlier begged Nixon to depose Allende, flayed the United States for opposing Pinochet.

In 1988, Pinochet finally authorized a plebiscite so that the Chilean people could decide if he should serve as president for another eight years. If Pinochet lost this contest, a second election would choose a successor. Given Pinochet's brutality and his regime's economic policies, permitting a plebiscite seemed an audacious, if not foolhardy, act.[29] Economically, however, Chile had prospered. Since 1984 the nation's economy had grown at an annual rate of 5 percent; unemployment had declined. Chile had diversified its economy, reducing its dependence upon copper; nontraditional exports had risen by 400 percent since 1973. The nation not only enjoyed a trade surplus, but it had also managed to reduce some of its foreign debt.

To ensure his electoral triumph, Pinochet used his office to distribute patronage, promising voters housing subsidies as well as free electrical power.[30] The general also shrewdly played on divisions within the antigovernment forces, which consisted of sixteen parties that shared little in common other than their loathing of Pinochet. Many Chileans doubted that these disparate elements could bridge the ideological gaps in order to forge a coalition. The still powerful Communist party, for example, initially refused to support a plebiscite, and its paramilitary surrogate, the Frente Popular Manuel Rodríguez, also reaffirmed its commitment to armed struggle. Predictably Pinochet used this threat to validate his claim that chaos would engulf Chile if the nation repudiated his government.[31]

The general had miscalculated. The proliferation of television sets and automobiles had deceived him. Despite appearances, Chile's economy had suffered: real wages had fallen, 20 percent of the population controlled 80 percent of the national income, and more than a third of the nation remained impoverished. Public opinion surveys indicated that Chileans wanted a change in government, and when the multiparty opposition agreed to suspend their political infighting until after they unseated Pinochet, the general lost additional ground.[32]

Washington, which earlier had increased tariffs on Chilean imports and refused to allow OPIC to insure U.S. investments in Chile to protest some of Pinochet's policies, increased the pressure by funneling more money to Pinochet's opposition. The United States also warned the general that he should not attempt either to prevent the election or to tamper with the vote count. To reinforce this threat, Washington sent poll watchers to observe the electoral process. In October 1988, 55 percent of the nation refused to renew Pinochet's mandate.[33] Surprisingly, the general accepted the results. In fact, he had little choice: elements within the armed forces had indicated that they would abide by the popular vote even if Pinochet would not. Confronted with a split in his supporters—who apparently announced the election results without his permission—Pinochet had to acquiesce. Democracy would return to Chile in 1989.

Given their ideological differences, the general's foes initially had difficulty coalescing around a single candidate. Eventually, a coalition of seventeen political parties nominated Patricio Aylwin, former senator and head of the Christian Democratic party. Conservative diehards predictably refused to support the PDC candidate. As is perhaps typical of Chile, Aylwin's opposition divided into two blocs. The pro-Pinochet forces, the Unión Demócrata Independiente (UDI), nominated Hernán Büchi, the general's wunderkind former minister of finance, and the more centrist conservatives, the Renovación Nacional (RN), selected Francisco Javier Errázuriz, a businessman who promised to resolve the nation's problems "in five minutes' time."[34] Even without this division in the opposition ranks, Aylwin's broad-based coalition easily won the election, receiving 55 percent of the election of December 1989. Chile's longest-lasting, if least-beloved regime, had finally ended.

The December elections, in addition to selecting Pinochet's replacement, also gave the nation an opportunity to elect both houses of the legislature. The race for the seats in the congress was more crowded than the presidential contest: Chile's approximately twenty political parties created eight coalitions, which in turn nominated 529 candidates for 158 seats in the Chamber of Deputies and the Senate. Given the number of competing factions, it seemed unlikely that one party would dominate the congress.

These expectations materialized: although the PDC emerged as Chile's most popular party—winning thirty-nine seats in the Chamber of Deputies and thirteen in the Senate—it did not enjoy a parliamentary majority in either the lower house or the upper house. The rightist coalition garnered forty-eight places in the lower house and sixteen in the senate. (Thanks to a skewed electoral system, the Communist party, for years Latin America's strongest and largest, failed to win a single legislative seat.)[35] Thus, the PDC had to forge an alliance with the center-Left, creating a coalition of seventy-two legislators and twenty-two senators, enough for a majority in the 120-seat Chamber of Deputies but insufficient to control the Senate, which numbered forty-seven. (The 1980 constitution permitted Pinochet, the heads of the armed forces, the council of state, the judiciary, and the controller of the republic to appoint nine senators.)

The fact that Aylwin's coalition does not dominate both legislative houses hampers his ability to institute change. Although the 1980 constitution required a 60 percent or two-thirds majority (the amount varied depending on the issue) before the Chamber of Deputies could abrogate the laws or decrees of the Pinochet government, only a simple majority was needed to achieve this same goal in the upper house. Although Aylwin might convince two-thirds of the lower house to support his proposals, winning half of the Senate's votes appears unlikely. The nine appointed senators plus those of the Right number twenty-five, more than enough to abort any reform measure in the upper house.[36]

Regrettably, crucial issues remain unresolved. The Chilean armed forces will not obediently return to their barracks unless certain that the new government will not prosecute them for acts committed during the Pinochet interregnum. Many Chileans, particularly those whose families suffered, naturally seek retribution. Elements of the anti-Pinochet coalition have already demanded that the new congress abrogate the 1978 law which amnestied those involved in overturning the Allende government and the subsequent "dirty war." They also wish to extend the statute of limitations on certain crimes. Yet, General Fernando Matthei has already warned, "If they are going to try to put us in the pillory, as in Argentina, that is going to bring the most grave consequences."[37] Clearly the armed forces are angry. Divisions are already appearing in the governing coalition over this issue. The situation is complicated by the fact that Pinochet and his comrades still control the armed forces. Aylwin, though willing to retain the present commanders of the air force and the national police, had asked Pinochet to resign. (The head of the navy, Admiral José Merino, will voluntarily retire.) The general's refusal may cause future problems: Aylwin had earlier opposed granting amnesty to members of the armed forces who committed human rights crimes during Pinochet's administration. Faced with a potentially rebellious military still under the command of Pinochet, Aylwin may have to compromise. Although this solution may calm the armed forces, it will not endear the new president to some of his followers.

Economic issues also remain divisive. Aylwin had promised economic stability while instituting social and political changes.[38] Such goals seem difficult, if not impossible, to realize because the very reforms Aylwin's supporters seek—increased state involvement in the economy and changes in labor laws—may disrupt the delicate economic balance. Certainly the government will have to address outstanding social issues. Reconciliation of the two forces—one demanding change and the other favoring the status quo—may prove extremely difficult to achieve.

A democratic government that seeks to obtain a national consensus might prove more hostile to the United States than did the Pinochet administration, which did not have to satisfy domestic public opinion. The Left may attempt to punish Washington for first deposing Allende and then protecting Pinochet. Conversely the Right may chastise the United States for abandoning the general. Similarly, domestic political pressure or ideology may force any Aylwin government to demonstrate its independence by confronting the United States on such volatile issues as the 1989 invasion of Panama, which revived bitter memories of Washington's involvement in the War of the Pacific and the *Baltimore* incident.

Economic differences between the United States and Chile could also produce conflict. Santiago is heavily in debt. It may be politically expedient and economically attractive for the Moneda to repudiate its obligations to U.S. banks. Since Washington seems willing to back some plan of debt forgiveness, Chile might not have to take such a drastic step. The Moneda, however, will doubtless return to increased state participation in the economy. If so, the government might nationalize American-owned companies to create national industries. The

Moneda might also erect tariff barriers to protect local economic interests. In either case, American corporations might well press Washington for help, precipitating yet another rift with the White House.
Santiago might seek additional aid from the United States, though,
given the current world demands on American foreign aid, the White
House may have to reject Chile's request. If so, the Chileans may
accuse the U.S. of niggardliness.

Aylwin's agenda, particularly in relation to the United States, seems
unclear. He may attempt to resurrect Frei's policy of seeking diplomatic independence and economic development by distancing himself
from Washington. Chile, for example, joined other Latin American
nations in attacking Bush's invasion of Panama. This denunciation
may not be enough. Elements within the Communist party had earlier
described Patricio Aylwin as "the card of imperialism and the Right." [39]
The Moneda might have to become more anti-American in order to
demonstrate to its leftist supporters that Santiago is not under the
American thumb. Whatever the outcome, little has changed: Chile and
the United States still entertain expectations of the other, expectations
that neither nation can fulfill.

Conclusion:
From Darwin to Marx

After 1891, Chile's relations with the United States co-alesced into three overlapping periods. From 1891 to 1929, the Moneda nurtured its residual rancor over the *Baltimore* incident and the Alsop claims. President Wilson's pious but hypocritical mouthings about the Pan-American movement, in conjunction with his attempt to force Santiago into a war in which it had no stake, merely provided new justifications for the old enmity. During this initial period, moreover, the Moneda tended to see the United States as seeking to deprive it of Tacna and Arica.

While the level of Chile's anger toward the United States deepened after 1929, the cause had changed: hostility toward the U.S. economic presence—particularly following the collapse of the nitrate industry —replaced Santiago's pique over the Tacna-Arica issue. The Moneda doubtless believed that it was sandwiched between Washington and Wall Street: Americans owned the nation's national resources and a good share of the Moneda's international debt. Although continuing to describe itself as the eternal victim, Santiago could and did retaliate. The Moneda browbeat its creditors, periodically threatened to seize American assets, and did indeed take some U.S.-owned property while reducing its trade with the United States. Thus, even in the 1930s, Chile consistently demonstrated its independence. This activity increased in the 1940s, when Santiago toyed with Washington, extracting piecemeal concessions in return for its participation in the Second World War. Chile eventually broke with the Axis powers, not in deference to Washington but because it coveted a place in the United Nations. Yet at the war's end Chile's economy and political destiny seemed linked to the United States. Henceforth, Chile might frustrate the United States but could not openly challenge it. Gone were the days when Santiago's fleet could cow Washington's. How had this once powerful nation lost its place as the premier power on the hemisphere's Pacific Coast?

Even during the early twentieth century, most Chileans recognized that a malaise paralyzed their once-powerful country. Remembering the nation's expansion into the south—its 1836 and 1879 wars fought to guarantee the economic supremacy of the nation's wheat dealers, Valparaíso's commercial elite, and miners; its annexation of the *salitreras* and Easter Island; its abortive attempt to absorb Patagonia; the investment of Chilean capital in the silver and copper mines of Peru and Bolivia or in the *estancias* of the Argentine; and its aggressive naval policy—some found Chile's decline puzzling.

Clearly racial factors could not have caused this fall. Chileans believed that their ruling elite was "more or less" pure European. Hence, if its lower classes were mestizo, then "the mental and moral characteristics of the superior race have prevailed."[1] And because their homeland had escaped the turmoil so often associated with societies containing "blacks or mulattoes," Chileans could not comprehend how their supremacy had evaporated—how former enemies such as Argentina had grown stronger and wealthier or how foreigners, particularly Americans, came to own the nation's most precious assets. While many attributed these problems to defects in the political system or the corrupting influence of the nitrate money, others sought a more basic answer.

In 1904, Dr. Nicolás Palacios's *La raza chilena* argued that Chileans were a race created by the fusion of the Araucanian Indian woman and the Spanish conquistador. Although this observation was not particularly new, Palacios provided a novel twist: unlike its neighbors, Chile was not a Latin nation. Although the conquistadores appeared to be Spanish, they were in fact Germans—descendants of the barbarian Visigoths—who had gravitated to Chile, drawn by the prospect of war and conquest. Hence, the "Chilean race" was not the despised Andean *cholo*, but a mixture of Teutons and Amerindians.

Palacios, like Joseph Arthur de Gobineau, attributed to racial groups certain unique characteristics. Because the Germans—whom Palacios called Goths—and the Araucanians were natural warriors, their offspring seemed genetically qualified for military endeavors. Such virtues, while ideal for a frontier society, became less useful during the late nineteenth and early twentieth centuries, when the plowshare became more prized than the sword. But just as Chileans were preparing themselves to confront the changing economic environment, a wave of foreigners poured into the nation. These immigrants, many of whom were Spaniards, took over the nation's commercial life, thereby aborting the process of converting the naturally warlike Chileans into merchants or farmers. To compound the problem, Jews had introduced alien ideas that undermined a sense of Chilean nationalism. By depriving Chileans of the opportunity to acquire a commercial/industrial/agrarian mentality, the foreigners relegated Chile to the backwater of the world economy.

The twentieth-century historian Francisco A. Encina advanced a similar thesis. He too believed that Chileans, as a race of Gothic-Araucanian warriors, were initially unfit for trade and industry. Fortunately, they could learn. Thus, while England and the United States honed their mercantile skills, Chile concentrated on creating an agrarian economy. But because the Chilean mestizo eschewed commerce, the hated Europeans gained control of the nation's resources and trade. Besides ensuring Chile's economic servitude, this foreign economic penetration produced an unfortunate dividend: it eroded traditional values. Chileans, for example, mindlessly rushed to adopt European customs and products, without first determining if the goods and practices applied to their national experience. Thus Encina, like Palacios, believed that European influence had prevented Chile from completing the process of modernization.[2]

The nation's genetic culture, in short, had limited its capacity to compete in the modern world. As the descendants of conquistadores, Chileans could conquer ferocious enemies but could not master the banal intricacies of capitalism. Unfortunately, Palacios and his followers suffered from a sense of racial determinism. The modern Chilean, noted one observer, lacked business acumen because the Goth and the Indian loathed commerce. Conversely, Americans triumphed because of what they had "inherited from the austere and hardworking Puritans of the North and the audacious cotton farmers of the South, ancestors of the present Yankees who do not have a drop of Indian blood."[3] Paradoxically the same Indian heritage, which had assured Chile's nineteenth-century victories against Peru and Bolivia, condemned the nation to lose its twentieth-century struggle against American mammon.

This analysis appalled many in Chile, because it virtually condemned the culturally deficient Chileans to perpetual peonage. Indeed some even argued that it was pointless to resist the inevitable foreign domination. Rather than the Yankee, who is "conquering us, overwhelming us, through our own fault, because of our torrid languor, our Indian fatalism," noted Gabriela Mistral, Chile's Nobel laureate in literature, "let us hate that in ourselves which renders us vulnerable to his spike of steel and gold, his will and his wealth."[4]

Happily some of Mistral's countrymen preferred to believe that Chileans could change the situation. A few tried the time-honored antidote of nationalism, without which "the Chilean people will disappear."[5] It was during the post-1900 period, for example, that the cult of the naval hero Arturo Prat became so widespread.[6] Chilean nationalism, however, turned to xenophobia, whose virulence increased almost in direct proportion to the amount of foreign economic and cultural penetration.

Pride alone could not overcome post-1900 Chile's desperate economic and political problems. The nationalists needed a theory that simultaneously vitiated their supposed racial inequality and explained the nation's failure to progress. Chileans faced a choice: accept passively their genetically engineered destiny, or discover some external cause for their decline. Given the alternatives of wallowing in self-hate or discovering a scapegoat, Chileans reasonably chose the latter.

Domestic scapegoats were few. Of course, Chileans could have focused on their own oligarchy: the men who sold the nation's natural resources to foreigners; the men who, by mortgaging the nation's future, ran the national government as if it were a pawnshop; the men who sweated the workers in the factories and the *inquilinos* in the fields. Such explanations, however, required Chileans to blame their own ancestors. The United States provided a splendid alternative target. Americans were so racially and culturally alien that they could not be confused with the local leaders. The United States also represented everything that the Chileans admired but hated. Consequently, Chileans turned on the same nation that it once regarded as the bearer of technology, denouncing Americans for investing in the copper industries and accusing them of maltreating Chilean workers, clearly a sin which the Chilean upper class did not commit. They emphasized the lack of elegance and grace in the United States, its excessive divorce rate, its crass materialism, and its pandemic sexuality. Ignoring their own rampant disease rates, the high level of illiteracy and illegitimacy, and the low life expectancy, Chileans rejoiced in their mythical bucolic life: the humble but invariably content *roto*, the austere but paternal *patron*. Do not be misled, noted Alberto Cabrero, "for the Americans, quantity is everything; quality is unimportant."[7]

Scientific socialism reinforced these romantic notions. Palacios's mysticism, embellished by Marx and fleshed out by Lenin, blamed foreign capital and foreign nationals for stunting Chile's economic development. The two ideologies, while agreeing about the cause, differed on the solution: Palacios and his band called for a return to national values, whatever these might be; Marxists sought to revamp the world economic order. Regardless of the solution, the romantics, the Marxists, and, later, the structuralists and their cohorts, the *dependistas*, agreed that the United States, as the premier economic power in the hemisphere, constituted Chile's principal adversary.

What Chileans found difficult to accept was that neither they nor the United States bore the responsibility for the nation's decline. Granted, the parliamentary regime was incompetent, if not venal. So, however, was gilded-age America, despite which the United States nevertheless managed to become a world power. The truth was that Chile possessed a small population and limited physical resources. Due to certain conditions—geographical isolation, weak neighbors, and better government—Santiago managed to reach the forefront of nineteenth-century Latin America. By the early twentieth century, however, the world changed. Chile's small agrarian sector could not compete effectively with the cereal producers like Russia and Argentina, let alone the United States. The Haber process subsequently rendered valueless the Moneda's most important economic asset, nitrates. Santiago had little to hawk on the world market.

Chile's neighbors possessed larger populations and superior economic resources. By 1900, for example, Argentina had more inhabitants than Chile. The Platine republic's abundant and fertile lands allowed it to produce enormous quantities of wheat and beef. Finally, Buenos Aires enjoyed easier access to the North Atlantic economy. If Santiago could not compete with twentieth-century Argentina, then any thought of vying with the United States seemed ludicrous. In a world of big battalions, Santiago was a platoon barely holding its own on the battlefield of world geopolitics.

When fantasy did not suffice, Santiago externalized its anger. Chileans focused on the United States, not so much because of what it did but because it was the world's preeminent economic power. Since Washington was responsible for every ill, it also bore the responsibility for resolving Chile's economic predicament. But Chileans disagreed about how the United States should act. Some demanded greater U.S. involvement in Chile; others opposed it. When the United States did intrude, it accelerated the pace of change enough to antagonize the Right but not enough to satisfy the Left. The result was inevitably frustrating for both governments: Washington should not order but only advise; it should provide financial assistance but never determine how funds were spent; it should be supportive in time of need but never intrusive.

Washington and Santiago still disagree profoundly about each other. Chile continues to regard the United States as an Anglo-Saxon, Protestant nation whose technical skills dwarf its humanist values. The United States sees Chile as just another Latin American nation continuously demanding a sensitivity and consideration that Washington does not believe it merits. The once antagonistic relationship between Santiago and Washington may have moderated, but it has not disappeared.

Notes

Introduction

1. Benjamín Vicuña Mackenna, *Páginas de mi diario durante tres años de viaje*, in *Obras completas*, 2 vols. (Santiago, 1936), 1: 245, 247, 250, 261.
2. Quoted in Reginald Horsman, *Race and Manifest Destiny* (Boston, 1981), 280.

1. Imperial Republics

1. Julio Heise González, *Historia constitucional de Chile* (Santiago, 1950), 53.
2. George McBride, *Chile: Land and Society* (Port Washington, N.Y., 1971), 3.
3. Quoted in E. Marcus, "Chile and Hispanic American Solidarity," *The Americas* 9 (1952): 181.
4. Benjamín Vicuña Mackenna, *Don Diego Portales*, 3rd ed. (Santiago, 1974), 238, 184.
5. Santa Cruz quoted in Robert N. Burr, *By Reason or Force* (Berkeley, 1965), 41. For a stronger statement on Chile's supposed economic motivations, see Valentín Abecia, *Las relaciónes internacionales en la historia de Bolivia*, 2d ed., 3 vols. (La Paz, 1986), 1: 434–35. Portales quoted in Burr, *By Reason or Force*, 40.
6. Burr, *By Reason or Force*, 38.
7. Benjamín Vicuña Mackenna, quoted in Henry C. Evans, *Chile and Its Relations with the United States* (Durham, 1927), 28.
8. Quoted in Alberto Cruchaga Ossa, "Impressions of the First Chilean Minister to Washington," *Pan American Magazine* 39 (1926): 157.
9. Jay Kinsbruner, "The Political Influence of the British Merchants Resident in Chile During the O'Higgins Administration, 1817–1823," *The Americas* 27 (1970): 27.
10. Carl A. Ross, Jr., "Chile and Its Relations with the United States During the Ministry of Thomas Henry Nelson, 1861–1866," Ph.D. diss., University of Georgia, 1966, p. 21; Sergio Sepulveda, *El trigo chileno en el mercado*

mundial (Santiago, 1959), 52–53; Arnold J. Bauer, *Chilean Rural Society from the Spanish Conquest to 1930* (Cambridge, Eng., 1975), 64–65.

11. Vicuña Mackenna, *Páginas de mi diario* 1: 254, 250–51, 259; Abdón Cifuentes, *Memorias*, 2 vols. (Santiago, 1936), 1: 338–41; Vicuña Mackenna, *Páginas de mi diario* 1: 260.

12. Quoted in Ernesto de la Cruz and Guillermo Feliú Cruz, *Epistolario de Don Diego Portales, 1811–1837*, 3 vols. (Santiago, 1936–37), 1: 76–77.

13. Evans, *Chile and Its Relations with the United States*, 46.

14. Quoted in Carolyn A. Richards, "Chilean Attitudes Toward the United States, 1860–1867," Ph.D. diss., Stanford University, 1970, p. 26; Carlos Mery Squella, *Las relaciónes diplomáticas entre Chile y los Estados Unidos de America, 1829–1841* (Santiago, 1965), 105.

15. Quoted in Horsman, *Race and Manifest Destiny*, 226.

16. Quoted in Richards, "Chilean Attitudes," 244.

17. Francisco Bilbao, *Obras completas*, 2 vols. (Santiago, 1897), 2: 160, 162.

18. Vicente Pérez Rosales, "Viaje a California: Recuerdos de 1848, 1849, 1850," in *We Were 49ers: Chilean Accounts of the California Gold Rush*, ed. Edwin A. Beilharz and Carlos U. López (Pasadena, 1976), 68.

19. Quoted in Richards, "Chilean Attitudes," 41; Jay Monahan, *Chile, Peru, and the California Gold Rush of 1849* (Berkeley, 1973), 198; Ross, "Chile and Its Relations with the United States," 22.

20. Quoted in Hernán Ramírez Necochea, *Historia del imperialismo en Chile*, 2d. ed. (Santiago, 1970), 82.

21. Mario Barros Van Buren, *Historia diplomática de Chile, 1541–1938*, (Barcelona, 1970), 185.

22. Bilbao, *Obras completas* 1: 168, 171; *El Mercurio* (Valparaíso), 13 February 1856.

23. Richards, "Chilean Attitudes," 68; *El Mercurio*, 25 February 1860.

24. Quoted in Daniel J. Hunter [Benjamín Vicuña Mackenna], *Chili, the United States, and Spain* (New York, 1866), 61.

25. Quoted in Stephen D. Brown, "The Power of Influence in United States–Chilean Relations," Ph.D. diss., University of Wisconsin, 1983, 135.

26. Ibid., 142.

27. Richards, "Chilean Attitudes," 200, 231.

28. Bilbao, *Obras completas* 1: 163.

2. War of the Pacific

1. Statement by a Chilean legislator, quoted in William F. Sater, *Chile and the War of the Pacific* (Lincoln, 1986), 202.
2. Alan Peskin, "Blaine, Garfield and Latin America: A New Look," *The Americas* 36 (1979): 82.
3. Quoted in James W. Pierce, *Life of James G. Blaine* (Baltimore, 1893), 440–41, in Richard C. Winchester, "James G. Blaine and the Ideology of American Expansionism," Ph.D. diss., University of Rochester, 1966, p. 74.
4. Winchester, "James G. Blaine," 83.
5. David M. Pletcher, *The Awkward Years: American Foreign Policy Under Garfield and Arthur* (Columbia, Mo., 1962), 42.
6. Peskin, "Blaine, Garfield and Latin America," 83.
7. Pletcher, *Awkward Years,* 46; Herbert Millington, *American Diplomacy and the War of the Pacific* (New York, 1948), 86.
8. Russell H. Bastert, "A New Approach to the Origins of Blaine's Pan American Policy," *Hispanic American Historical Review* 39 (August 1959): 400.
9. *La Patria* (Valparaíso), 20, 27 January, 30 June 1883; *Los Tiempos* (Santiago), 1 February 1883.
10. Quoted in Pletcher, *Awkward Years,* 79.
11. *El Ferrocarril* (Santiago), 18 November 1880; *La Patria,* 10 January 1880.
12. *La Patria,* 5 September 1882.
13. *El Estandarte Católico* (Santiago), 21, 22 April 1881.
14. *El Ferrocarril,* 24 March 1881, 4 November 1883; *El Ñuble* (Chillán), 23 November 1881; *El Padre Cobos* (Santiago), 23 July 1881; *El Constituyente* (Copiapó), 20 January 1882; *La Patria,* 11 February, 5 September 1882; *El Comercio* (San Felipe), 8 March 1883.

3. Chile Confronts the United States, 1884–1891

1. "The Growing Power of the Republic of Chile," *Atlantic Monthly* 54 (July 1884): 111; William E. Curtis, "The South American Yankee," *Harper's Magazine* 75 (1887): 564.
2. James Douglas, Jr., *Chile: Its Geography, People, and Institutions* (New York, 1881), 91.

3. Albert G. Browne, "The Growing Power of the Republic of Chile," *Journal of the American Geographical Society of New York* 16 (July 1884): 64.

4. "Growing Power," 111.

5. See *Congressional Record*, 47th Cong., 1st sess., 28 June 1882, p. 5474; 2d sess., 20 January 1883, p. 1404. A Mr. Berry stated: "The little ironclads of the Government of Chili [*sic*] could come and levy tribute upon the metropolis of our great western country," *Cong. Rec.*, 47th Cong., 2d. sess., 24 January 1883, p. 1557. Browne, "Growing Power," 80, 82.

6. *Army and Navy Journal* (Washington, D.C.), 1 August 1885; Balmaceda quoted in Francisco A. Encina, *La Presidencia de Balmaceda*, 2 vols. (Santiago, 1952), 1: 336.

7. Rodrigo Fuenzalida Bade, *Marinos ilustres y recuerdos del pasado* (Santiago, 1985), 111–12; Benjamín Vicuña Mackenna, "El reparto del Pacífico la posesión de la Isla de Pascua," *Revista de Marina* 100 (1985): 292.

8. Vicuña Mackenna, "El reparto," 290–92. See also J. Douglas Porteos, "The Annexation of Eastern [*sic*] Island: Geopolitics and Environmental Perception," *North-South* 6 (1981): 79.

9. Harold Blakemore, *British Nitrates and Chilean Politics, 1886–1896: Balmaceda and North* (London, 1974), 80.

10. Osgood Hardy, "The *Itata* Incident," *Hispanic American Historical Review* 5 (1922): 195–225.

11. Fredrick B. Pike, *Chile and the United States, 1880–1962: The Emergence of Chile's Social Crisis and the Challenge to United States Diplomacy* (Notre Dame, 1963), 68.

12. Lawrence A. Clayton, *Grace* (Ottawa, Ill., 1985), 213.

13. Ibid., 215.

14. Joyce Goldberg, *The Baltimore Affair* (Lincoln, 1986), 56.

15. Clayton, *Grace*, 219.

16. Quoted in Barros Van Buren, *Historia diplomática de Chile*, 492.

17. Quoted in Goldberg, *Baltimore Affair*, 107.

18. "The Chilian Trouble," *Harper's Weekly* 36 (30 January 1892): 110.

19. Quoted in Brown, "Power of Influence," 482.

20. Quoted in Emilio Meneses Ciuffari, *El factor naval en las relaciónes entre Chile y los Estados Unidos, 1881–1951* (Santiago, 1989), 83.

21. Ventura Blanco Viel, quoted in Oscar Espinosa Moraga, *La postguerra del Pacífico y la Puna de Atacama* (Santiago, 1958), 287.

22. Barros Van Buren, *Historia diplomática de Chile*, 492–93.

4. Chile's Long Descent, 1892–1920

1. Enrique Mac-Iver, *Discurso sobre la crisis moral de la república* (Santiago, 1900), 27.
2. In retaliation for the Alsop incident, Chile refused to purchase U.S.-made warships. Meneses Ciuffari, *El factor naval*, 127.
3. Gonzalo Vial, *Historia de Chile, 1891–1973*, 4 vols. (Santiago, 1981–87), 2: 174. President Jorge Montt, for example, refused to attend a banquet unwisely given aboard the *Baltimore* in 1892. When he left the presidency, he continued to control the navy. He used this position to demonstrate his anger toward the United States. See Meneses Ciuffari, *El factor naval*, 86–87. Chile also refused to send a naval vessel to celebrate the inauguration of Grant's tomb.
4. Pike, *Chile and the United States*, 137; Galvarino Gallardo Nieto, *Panamericanismo* (Santiago, 1941), 30.
5. *El Ferrocarril*, 8 November 1899, in Ramírez Necochea, *Historia del imperialismo en Chile*, 182. Chile may have disliked American imperialism, but it also wanted to avoid a confrontation with Washington. Some Spanish residents of Chile wanted to destroy two U.S. naval vessels docked in Chilean waters. Fearing another *Maine* incident, the Moneda intervened and crushed the bomb plot. Meneses Ciuffari, *El factor naval*, 89.
6. Ramírez Necochea, *Historia del imperialismo en Chile*, 183; Tancredo Pinochet Le Brun, *La conquista de Chile en el siglo XX* (Santiago, 1909), 20. The United States, conversely, feared that the Chilean fleet might attempt to stop the Panamanian rebellion from succeeding. Meneses Ciuffari, *El factor naval*, 104.
7. Ramírez Necochea, *Historia del imperialismo en Chile*, 187; Vial, *Historia de Chile* 2: 174–75; Meneses Ciuffari, *El factor naval*, 88.
8. Jaime Eyzaguirre, *Chile durante el gobierno de Errázuriz Echaurren, 1896–1901*, 2d. ed. (Santiago, 1957), 372.
9. Seward Livermore, "American Strategy [*sic*] Diplomacy in the South Pacific, 1890–1914," *Pacific Historical Review* 12 (1943): 49.
10. Quoted in William L. Kreig, *Legacy of the War of the Pacific* (Washington, D.C., 1974), 47.
11. Quoted in Mark T. Gilderhus, *Pan American Visions: Woodrow Wilson in the Western Hemisphere, 1913–1921* (Tucson, 1986), 24.
12. Cristián Guerrero Yoacham, *Las conferencias del Niagara Falls* (Santiago, 1966), 66–67.

13. Ibid., 83, 156, 163–64.

14. Samuel Bemis, *The Latin American Policy of the United States* (New York, 1967), 196.

15. Quoted in Gilderhus, *Pan American Visions*, 67.

16. Gallardo Nieto, *Panamericanismo*, 95–105.

17. Juan Ricardo Couyoumdjian, *Chile y Gran Bretaña durante la Primera Guerra Mundial y la postguerra, 1914–1921* (Santiago, 1986), 27, 41–42.

18. Ibid., 30.

19. Enrique Roucant, *La neutralidad de Chile* (Valparaíso, 1919), 11; *El Mercurio* quoted in Couyoumdjian, *Chile y Gran Bretaña*, 49.

20. Couyoumdjian, *Chile y Gran Bretaña*, 122, 69–80.

21. Quoted in Evans, *Chile and Its Relations with the United States*, 177.

22. Carlos Gutiérrez U., *El peligro yanqui* (Valparaíso, 1917), 26.

23. Quoted in Evans, *Chile and Its Relations with the United States*, 176; Gallardo Nieto, *Panamericanismo*, 104.

24. Quoted in Pike, *Chile and the United States*, 156.

25. Couyoumdjian, *Chile y Gran Bretaña*, 153.

26. Gallardo Nieto, *Panamericanismo*, 241, 136.

27. Gilderhus, *Pan American Visions*, 85.

28. Juan Ricardo Couyoumdjian, "En torno a la neutralidad de Chile durante la Primera Guerra Mundial," in *150 años de política exterior chilena*, ed. W. Sanchez and T. Pereira (Santiago, 1977), 188, 190.

29. Couyoumdjian, *Chile y Gran Bretaña*, 166–69; Vial, *Historia de Chile* 2: 640–41.

5. The Social Crisis, 1920–1938

1. Couyoumdjian, *Chile y Gran Bretaña*, 273–75.

2. Ibid., 228, 104.

3. Juan Ricardo Couyoumdjian, "En torno al protocolo de Washington de 1922," *Boletín de la Academia Chilena de la Historia* 96 (1985): 104.

4. Ernesto Barros Jarpa, *Hacia la solución* (Santiago, 1922), 52–58; Ibid., 105.

5. Kreig, *Legacy*, 52; Kenneth J. Grieb, *The Latin American Policy of Warren G. Harding*, (Fort Worth, 1976), 160.

6. Couyoumdjian, "En torno," 109.

7. Joe F. Wilson, *The United States, Chile and Peru in the Tacna and Arica Plebiscite* (Washington, 1979), 32.

8. Grieb, *Latin American Policy*, 166.

9. Agustín Edwards, *Recuerdos de mis persecución* (Santiago, n.d.), 26–27; Arturo Alessandri, *Recuerdos de gobierno*, 3 vols. (Santiago, 1967), 1: 159, 187.

10. Quoted in Wilson, *United States, Chile and Peru*, 52–53, 63–66.

11. Ibid., 70, 231–32.

12. Ibid., 231, 233.

13. Domingo Arturo Garfía, *El proceso plebiscitario de Tacna y Arica* (Santiago, n.d.), 46–47, 96; Pike, *Chile and the United States*, 219, 398 n. 36; Wilson, *United States, Chile and Peru*, 219.

14. Carlos Vicuña, *La libertad de opiniar y el problema de Tacna y Arica*, (Santiago, 1922), 324.

15. Robert Alexander, *Alessandri*, 2 vols. (Ann Arbor, 1977), 1: 376, 381, 383.

16. Meneses Ciuffari, *El factor naval*, 167–70. In 1938 Chile would again attempt to sell Easter Island. Japan was interested, but the Moneda refused to sell the island to Tokyo, knowing that such a sale would distress the United States (190).

17. At the last moment, Bolivia almost derailed the compromise. The treaty between Peru and Chile stipulated that neither nation could cede any of the once-disputed territory to a third party without the other signatory's permission. Bolivia, fearing that it would forever be landlocked, asked the United States to convince Peru and Chile to strike this clause from the treaty. Secretary of State Henry Stimson agreed that the settlement hamstrung La Paz. Consequently, when Stimson urged Leguía and Ibáñez to delete the offending section from the treaty, both nations complied. The two countries, in fact, simply made the offending clause a secret protocol, attaching it to the treaty. The U.S. ambassador learned of this action only after the Chilean senate had ratified the treaty with the secret provision.

18. Augusto Santelices, *El imperialismo yanqui y su influencía en Chile* (Santiago, 1926), 40; Clark Reynolds, "Development Problems of an Export Economy," in *Essays on the Chilean Economy* (Homewood, Ill., 1965), 222.

19. Alejandro Fuenzalida, *El trabajo i la vida en el mineral "El Teniente"* (Santiago, 1919), 94.

20. Ramírez Necochea, *Historia del imperialismo en Chile*, 229–30.

21. Quoted in Reynolds, "Development Problems," 220.

22. Joseph Tulchin, *The Aftermath of World War I and U.S. Policy Toward Latin America* (New York, 1971), 48–49.

23. Culbertson quoted in Richard J. Snyder, "William S. Culbertson in Chile:

Opening the Door to a Good Neighbor, 1928–1933," *Interamerican Economic Affairs* 26 (1972): 84; Ramírez Necochea, *Historia del imperialismo en Chile,* 230–32; Snyder, "William S. Culbertson," 92.

24. Dávila quoted in Ramírez Necochea, *Historia del imperialismo en Chile,* 242; Paul W. Drake, *Socialism and Populism in Chile, 1932–1952* (Urbana, 1978), 81.

25. Dick Steward, *Trade and Hemisphere: The Good Neighbor Policy and Reciprocal Trade* (Columbia, Mo., 1975), 224–26.

26. Ibid., 228–29.

6. The Radical Presidents, 1938–1952

1. Quoted in Boris Yopo, *El partido radical y Estados Unidos: 1933–1946* (Santiago, 1984), 25, 36–37.

2. Reynolds, "Development Problems," 238.

3. Drake, *Socialism and Populism,* 199.

4. Anthony O'Brien, "The Politics of Dependency: A Case Study of Dependency—Chile, 1939–45," Ph.D. diss., Notre Dame, 1977, pp. 217–18.

5. Reynolds, "Development Problems," 239.

6. Enrique Bernstein Carabantes, *Recuerdos de un diplomático* (Santiago, 1984), 71. Immediately after the bombing of Pearl Harbor, the United States requested that Chile sell the battleship *Latorre,* some of its destroyers, and a submarine tender. Santiago's refusal, although quite logical from Chile's point of view, nonetheless angered Washington. (See Meneses Ciuffari, *El factor naval,* 195.)

7. Bernstein Carabantes, *Recuerdos de un diplomático,* 71.

8. Ernesto Barros Jarpa, "Historia para olvidar: Ruptura con el Eje, 1942–1943," in *Homenaje a Guillermo Feliú Cruz,* ed. Neville Blanc Renard (Santiago, 1973), 56.

9. Michael J. Francis, *The Limits of Hegemony* (Notre Dame, 1977), 95, 107.

10. Bryce Wood, *The Dismantling of the Good Neighbor Policy* (Austin, 1985), 214.

11. Francis, 109.

12. Tobías Barros Ortiz, *Recogiendo los pasos* (Santiago, 1988), 418, 429.

13. Francis, 110.

14. British diplomat quoted in Wood, *Dismantling of the Good Neighbor Policy,* 214.

15. Barros Jarpa, "Historia para olvidar," 73.
16. Ibid., 92–93.
17. O'Brien, "Politics of Dependency," 226–27, 297–99.
18. Andrew Barnard, "Chilean Communists, Radical Presidents and Chilean Relations with the United States, 1940–1947," *Journal of Latin American Studies* 13 (1981): 360–61.
19. Gabriel González Videla, *Memorias*, 2 vols. (Santiago, 1975), 1: 558, 563.
20. Quoted in Boris Yopo, *Los partidos radical y socialista y Estados Unidos: 1947–1958* (Santiago, 1985), 14.
21. Jorge González von Marés, *El mal de Chile* (Santiago, 1940), 171.
22. Quoted in Yopo, *Los partidos radical y socialista y Estados Unidos: 1947–1958*, 32.

7. From Caudillos to Christian Democracy, 1952–1970

1. Quoted in René Montero Moreno, *La verdad sobre Ibáñez* (Santiago, 1952), 201.
2. Quoted in Arturo Olavarría Bravo, *Chile entre dos Alessandri*, 4 vols. (Santiago, 1962–65), 1: 390–91.
3. Quoted in Yopo, *Los partidos radical y socialista y Estados Unidos: 1947–1958*, 36.
4. Quoted in Otto Boye Soto, "Chile y el interamericanismo en las dos últimas decadas," *Mensaje* 20 (1971): 74–75.
5. Quoted in Albert Hirschman, "Inflation in Chile," in *Journeys Toward Progress* (New York, 1965), 260.
6. Reynolds, "Development Problems," 247.
7. William G. Tyler, "An Evaluation of the Klein and Saks Stabilization Program in Chile," *America Latina* (January 1968): 47–71.
8. R. Tarud, *Contra el despojo de los reajustes* (Santiago, n.d.), 6, 26.
9. Tyler, "Evaluation," 62–63.
10. Quoted in Yopo, *Los partidos radical y socialista y Estados Unidos: 1947–1958*, 45.
11. Heraldo Muñoz and Carlos Portales, *Una amistad esquiva: Las relaciónes de Estados Unidos y Chile* (Santiago, 1987), 53–56.
12. Ricardo Cruz Coke, *Geografía electoral de Chile* (Santiago, 1952), 63.
13. Miles D. Wolpin, *Cuban Foreign Policy and Chilean Politics* (Lexington, Mass., 1972), 109, 130–31.

14. *Hispanic American Report* 15, no. 7 (1962): 645; 15, no. 8 (1962): 744; 16, no. 2 (1963): 164; 16, no. 5 (1963): 492; 16, no. 11 (1963): 1091; 17, no. 3 (1964): 163; Ricardo Ffrench-Davis, *Políticas económicas en Chile, 1952–1970* (Santiago, 1973), 41–50.

15. Manfred Wilhelmy, "Hacia una análisis de la política exterior chilena contemporánea," *Estudios Sociales* 12 (1979): 456–59.

16. Quoted in *El Mercurio*, 5 November 1957, in Manfred Wilhelmy, "Chilean Foreign Policy: The Frei Government, 1964–1970," Ph.D. diss., Princeton University, 1973, p. 84.

17. Quoted in *Hispanic American Report* 13, no. 7 (1960): 477.

18. Joaquín Fermandois Huerta, "Chile y la 'Cuestión Cubana,' 1959–1964," *Historia* 17 (1982): 127–30.

19. Ibid., 149.

20. Ibid., 150–53.

21. Ibid., 166, 168.

22. Ibid., 173–75, 179–81.

23. Ibid., 184–93; Wolpin, *Cuban Foreign Policy*, 120.

24. Fermandois Huerta, "Chile y la 'Cuestión Cubana,'" 193–95.

25. Brian Loveman, *Struggle in the Countryside* (Bloomington, 1976), 223–40.

26. *Hispanic American Report* 13, no. 7 (1960): 408–9; 13, no. 7 (1960): 476–77; 14, no. 4 (1961): 354; 14, no. 7 (1961): 638–39; Theodore H. Moran, *Multinational Corporations and the Politics of Dependence: Copper in Chile* (Princeton, 1974), 200.

27. *Hispanic American Report* 14, no. 7 (1961): 638–39; Moran, *Multinational Corporations*, 202.

28. Robert Alexander, *The Tragedy of Chile* (Westport, Conn., 1978), 50.

29. Eduardo Frei, *La verdad tiene su hora*, 3rd ed. (Santiago, 1955), 129.

30. Otto Boye Soto, "La política exterior chilena entre 1964 y 1970," *Estudios Sociales* 2 (April 1974): 49; Wilhelmy, "Chilean Foreign Policy," 135–38, 59–60, 87.

31. Wilhelmy, "Chilean Foreign Policy," 62–63.

32. Manfred Wilhelmy, "Christian Democratic Ideology in Inter-American Politics: The Case of Chile, 1964–1970," in *Terms of Conflict: Ideology in Latin American Politics*, ed. Morris Blachman and Ronald Hellman, (Philadelphia, 1977), 138–41.

33. J. Levinson and J. Onis, *The Alliance That Lost Its Way: A Critical Report on the Alliance for Progress* (Chicago, 1970), 238.

34. Wilhelmy, "Chilean Foreign Policy," 189, 197; Moran, *Multinational Corporations*, 127–44.

35. David Berteau, "The Harriman-Solomon Mission and the 1966 Chilean Copper Agreement," in *Economic Coercion and U.S. Foreign Policy*, ed. S. Weintraub, (Boulder, 1982), 173–214.

36. Moran, *Multinational Corporations*, 144–46; Albert L. Michaels, "The Alliance for Progress and Chile's 'Revolution in Liberty,' 1964–1970," *Journal of Interamerican Studies and World Affairs* 18 (1976): 81.

37. Irving L. Horowitz, "The Life and Death of Project Camelot," *American Psychologist* 21 (May 1966): 445–48.

38. Wilhelmy, "Chilean Foreign Policy," 238–48.

39. Gonzalo Quezada, "Política exterior chilena, 1958–1973," *Revista de Ciencia Politica* 1 (1983): 55–56.

40. Wilhelmy, "Chilean Foreign Policy," 237–38.

41. Ibid., 297–311.

42. Ibid., 304.

43. Ibid., 306.

44. Ibid., 251–55, 260–70.

45. Ibid., 325.

46. Ibid., 328–35.

47. Ibid., 405–17; Manfred Wilhelmy, "La política exterior chilena y el grupo andino," *Estudios Sociales* 10 (1976): 16–37.

48. Wolpin, *Cuban Foreign Policy*, 170.

49. Wilhelmy, "Chilean Foreign Policy," 433–44.

50. Eduardo Frei, *The Mandate of History and Chile's Future*, (Athens, Ohio, 1977), 27.

8. Socialism Triumphant: Allende Versus Nixon

1. Paul E. Sigmund, *The Overthrow of Allende and the Politics of Chile, 1964–1976* (Pittsburgh, 1977), 103–4; U.S. Congress, Senate Select Committee to Study Governmental Operations with Respect to Intelligence Activities, *Covert Action in Chile, 1963–1973* 94th Cong., 1st sess., 1975, 20.

2. Sigmund, *Overthrow of Allende*, 111.

3. Ibid., 113.

4. Joaquín Fermandois Huerta, *Chile y el mundo, 1970–1973* (Santiago, 1985), 40, 42, 44.

5. Carlos Fortin, "Principled Pragmatism in the Face of External Pressure: The Foreign Policy of the Allende Government," in *Latin America: The Search for a New International Role*, ed. Ronald Hellman and H. Jon Rosenbaum (New York, 1975), 220.

6. Ibid., 223.

7. Ibid., 231.

8. Clodomiro Almeyda Medina, "The Foreign Policy of the Unidad Popular Government," in *Chile, 1970–1973*, ed. S. Sideri (The Hague, 1979), 117.

9. Fortin, "Principled Pragmatism," 223; Edy Kaufman, "La política exterior de la unidad popular chilena," *Foro Internacional* 167 (1976): 253–54.

10. Fermandois Huerta, *Chile y el mundo*, 133, 134.

11. Almeyda Medina, "Foreign Policy," in *Chile, 1970–1973*, 123.

12. Fermandois Huerta, *Chile y el mundo*, 115.

13. Fortin, "Principled Pragmatism," 225.

14. Ibid., 223.

15. Fermandois Huerta, *Chile y el mundo*, 44, 57; Almeyda Medina, "Foreign Policy," in *Chile, 1970–1973*, 108, 110.

16. Moran, *Multinational Corporations*, 204.

17. Eduardo Novoa, *La batalla por el Cobre* (Santiago, 1972), 155.

18. Carlos Fortin, "Chile Economic News, 21:43," cited in Eric N. Baklanoff, *Expropriation of U.S. Investments in Cuba, Mexico, and Chile* (New York, 1975), 127.

19. Baklanoff, *Expropriation of U.S. Investments*, 92–94; Paul E. Sigmund, *Multinationals in Latin America: The Politics of Nationalization* (Madison, 1980), 157–58.

20. Fortin, "Principled Pragmatism," 235; Sigmund, *Multinationals*, 152.

21. Jorge Edwards, *Persona non grata* (Barcelona, 1973), 454.

22. U.S. Congress, *Covert Action*, 33.

23. Paul E. Sigmund, "The 'Invisible Blockade' and the Overthrow of Allende," in *Chile: The Balanced View*, ed. Francisco Orrego Vicuña (Santiago, 1975), 112.

24. Ibid., 113.

25. Sigmund, *Overthrow of Allende*, 174.

26. J. Farrell, *The National Unified School in Allende's Chile* (Vancouver, 1986), 96–97.

27. Allende's supporters adamantly insist that he died fighting the junta's troops. Ian Roxborough, Phil O'Brien, and Jackie Roddick, *Chile: The State and Revolution* (New York, 1977), 231. Survivors of the event, however,

allege that the president did indeed shoot himself. For a recent discussion of this debate, see *Análisis* 180 (22–29 June 1987). The argument appears academic: people who shoot themselves rather than surrender are no less heroic than those who die fighting. Allende's widow, who seems to be backing away from her belief that Allende was shot, recently made this same point (*New York Times* 5 June 1990).

28. Les Evans, *Disaster in Chile* (New York, 1974), 256; Robinsón Rojas Sandford, *The Murder of Allende and the End of the Chilean Way to Socialism* (New York, 1975), 122; Gary MacEoin, *No Peaceful Way* (New York, 1974), 169, 177.

29. Sigmund, "Invisible Blockade," 117.

30. Quoted in ibid., 115; Jonathan E. Sanford, "The Multilateral Development Banks and the Suspension of Lending to Allende's Chile," in *Chile: The Balanced View*, ed. Orrego Vicuña, 126.

31. Sigmund, "Invisible Blockade," 116; Sanford, "Multilateral Development Banks," 125.

32. Fermandois Huerta, *Chile y el mundo*, 264.

33. Quoted in ibid., 263.

34. Ibid., 379 n. 73.

35. Kaufman, "La política exterior," 252.

36. Almeyda quoted in Fermandois Huerta, *Chile y el mundo*, 395 n. 52; Manuel Cantero, "Chile: The Role and Character of External Factors," *World Marxist Review* 20 (August 1977): 51.

37. U.S. Congress, Senate Select Committee to Study Governmental Operations with Respect to Intelligence Activities, *Alleged Assassination Plots Involving Foreign Leaders* 94th Cong., 1st sess., 1975, 254. Secretary of State Kissinger denied Karamessines's charges.

The issue of U.S. involvement, like assessing contributory negligence, becomes an exercise in judgment. William E. Colby's *Honorable Men: My Life in the CIA* (New York, 1978), Henry Kissinger's *Years of Upheaval* (Boston, 1982), and Nathaniel Davis's *The Last Two Years of Salvador Allende* (New York, 1985), for example, deny Washington fomented or participated in the coup. Seymour M. Hersh's *The Price of Power: Kissinger in the Nixon White House* (New York, 1983) and Thomas Hauser's *The Execution of Charles Homan* (New York, 1978), as well as other commentators, including Allende's widow, Hortensia Allende, have argued that U.S. military personnel participated in the coup or provided logistical support. See Gabriel Garcia Marquez, "The Death of Salvador Allende," *Harper's*, March 1974;

Robinsón Rojas Sandford, *The Murder of Allende* (New York, 1976); Laurence Birns, *The End of Chilean Democracy* (New York, 1974); James Petras and Morris Morley, *The United States and Chile: Imperialism and the Overthrow of the Allende Government* (New York, 1975); and Gary MacEoin, *No Peaceful Way* (New York, 1974). For a detailed and relatively objective analysis, see Nathaniel Davis's *The Last Two Years of Salvador Allende,* 345–66. Invariably, individuals will believe what and whom they want to believe. As the Rosenberg case indicates, opening archives more often fans the fires of controversy than quenches them.

38. Almeyda Medina, "Foreign Policy," in *Chile, 1970–1973,* 128–29.

9. The Corporate Caudillos and the Return of Democracy, 1973–1990

1. Sigmund, *Overthrow of Allende,* 253. The most recent estimate is one thousand killed; seven hundred subsequently "disappeared," and approximately seven thousand jailed and later released. *New York Times,* 1 August 1989.

2. Lars Schoultz, *Human Rights and United States Policy Toward Latin America* (Princeton, 1981), 170.

3. Genaro Arriagada, *Pinochet: The Politics of Power* (Boston, 1988), 14.

4. Ibid., 185.

5. Heraldo Muñoz, *Las relaciónes exteriores del gobierno militar chileno* (Santiago, 1986), 19; Muñoz and Portales, *Una amistad esquiva,* 47.

6. The only time a diplomatic problem developed was in 1975. Pinochet, hoping to end his government's diplomatic isolation, tried to ingratiate his regime with the Arab states. Consequently he ordered his diplomats to vote for the UN resolution equating Zionism with racism. When the U.S. State Department complained, General Pinochet ordered his delegation to abstain on the issue.

7. Schoultz, *Human Rights,* 19.

8. Muñoz, *Las relaciónes exteriores,* 26.

9. Augusto Varas, *Los militares en el poder* (Santiago, 1987), 115.

10. Muñoz, *Las relaciónes exteriores,* 168. Cardoen Industries apparently sold bombs to Iran, as did Ferrimar, an arms firm with ties to FAMAE. *Latin American Weekly Report,* 29 January 1987.

11. Schoultz, *Human Rights*, 133.

12. Taylor Branch and Eugene M. Propper, *Labyrinth* (New York, 1983), 35.

13. Although unwilling to extradite the Chilean conspirators, the Chilean courts expelled Townley. Once in the United States, Townley confessed his role in the Letelier assassination, implicating General Manuel Contreras—the head of DINA, the security service, and a friend of the Pinochet family—as well as Colonel Espinoza and Captain Fernández Larios. In a civil suit brought by the Moffitt family, a federal court found Contreras and the others responsible for the death of the Moffitts' daughter, awarding almost $5 million in damages and ordering the Chilean government to pay $2.9 million. Citing the doctrine of sovereign immunity, the Moneda refused to pay the court-imposed damages. The United States recently adopted the cause of Letelier and Moffitt by demanding that Chile pay $12 million. This sum would not only include the $5 million judgment for the wrongful deaths but would also compensate Washington for the cost of investigating and adjudicating the case. *New York Times*, 13 October 1988. Since Aylwin's election, Chile has agreed to pay compensation to the Moffitt family. As of June 1990 Chile would not extradite Contreras and the others accused of the crime.

14. Arriagada, *Pinochet*, 34, 44.

15. Schoultz, *Human Rights*, 298.

16. Arriagada, *Pinochet*, 41.

17. Heraldo Muñoz, "Las relaciónes exteriores del gobierno militar chileno," in *Chile, 1973–198?* ed. Manuel Garretón (Santiago, 1983), 246.

18. Arriagada, *Pinochet*, 46.

19. Muñoz and Portales, *Una amistad esquiva*, 108.

20. *New York Times*, 25 August 1983.

21. Pinochet's government also had the bad taste to nominate to the post of ambassador to the United States Mario Barros Van Buren, the former editor of an anti-Semitic journal. Some believe that the Moneda deliberately acted in a provocative manner. The United States responded by requesting that Santiago withdraw the nomination.

22. Muñoz and Portales, *Una amistad esquiva*, 112, 114.

23. Arriagada, *Pinochet*, 63.

24. Muñoz and Portales, *Una amistad esquiva*, 117–19, 131.

25. *Latin American Weekly Report*, 20 August 1987; *Insight*, 16 November 1987.

26. *New York Times*, 18 November 1988.

27. Tina Rosenberg, "Pinochet's Chile: Order and Chaos," *Present Tense* 15 (1987): 22. A poll conducted in 1985 noted that 39 percent of residents of slums preferred a government like that of Frei; 14 percent wanted a more conservative one, like that of Jorge Alessandri; 7 percent favored the military; 6 percent hoped for an Allende-type government; and 20 percent did not respond. *Latin American Weekly Report* 22 January 1987.

28. *Las Noticias* (Los Angeles), 9 September 1988.

29. *New York Times*, 25 September 1988; *Latin American Economic Report*, 30 September 1988; *Latin American Weekly Report*, 28 April 1988.

30. *New York Times*, 3 October 1988.

31. *Latin American Weekly Report*, 11 February, 30 June 1988.

32. *Latin American Weekly Report*, 17 September 1987.

33. *Latin American Weekly Report*, 13, 27 October 1988.

34. *New York Times*, 13 December 1989.

35. *The Economist*, 23 December 1989.

36. *El Pais* (Madrid), 18 December 1989.

37. *New York Times*, 1 August 1989.

38. *Washington Post*, 6 January 1990.

39. *Latin American Weekly Report*, 27 April 1989.

Conclusion: From Darwin to Marx

1. Julio Pérez Canto, *Chile* (London, 1912), 141, 148.

2. Francisco A. Encina, *Nuestra inferioridad económica* (Santiago, 1912).

3. Santelices, *El imperialismo yanqui*, 29–30, 45.

4. Gabriela Mistral, *Inter-America*, 6 (1922), quoted in John T. Reid, *Spanish American Images of the United States* (Gainesville, Fla., 1977), 161.

5. Nicolás Palacios, *Decadencia del espiritu de nacionalidad* (Santiago, 1908), 23.

6. William F. Sater, *The Heroic Image in Chile* (Berkeley, 1973).

7. Alberto Cabrero, *Chile y los Chilenos* (Santiago, 1926), 27.

Bibliographical Essay

Regrettably no single volume discusses the entire scope of Chilean-American diplomatic relations from Chile's independence to the 1980s. Of the existing works, Fredrick B. Pike, *Chile and the United States, 1880–1962: The Emergence of Chile's Social Crisis and the Challenge to United States Diplomacy* (Notre Dame, 1963), is certainly the best and most comprehensive; it is a well-written monument of detailed research. Arthur Whitaker, *The United States and the Southern Cone: Argentina, Chile, and Uruguay* (Cambridge, Mass., 1976), focusing on the post–World War II period, does not devote much space to Chile. Henry C. Evans, *Chile and Its Relations with the United States* (Durham, 1927), which concentrates on the nineteenth century, is hopelessly outdated, limited, and narrow in perspective. Mario Barros Van Buren, *Historia diplomática de Chile, 1541–1938* (Barcelona, 1970), stresses Santiago's dealings with the world rather than Chilean-American relations; moreover, the work ends with the Popular Front. Robert N. Burr, *By Reason or Force* (Berkeley, 1965), focuses on Chile's attempt to create a balance of power in nineteenth-century Latin America. Consequently, while Burr's volume is essential to obtaining an understanding of the Moneda's motives, it does not deal extensively with Santiago's relations with Washington. Two historians have attempted to forge comprehensive studies, but their works suffer from ideological biases: the Marxist Hernán Ramírez Necochea's *Historia del imperialismo en Chile*, 2d. ed. (Santiago, 1970), ecumenically attacks capitalism and Great Britain before zeroing in on the United States, which, predictably, emerges as the bogeyman. Luis Vitale's multivolume *Interpretación marxista de Chile* (Santiago, 1965–), which denounces the United States more stridently than Ramírez's work, expresses a similar view.

Since few scholars have comprehensively studied Chilean-American relations, students should consult those monographs and articles that have stressed either a particular issue or, as is generally the case, a specific period of time. Cristián Guerrero Yoacham's recent essay, "Chile y Estados Unidos: Relaciones y problemas, 1812–1916," in *150 años de política exterior chilena*, edited by W. Sanchez and T. Pereira, 66–83 (Santiago, 1977), provides a tantalizing introduction to the often-conflicted relationship between the Moneda and the

White House. Perhaps the best of the studies on the earlier period is Eugenio Pereira Salas, *La influencia norteamericana en las primeras constituciones de Chile* (Santiago, 1945), and his *Los primeros contactos entre Chile y los Estados Unidos, 1778–1809* (Santiago, 1974).

The dean of Chilean diplomats, Alejandro Alvarez, in his *La diplomácia de Chile durante la emancipacion* (Santiago, 1916), concentrated on Chile's earlier period, as did Ricardo Montaner, *Historia diplomática de la independencia de Chile* (Santiago, 1961). John J. Johnson's "Early Relations of the United States with Chile," *Pacific Historical Review* 13 (1944): 260–70, provides a view of the United States. An interesting doctoral dissertation is that of W. L. Neumann, "The Role of the United States in the Chilean Wars of Independence," University of Michigan, 1948. Julio Heise González, *Años de formacion y aprendizaje políticos, 1810–1830* (Santiago, 1978), briefly describes U.S. influence on Chile's earliest political institutions.

Carlos Mery Squella, *Las relaciones diplomáticas entre Chile y los Estados Unidos de America, 1829–1841* (Santiago, 1965), covers the crucial period of the 1830s and 1840s. Luis Carcovic, *Portales y la política international hispanoamericana* (Santiago, 1937), stresses the views of the guiding force in Chile. Thomas R. Shurbutt, "United States Chargés d'Affaires to Chile, 1835–1848," Ph.D. diss., University of Georgia, 1971, provides an interesting, albeit short, glimpse of the various men who served as Washington's ministers to Santiago. Some historians have studied the impact of American entrepreneurs. Jay Kinsbrunner wrote about William Wheelwright, who provided Chile with potable water and steamship service, in "Water for Valparaíso: A Case of Entrepreneurial Frustration," *Journal of Interamerican Studies and World Affairs* 10 (1968): 653–61, and in "The Business Activities of William Wheelwright in Chile, 1829–1860," Ph.D. diss., New York University, 1965. Watt Stewart, *Henry Meiggs, Yankee Pizarro* (Durham, 1946), provides a biography of the man who built Chile's first railroads. Augusto Marambio Cabrera's *La cuestión del Macedonian* (Santiago, 1989), is a well-prepared monograph studying the *Macedonian* claims, which constituted one of the most long-lasting, if not most vexing, problems to bedevil the United States and Chile.

Works on Chile's involvement in the California gold rush have recently appeared. Sergio Sepulveda, *El trigo chileno en el mercado mundial* (Santiago, 1959), discusses the impact of the gold rush on agriculture. Jay Monahan, *Chile, Peru, and the California Gold Rush of 1849* (Berkeley, 1973), relates how the discovery of gold affected Chile and California. Edwin A. Beilharz and

Carlos U. López, eds., *We Were 49ers: Chilean Accounts of the California Gold Rush* (Pasadena, 1976), fleshes out the Chilean point of view, supplementing the more traditional work of Vicente Pérez Rosales, *Recuerdos del Pasado*, 3rd. ed. (Santiago, 1886).

Washington's abortive involvement in the Spanish intervention is well documented in Carolyn A. Richards, "Chilean Attitudes Toward the United States, 1860–1867," Ph.D. diss., Stanford University, 1970. The classic study of this event in English remains William C. Davis, *The Last Conquistadores: The Spanish Intervention in Peru and Chile, 1863–1866* (Athens, Ga., 1950). Also of some interest is Cristián Guerrero Yoacham's description of Benjamín Vicuña Mackenna's activities in the United States during the Spanish incursion into Chile, "La misión de Vicuña Mackenna a los Estados Unidos, 1865–1866," *Atenea* 454 (1986): 239–75.

The U.S. Civil War constituted a diplomatic watershed in relations between Washington and Santiago. Cristián Guerrero Yoacham, "Chile y la guerra de secesión de los Estados Unidos, 1861–1865," *Boletín de la Academia Chilena de Historia* 39 (1975–76), 97–167, provides one of the most comprehensive accounts of that period. See also Carl A. Ross, Jr., "Chile and Its Relations with the United States During the Ministry of Thomas Henry Nelson, 1861–1866," Ph.D. diss., University of Georgia, 1966. Richards's dissertation is also a valuable, albeit less comprehensive, source of information about the period.

Washington's clumsy involvement in the War of the Pacific has been the subject of various works. Herbert Millington, *American Diplomacy and the War of the Pacific* (New York, 1948), provides more data than analysis. A particularly trenchant but woefully biased interpretation is that of the Russian historian V. Smolenski, "Los Estados Unidos y la Guerra del Pacífico," *Boletín de la Academia Chilena de la Historia* 78 (1968): 96–120. Smolenski adroitly manipulates not only the facts but also his sources to prove to his satisfaction that Washington caused the War of the Pacific. Neither V. Kiernan, "Foreign Interests in the War of the Pacific," *Hispanic American Historical Review* 35 (1955): 14–36, nor Peter Sehlinger, "Las armas diplomáticas de inversionistas internacionales durante la Guerra del Pacífico," in *150 años de política exterior chilena*, edited by W. Sanchez and T. Pereira, 45–65 (Santiago, 1977), share either Smolenski's views or his dexterity in footnoting. (For a rejoinder to Smolenski, see William F. Sater, "La intervención norteamericana durante la Guerra del Pacífico," *Boletín de la Academia Chilena de la Historia* 83–84 (1970): 185–206. Additional information on Chile's attitudes toward U.S. intervention can be found in William F. Sater, *Chile and the War of the Pacific* (Lincoln, 1986). For a study of the situation in the United States, see David M. Pletcher, *The Awkward Years: American Foreign Policy Under Garfield and Arthur* (Columbia, Mo., 1962).

The 1891 revolution constitutes one of the nodal points in Chilean historiography. Those interested in learning about the causes and the course of the revolution should begin with Harold Blakemore's "The Chilean Revolution of 1891 and Its Historiography," *Hispanic American Historical Review* 45 (1965): 393–421, and his *British Nitrates and Chilean Politics, 1886–1896: Balmaceda and North* (London, 1974). Based on extensive archival materials, Blakemore's works explain the events that precipitated the 1891 civil war as well as the war's outcome. Another particularly useful work is Stephen D. Brown, "The Power of Influence in United States–Chilean Relations," Ph.D. diss., University of Wisconsin, 1983. Brown's work carefully traces the interchange between the United States and Chile that culminated in the 1891 *Baltimore* crisis, demonstrating how Santiago's naval might provided Washington's naval buffs with a reason to acquire a fleet of their own. Another monograph dealing with this topic is Emilio Meneses Ciuffari, *El factor naval en las relaciónes entre Chile y los Estados Unidos, 1881–1951* (Santiago, 1989). Meneses not only analyzes some of the same issues, from the Chilean perspective, that Brown discussed, but he also extends his study into the twentieth century.

Osgood Hardy's doctoral dissertation, "The United States and Chile: A Study in Diplomatic Relations, with Special Emphasis on the Period of the Chilean Civil War of 1891," University of California, 1925, and his article, "The *Itata* Incident," *Hispanic American Historical Review* 5 (1922): 195–226, exhaustively study American involvement in the 1891 revolution. Joyce Goldberg, *The Baltimore Affair* (Lincoln, 1986), describes particularly well the United State's response to the clash in Valparaíso. Patricio Estelle, "La controversia chileno-americano de 1891 a 1892," *Estudios de la Historia de las Instituciónes Políticas y Sociales* 1 (1967): 149–277, emphasizes the Chilean reaction.

In order to gain some understanding of Blaine, his policies, and the prevailing American attitudes during the late nineteenth century, see Richard C. Winchester, "James G. Blaine and the Ideology of American Expansionism," Ph.D. diss., University of Rochester, 1966; Philip W. Kennedy, "The Concept of Racial Superiority and United States Imperialism, 1890–1910," Ph.D. diss., St. Louis University, 1963; and Arthur H. Ogle, Jr., "Nationalism and American Foreign Policy, 1898–1920: A Series of Case Studies on the Influence of an Idea," Ph.D. diss., University of Virginia, 1971.

Historians have devoted little effort to discussing the years leading up to the First World War. Gonzalo Vial's multivolume *Historia de Chile, 1891–1973,* 4 vols. (Santiago, 1981–87), however, does contain material on Chile's diplomatic relations with other nations, including the United States. In addition, various monographs, while tracing the presidential regimes of the Parliamentary period, also discuss diplomacy: these include Jaime Eyzaguirre, *Chile durante el gobierno de Errázuriz Echaurren, 1896–1901,* 2d. ed. (Santiago, 1957), and Germán Riesco, *Presidencia de Riesco, 1901–1905* (Santiago, 1950). Cristián Guerrero Yoacham, *Las conferencias del Niagara Falls* (Santiago, 1966), explains the role of the ABC powers in mediating Washington's struggle with revolutionary Mexico.

Predictably the Tacna-Arica dispute emerged as one of the principal issues vexing Washington and Santiago. Both Peru and Chile produced massive monographs and collections of documents, invariably justifying their respective positions. Perhaps the best works in English are the two studies of W. Dennis, *Documentary History of the Tacna-Arica Dispute* (Iowa City, 1927), and *Tacna and Arica: An Account of the Chile-Peru Boundary Dispute and of the Arbitrations by the United States* (New Haven, 1931). Joe F. Wilson, *The United States, Chile and Peru in the Tacna and Arica Plebiscite* (Washington, 1979), superbly describes the ill-fated involvement of the United States in the abortive plebiscite. A new addition to the literature is Juan Ricardo Couyoumdjian, "En torno al protocolo de Washington de 1922," *Boletín de la Academia Chilena de la Historia* 96 (1985): 77–123.

For analysis of Chile's involvement in the First World War, the latest and perhaps the best work is Juan Ricardo Couyoumdjian, *Chile y Gran Bretaña durante la Primera Guerra Mundial y la postguerra, 1914–1921* (Santiago, 1986), and his "En torno a la neutralidad de Chile durante la Primera Guerra Mundial," in *150 años de política exterior chilena,* edited by W. Sanchez and T. Pereira, 180–207 (Santiago, 1977). Couyoumdjian's book, while emphasizing the relationship between England and Chile, nonetheless includes valuable material on Washington's interaction with Santiago. Also of great value is Mark T. Gilderhus, *Pan American Visions: Woodrow Wilson in the Western Hemisphere, 1913–1921* (Tucson, 1986). Enrique Roucant, *La neutralidad de Chile* (Valparaíso, 1919), provides an excellent rationalization for Chile's refusal to become involved in the war.

Events in post–World War I Chile, other than the Tacna-Arica dispute, have not attracted many scholars. Many works, such as Claude Bower, *Chile Through Embassy Windows, 1939–1953* (New York, 1958), like the ambassador himself, tend to be charming but not very illuminating. Some historians have discussed Chile while describing the diplomatic policies of various presidential regimes: for example, Kenneth J. Grieb, *The Latin American Policy of Warren G. Harding* (Fort Worth, 1976), indicates, at least, that Harding did indeed have policy. See also Alexander DeConde, *Herbert Hoover's Latin American Policy* (Stanford, 1951).

The 1930s, of course, proved chaotic for Chile. Regrettably, little has appeared about these crucial times. Arturo Alessandri, *Recuerdos de gobierno,* 3 vols. (Santiago, 1967), provides the author's version of events, a version that does not conform to those of his opponents or even to those of some of his friends. For examples of the former, see Ricardo Donoso, *Alessandri, agitador y demoledor,* 2 vols. (Mexico, 1952), and Carlos Charlin, *Del avión rojo a la república socialista* (Santiago, 1972). J. R. Stevenson, *The Chilean Popular Front* (Philadelphia, 1942), and P. T. Ellsworth, *Chile, an Economy in Transition* (New York, 1945), are important for understanding Chile during the 1930s and 1940s. Richard J. Snyder, "William S. Culbertson in Chile: Opening the Door to a Good Neighbor, 1928–1933," *Interamerican Economic Affairs* 26 (1972): 81–98, is one of the few works emphasizing the role of a U.S. diplomat to Chile. Paul W. Drake, *Socialism and Populism in Chile, 1932–1952* (Urbana, 1978), while concentrating on the evolution of the Socialist party, also contains some useful material.

Chile's involvement, or rather noninvolvement, in the Second World War is extremely well covered in Michael J. Francis, *The Limits of Hegemony* (Notre Dame, 1977). R. A. Humphreys, *Latin America and the Second World War, 1939–1942* (London, 1981), discusses Chile's policies within the context of the entire continent. For a Chilean perspective, see Ernesto Barros Jarpa, "Historia para olvidar: Ruptura con el Eje, 1942–1943," in *Homenaje a Guillermo Feliú Cruz,* edited by Neville Blanc Renard, 31–96 (Santiago, 1973); Enrique Bernstein Carabantes, *Recuerdos de un diplomático* (Santiago, 1984); and Joaquín Fermandois Huerta, "Guerra y hegemonia, 1939–1943: Un aspecto de las relaciónes chileno-norteamericanas," *Historia* 23 (1988): 5–51.

Little has appeared about Chile's post–World War II relations with Washington. Bryce Wood, *The Dismantling of the Good Neighbor Policy* (Austin, 1985), traces U.S. policies during the latter part of the Second World War and the early cold war. Frederick B. Pike and Donald Bray, "A Vista of Catastrophe: The Future of United States-Chilean Relations," *The Review of Politics* 22 (1960): 393–418, ably describes the various cultural impediments to mutual understanding. As the authors note, Chileans have preconceived notions about the United States that, in conjunction with Washington's misguided vision of Chile, created an environment of misunderstanding.

Santiago's branch of FLACSO has published piecemeal a series of essays by Boris Yopo: *El partido socialista chileno y Estados Unidos: 1939–1946* (Santiago, 1984); *Los partidos radical y socialista y Estados Unidos: 1947–1958* (Santiago, 1985); *El partido radical y Estados Unidos: 1933–1946* (Santiago, 1984); and *El partido socialista, el partido radical y Estados Unidos, 1959–1973* (Santiago, 1985). Although based largely on secondary sources, Yopo's essays explain the attitudes of the Radical and Socialist parties toward the United States.

Manfred Wilhelmy's "Hacia una análisis de la política exterior chilena contemporánea" *Estudios Internacionales* 48 (1979): 441–71 and his "Política, burocracia y diplomácia en Chile," *Estudios Sociales* 35 (1983): 13–19, also contain excellent overviews of the period from González Videla through Allende. In the latter work, the author analyzes the impact of individual presidents and the bureaucracy on the formulation of Chile's foreign policy. A more ambitious work, Heraldo Muñoz and Carlos Portales, *Una amistad esquiva: Las relaciónes de Estados Unidos y Chile* (Santiago, 1987), emphasizes the post-1945 period, particularly the Carter and Reagan regimes. Alberto Sepúlveda A., *La nueva política exterior de Chile* (Caracas, 1971), provides a general but more limited overview. Otto Boye Soto's "Chile y el interamericanismo en las dos últimas decadas," *Mensaje* 20 (1971): 67–86, is a more descriptive work explaining Santiago's involvement in the inter-American movement. Lars Schoultz, *Human Rights and United States Policy Toward Latin America* (Princeton, 1981), traces Washington's vacillating post-1945 Latin American human rights policy.

One of the few studies examining the supposed ability of Washington to shape the Moneda's domestic policies is Andrew Barnard, "Chilean Communists, Radical Presidents and Chilean Relations with the United States, 1940–1947," *Journal of Latin American Studies* 13 (1981): 347–74. A more personal perspective on the same period can be found in Gabriel González Videla, *Memorias*, 2 vols. (Santiago, 1975).

Jorge Alessandri's administration has attracted little scholarly attention. L. Littwin's doctoral dissertation, "An Integrated View of Chilean Foreign Policy," New York University, 1967, discusses Alessandri's Cuban policy. Joaquín Fermandois Huerta, "Chile y la 'Cuestión Cubana,' 1959–1964," *Historia* 17 (1982): 113–20, and Miles D. Wolpin, *Cuban Foreign Policy and Chilean Politics* (Lexington, Mass., 1972), explain the various forces shaping Santiago's attitude toward Havana. Wolpin, unlike Fermandois, does not confine himself solely to the Alessandri period but also includes material on Frei.

If Alessandri's presidency seems to remain unexamined, his successor's term of office came to be dubbed what Leonard Gross called "the last best hope"; see Gross, *The Last Best Hope: Eduardo Frei and Chilean Democracy* (New York, 1967). Michael Fleet, *The Rise and Fall of Chilean Christian Democracy* (Princeton, 1985), attempts to provide theoretical analysis of the PDC and its ideology. Arturo Olavarría Bravo, *Chile bajo la Democracia Cristiana*, 6 vols. (Santiago, 1966–71), offers an uninspired factual account. Ernest Halperin, *Nationalism and Communism in Chile* (Cambridge, Mass., 1965), written after Frei's victory, offers insight into contemporary feelings, particularly those of the Socialist party.

The role of the United States has become the subject of numerous studies. Eduardo Labarca Goddard, *Chile invadido* (Santiago, 1969), and Miles D. Wolpin, *La intervención extranjera en las elecciones chilenas* (Buenos Aires, 1970), examined U.S. involvement in Frei's election. A less partisan account of that contest is Federico Gil and Charles Parrish, *The Chilean Presidential Election of September 4, 1964*, 2 vols. (Washington, D.C., 1965).

Albert L. Michaels, "The Alliance for Progress and Chile's 'Revolution in Liberty,' 1964–1970," *Journal of Interamerican Studies and World Affairs* 18 (1976): 74–99, analyzes the impact and consequences of U.S. aid on Chile, as does Eduardo Frei, "The Alliance That Lost its Way," *Foreign Affairs* 45 (April 1967): 437–48. A more pessimistic interpretation of that program is Philip O'Brien, "La Alianza para el Progreso y los préstamos por programa a Chile," *Estudios Internacionales* 2 (1969): 461–89. Irving L. Horowitz, ed., *The Rise and Fall of Project Camelot: Studies in the Relationship Between Social Science and Practical Politics*, rev. ed. (Cambridge, Mass., 1974), describes the Camelot fiasco.

Manfred Wilhelmy, "Chilean Foreign Policy: The Frei Government, 1964–1970," Ph.D. diss., Princeton University, 1973, remains the single best work on Frei's foreign policy. Also of great importance is Wilhelmy's "Christian Democratic Ideology in Inter-American Politics: The Case of Chile, 1964–1970," in *Terms of Conflict: Ideology in Latin American Politics*, edited by Morris Blachman and Ronald Hellman, 129–60 (Philadelphia, 1977). Wilhelmy discusses Chile's participation in the Andean Pact in his "La política exterior chilena y el grupo andino," *Estudios Sociales* 10 (1976): 16–37. Another useful work is Otto Boye Soto, "La política exterior chilena entre 1964 y 1970," *Estudios Sociales* 2 (April 1974): 48–66.

Salvador Allende and his regime generally inspire more frenzy than reason. The Right regards Allende as the Antichrist; the Left pictures him as a secular demigod. Consequently, finding a balanced approach is very difficult. The two works that best accomplish this goal are Paul E. Sigmund, *The Overthrow of Allende and the Politics of Chile, 1964–1976* (Pittsburgh, 1977), and Arturo Valenzuela, *The Breakdown of Democratic Regimes: Chile* (Baltimore, 1978). Robert Alexander, *The Tragedy of Chile* (Westport, Conn., 1978), is also useful. Devotees of the more ideological approach can read Robert Moss, *Chile's Marxist Experiment* (London, 1973), which offers a conservative perspective, while the more recent Hugo Cancino Troncoso, *Chile: La problemática del poder popular en el proceso de la vía chilena al socialismo, 1970–1973* (Aarhus, 1988), provides a leftist antidote. A useful biography and compilation of Allende's speeches is Juan Ligero and Juvencio Negrete, *Allende: La consecuencia de un líder* (Concepción, 1986). Carlos Altamirano, *Dialéctica de una derrota* (Mexico, 1977), is a useful supplement to the other works.

Works that specifically address Allende's foreign policy include Aníbal Palma, "The Popular Unity Government's Foreign Policy," and Jorge Arrate, "The Nationalization of Copper," both in *The Chilean Road to Socialism*, edited by J. Ann Zammit, 141–50 (Austin, 1973). Clodomiro Almeyda Medina, who served as Allende's minister of foreign relations, has written "The Foreign Policy of the Unidad Popular Government," in *Chile at the Turning Point: Lessons of the Socialist Years, 1970–1973*, edited by Federico Gil, Ricardo Lagos E., and Henry Landsberger, translated by John S. Gitlitz, 76–104 (Philadelphia, 1979), as well as "The Foreign Policy of the Unidad Popular Government," in *Chile, 1970–1973*, edited by S. Sideri, 104–34 (The Hague, 1979). Almeyda's *Pensando a Chile* (Santiago, 1976), while it does not deal with diplomatic topics, is nonetheless interesting. For other contributions see Leopoldo González Aguayo, *Teoría y praxis internacional del gobierno de Allende* (Mexico, 1971); Heraldo Muñoz, "La política internacional del partido socialista y las relaciónes exteriores de Chile," in *Entre la autonomía y la subordinación: Política exterior de los países latinoamericanos*, 174–222 (Buenos Aires, 1984); Edy Kaufman, "La política exterior de la unidad popular chilena," *Foro Internacional* 167 (1976): 244–74; and Carlos Fortin, "Principled Pragmatism in the Face of External Pressure: The Foreign Policy of the Allende Government," in *Latin America: The Search for a New International Role*, edited by Ronald Hellman and H. Jon Rosenbaum, 217–45 (New York, 1975). One of the best efforts dealing with Allende's foreign policy is Joaquín Fermandois Huerta, *Chile y el mundo,*

1970–1973 (Santiago, 1985). Using a variety of sources, the author explains Chile's attitude toward Cuba, Latin America, the United States, and the rest of the world. Fermandois's volume is an excellent study. Also of great value is Jorge Vera Castillo, *La política exterior chilena durante el gobierno del Presidente Salvador Allende, 1970–1973* (Santiago, 1987). This book contains the papers and comments of a recent conference that dealt with the Allende government's foreign policy, and it is particularly valuable because it includes statements by former participants in the UP regime.

Various studies deal exclusively with relations between Santiago and Washington. Richard Fagen, "The United States and Chile: Roots and Branches," *Foreign Affairs* 53 (1975): 297–313, provided one of the first examples of the "blame it on Washington" school of interpretation. A more recent, better documented study is that of the Dane, Poul Jensen, *The Garotte: The United States and Chile, 1970–1973*, 2 vols. (Aarhus, 1989). Other works sharing similar feelings are James Petras and Morris Morley, *The United States and Chile: Imperialism and the Overthrow of the Allende Government* (New York, 1975); Robinsón Rojas Sandford, *El imperialismo yanqui en Chile* (Santiago, 1971); and A. Uribe, *The Black Book of American Intervention in Chile* (Boston, 1974).

Paul E. Sigmund, "The 'Invisible Blockade' and the Overthrow of Allende"; Jonathan E. Sanford, "The Multilateral Development Banks and the Suspension of Lending to Allende's Chile"; and James Theberge, "U.S. Economic Policy Towards Chile During the Popular United Government," are reprinted in *Chile: The Balanced View*, edited by Francisco Orrego Vicuña, 21–38, 111–52, (Santiago, 1975). These works generally attribute Allende's fall more to his domestic policies than to U.S. intervention. Also worth reading are Federico Gil, "Socialist Chile and the United States," *Interamerican Economic Affairs* 27 (1973): 29–47, and Mark Falcoff, *Small Countries, Large Issues* (Washington, D.C., 1984). U.S. Congress, Senate Select Committee on Intelligence Activities, *Covert Action in Chile, 1963–1973*, 94th Cong., 1st sess., 1975, provides the results of an official congressional investigation. The works of two former U.S. ambassadors to Santiago, Edward Korry's "U.S. Politics in Chile Under the Allende Government," in *Chile: The Balanced View*, ed. Orrego Vicuña, 287–89, and Nathaniel Davis's *The Last Two Years of Salvador Allende* (Ithaca, N.Y., 1985), provide more personal perspectives.

Eric N. Baklanoff, *Expropriation of U.S. Investments in Cuba, Mexico, and Chile* (New York, 1975); Theodore H. Moran, *Multinational Corporations and the Politics of Dependence: Copper in Chile* (Princeton, 1974); and Paul E. Sigmund, *Multinationals in Latin America: The Politics of Nationalization* (Madison, 1980), deal with the nationalization of the copper mines. Moran's work is particularly useful because he explains the process within a broader framework of Chilean history.

The Pinochet administration engenders only slightly less controversy than the Allende regime. Since the general has antagonized so many people, there seems to be more of a consensus about him—that he is gratuitously brutal, a fool, or both—than about the UP, which some—particularly those who did not live in Chile—still regard as a golden age. Examples of those unimpressed with Pinochet are Genaro Arriagada, *Pinochet: The Politics of Power* (Boston, 1988), and Augusto Varas, *Los militares en el poder* (Santiago, 1987). When the general leaves the Moneda, we can expect a deluge of more anti-Pinochet volumes. Heraldo Muñoz, *Las relaciónes exteriores del gobierno militar chileno* (Santiago, 1986), and Muñoz, "Las relaciónes exteriores del gobierno militar chileno," in *Chile, 1973–198?*, edited by Manuel Garreton, 229–49 (Santiago, 1983), together provide one of the few studies of General Pinochet's foreign policy.

Index